Penal Era and Golden Age

PENAL ERA AND GOLDEN AGE

Essays in Irish History, 1690-1800

Edited by Thomas Bartlett and D. W. Hayton

Ulster Historical Foundation Belfast, 1979

Printed by
W. & G. Baird Ltd., Antrim, 1979

FOREWORD

Eight of the nine essays in this book (the exception being Dr Malcomson's[1]) originated as papers delivered at a symposium on eighteenth-century Ireland at the Institute of Irish Studies, The Queen's University of Belfast, in March 1975. The symposium was held in honour of Professor J. C. Beckett — to mark his retirement from the chair of Irish history at Queen's — and this volume is likewise intended as a tribute to Professor Beckett, one of the foremost historians of eighteenth-century Ireland.

The purpose of the book (as of the symposium which generated it) is to publish the results of new research on various aspects of the period, much of it making use of manuscript sources which have only recently come to light. The essays have been written with a view either to revising textbook orthodoxy or to exploring uncharted territory: new interpretations are offered of crucially important episodes in Irish political history, and there are pioneering ventures into hitherto neglected areas of study.

The topics covered reflect the interests of individual contributors and, perhaps, underlying trends in the current historiography of the period. There is a greater emphasis than is usual in books on eighteenth-century Ireland on the earlier part of the century and, although most of the essays are concerned with political history, some attention is paid to developments in the economy and in Irish society as a whole.

The editors and contributors would like to thank the Institute of Irish Studies, Queen's University, Belfast, and the Trustees of the Esme Mitchell Fund, without whose generous financial support this book would not have been published; Professor E. R. R. Green, Professor Edith M. Johnston, Dr P. J. Jupp and Professor J. L. McCracken, for encouragement and advice; the owners and custodians of the various collections of manuscripts from which items have been cited; and the officials of the institutional libraries and record offices in which research has been carried out, in particular Mr Brian Trainor, the Deputy Keeper, and his courteous and efficient staff in the Public Record Office of Northern Ireland.

March 1978   T.B., D.W.H.

---

1.   A revised version of a paper read at the eleventh Irish Conference of Historians at Galway in May 1973.

NOTES ON CONTRIBUTORS

THOMAS BARTLETT: Lecturer in History, University College, Galway. Sometime Senior History Master, Royal Belfast Academical Institution. Graduate of Queen's University, Belfast. Formerly a research student at the University of Michigan and a member of the Institute of Irish Studies, Queen's University, Belfast. Author of a doctoral thesis on the Townshend viceroyalty (Queen's Univ. Belfast), and of a forthcoming calendar of the Irish papers of Sir George Macartney (H.M.S.O.).

W. H. CRAWFORD: Assistant Keeper, Public Record Office of Northern Ireland. Graduate of the University of Dublin. His publications include *The Study of Local History in Northern Ireland* (1968), *Aspects of Irish Social History, 1750-1800* (with B. Trainor, 1969), *Domestic Industry in Ireland: The Experience of the Linen Industry* (1972) and several articles in *Ulster Folklife* and *Irish Economic and Social History*.

DAVID DICKSON: Junior Lecturer in Modern History, Trinity College Dublin. Graduate of the University of Dublin. Formerly a Junior Fellow at the Institute of Irish Studies, Queen's University Belfast. Author of a Doctoral thesis on the economy of the Cork region in the eighteenth century (Dublin Univ.), and of a number of articles in local historical journals. Joint-editor of *Irish Economic and Social History*.

MARIANNE ELLIOTT: Research Fellow, The University of Wales. Graduate of Queen's University Belfast. Formerly Lecturer in History, West London Institute of Higher Education. Is preparing for publication her doctoral thesis on 'The United Irishmen and France' (Oxford Univ.).

DAVID HAYTON: Research Assistant, The History of Parliament Trust. Graduate of Manchester University. Formerly a Junior Fellow at the Institute of Irish Studies, Queen's University Belfast. Author of a doctoral thesis on the government of Ireland in the early eighteenth century (Oxford Univ.), and of a collection of facsimile-documents entitled *Ireland after the Glorious Revolution* (1976).

JAMES I. McGUIRE: Assistant Lecturer in Modern Irish History University College, Dublin. Graduate of the National University of Ireland. Formerly Junior Lecturer in Irish History, University

College, Cork. Author of an M.A. thesis on Irish constitutional history in the period 1688-1707 (Nat. Univ. Ireland). Is working on a study of the Restoration settlement in Ireland.

A. P. W. MALCOMSON: Assistant Keeper, Public Record Office of Northern Ireland. Graduate of Cambridge University. Author of a doctoral thesis on Speaker John Foster (Queen's Univ. Belfast), which formed the basis of his recently published *John Foster: The Politics of the Anglo-Irish Ascendancy* (Oxford, 1978), and of numerous articles on eighteenth-century Irish politics.

DECLAN O'DONOVAN: A First Secretary in the Irish Department of Foreign Affairs. Graduate of the National University of Ireland. Author of a doctoral thesis on the Money Bill dispute of 1753 (Nat. Univ. Ireland).

P. D. H. SMYTH: Research Assistant, Public Record Office of Northern Ireland. Graduate of Queen's University Belfast. Author of a doctoral thesis on the Volunteer movement in Ulster (Queen's Univ. Belfast), and has edited and introduced a set of facsimile-documents on *The Volunteers* (1974).

PRINCIPAL ABBREVIATIONS USED IN FOOTNOTES

A.A.G.	Archives Administratives de la Guerre, Vincennes.
A.H.G.	Archives du Ministere des Affaires Etrangeres, Paris.
A.N.	Archives Nationales, Paris.
B.L.	British Library.
Bod.	Bodleian Library.
C.J.I.	*The Journals of the House of Commons of the Kingdom of Ireland* (19 vols., Dublin, 1796-1800).
C.S.P. Dom.	*Calendar of State Papers, Domestic.*
E.H.R.	*English Historical Review.*
H.M.C.	*Historical Manuscripts Commission.*
I.H.S.	*Irish Historical Studies.*
Lecky	W. E. H. Lecky, *A History of Ireland in the Eighteenth Century* (2nd. edn., 5 vols., London, 1892).
N.L.I.	National Library of Ireland.
Parliamentary History	William Cobbett, *The Parliamentary History of England* (26 vols., London, 1806-20).
P.R.O.	Public Record Office.
P.R.O.N.I.	Public Record Office of Northern Ireland.
R.I.A.	Royal Irish Academy.
R.O.	Record Office.
S.P.O.	State Paper Office, Dublin.
T.C.D.	Trinity College Dublin.

EDITORIAL NOTE

In all quotations, whether from printed works or manuscript sources, spelling, punctuation and capitalization have been modernized, in accordance with the conventions observed in the main body of the text, except in cases where the intention of the original is unclear. 'Old-Style' dates have been converted to 'New Style'. Where contributors have used the same source, in different editions, versions or locations, these differences have not been standardized.

CONTENTS

THE IRISH PARLIAMENT OF 1692

James I. McGuire

The parliament which met in Dublin on 4 October 1692 has an important place in the history of the Irish parliament and, more particularly, in the political and constitutional history of eighteenth-century Ireland. This may seem a surprising assertion for a parliament which sat for only four weeks and which contemporaries saw as a total failure.[1] But the issues raised in this parliament and the political acrimony which accompanied its prorogation led in time to a change in government policy, the adoption of a more sophisticated approach to Irish political management and the emergence of a constitutional *modus vivendi* between executive and parliament. The lessons learned from the failure of 1692 enabled parliament to become a regular part of government over the succeeding century.

Parliament had not been part of the normal governmental process in seventeenth-century Ireland. Indeed only four parliaments met before 1688 and these were convened to answer some particular requirement of government.[2] For the greater part of the century the executive in Dublin governed without the aid or hindrance of the representatives of the political nation and when Charles II's parliament voted a hereditary revenue of more than ample proportions, no new parliament was summoned between its dissolution in 1666 and the Glorious Revolution of 1688.[3] When the government decided to summon a parliament in 1692 it was the first time in over twenty-six years that a government had sought the advice of the Protestant political nation.

The situation in Ireland was in sharp contrast with the emerging constitutional practices of colonial America. By the late 1680s representative assemblies were providing the King's subjects in the colonies with a voice in the government of their territories, and on

1. The lord lieutenant opened parliament on 5 October and prorogued it on 3 November.
2. The following are the dates of the four seventeenth-century Irish parliaments: 1613-15; 1634-5; 1640-41 (47); 1661-6. The Jacobite parliament of 1689 falls into a special category. For an authoritative account see J. G. Simms, *The Jacobite Parliament of 1689* (Dundalk, 1966).
3. On the hereditary revenue, see T. J. Kiernan, *A History of the Financial Administration of Ireland to 1817* (London, 1930), p. 114.

a regular basis as well.[4] What was more remarkable was the fact that these assemblies were in the process of gaining the legislative initiative, an attribute formally denied the Irish parliament under the terms of Poynings' Law. This statute, which restricted the Irish parliament to rejecting or accepting without amendment bills already prepared by the Irish and English Privy Councils, ensured that the Irish legislature was but a pale shadow of its English counterpart.[5] Although a way round this Irish strait-jacket began to emerge in Charles II's parliament, with the drafting of heads of bills by either house for presentation to the Irish Privy Council, the fact that parliament did not meet again after 1666 arrested even this modest development and the letter of the law remained unchanged. The real power remained in the hands of the two Privy Councils, thus ensuring for the executive ultimate control even when parliament was sitting. Indeed, so advantageous were these controls imposed by Poynings' Law in the eyes of the government that an attempt was made in 1678, abortive as it turned out, to impose similar restrictions on the colonial legislatures.[6] By the last decade of the seventeenth-century, therefore, the colonial settlers in America had a greater *de facto* control over the internal government of their territories through the use they might make of their representative assemblies than had the King's loyal and Protestant subjects in Ireland, where the institution of parliament dated from the fourteenth century and the title and status of kingdom from 1541.

In 1691 there was no compelling reason why a parliament sitting in Ireland should be an instrument of the post-war settlement. Although William III, on a number of occasions during the war, had promised to summon an Irish parliament once peace was restored and his authority established, parliament at Westminster had been laying the legislative foundations for an Irish settlement since 1689.[7] Contemporaries assumed that this situation would

4.   Benjamin W. Labaree, *America's Nation-Time: 1607-1789* (Boston, Mass., 1972), pp 70-3.
5.   R. Dudley Edwards and T. W. Moody, 'The History of Poynings' Law: Part I, 1494-1615', *I.H.S.*, ii (1940-41), 415-24; Aidan Clarke, 'The History of Poynings' Law, 1615-41', *ibid.*, xviii (1972), 207-22.
6.   Leonard Woods Labaree, *Royal Government in America: a Study of the British Colonial System before 1783* (New York, 1964), p. 157.
7.   Two English statutes were particularly important. 1 William and Mary, c. 9, declared the acts of the Jacobite parliament to be null and void, while 3 William and Mary, c. 2, appointed new oaths to be taken in Ireland. This

continue. As John Pulteney (subsequently appointed clerk of the Irish Privy Council) put it, in a letter from London, 'a great part of that work [the settlement of Ireland] will be done by our parliament here'.8

There were sound political reasons why the King should think twice before honouring his promise to call a parliament in Dublin. The growing hostility of Irish Protestants towards the Articles of Limerick brought into question the political sense of leaving the ratification of the Articles to the representatives of the Protestant nation, who were increasingly worried both by the implications of the generous terms agreed at Limerick and by the generally tolerant policy of the Dublin government towards the Catholic church and its adherents. This Protestant unease was not unreasonable. With the war just over there was a quite genuine fear that Catholic power, given half a chance, would re-emerge as it had done in the Restoration period and that this might happen in conjunction with an attempt to reinstate James II. Government policy did not seem to offer any satisfactory guarantees against a Catholic revival nor did it seem punitive enough towards those who had put Protestant lives and property in jeopardy. This desire to settle old scores was what the lords justices in Dublin called 'that spirit of revenge'.

For their part the lords justices were endeavouring to uphold the King's treaty obligations to the Catholics, obligations made all the more important by William's anxiety not to damage his alliances with the Catholic states in the war against Louis XIV.9 As an earnest of the government's intention to maintain its policies, Bishop Dopping of Meath was suspended from the Irish Privy Council when he preached a sermon containing 'the most bitter invectives against the whole body of the Irish ... stirring up the people ... to continue their animosities against them'.10 In cir-

latter act precluded Catholics from sitting in any future Irish parliament. From 1689 several attainder bills were discussed in the English parliament but as late as 1694 none of these had been enacted. In this respect see J.G. Simms, *The Williamite Confiscation in Ireland, 1690-1703* (London, 1956), p. 82.
8.   P.R.O.N.I., D.638/15/1 (De Ros Mss.), John Pulteney to Richard Levinge, 29 Oct. 1691.
9.   *H.M.C. Finch*, iii, 305-6, the lords justices to the sheriffs, 19 Nov. 1691; proclamation by the lords justices and Privy Council of Ireland, 14 Oct. 1691.
10.   *H.M.C. Finch*, iii, 304-5, the lords justices to [Nottingham], 30 Nov. 1691; *C.S.P. Dom.*, 1691-2, p. 28, the King's warrant of suspension, 10 Dec. 1691.

cumstances where it was necessary to make an example of the bishop, it was more than likely that the members elected to an Irish parliament would reflect the general antipathy to Catholics in general and government policy in particular.

Every bit as serious were the growing allegations of corruption in the administration of the Irish revenue and of the estates forfeited by Jacobites.[11] These allegations cast even more doubt on the likelihood of the administration's summoning a parliament. James Bonnell, the Irish accountant-general, a devout and unyielding Protestant, implied as much in a letter to Robert Harley, one of the most prominent members of the 'Country party' in the English parliament:

> It is certain the courtiers of this kingdom would endeavour to prevent it [*i.e.* a parliament]; it would be too clamorous against them.[12]

Even after the decision to call a parliament was taken, it was assumed in London that certain members of the Dublin administration were trying to delay for as long as possible the day when parliament must actually convene.[13]

Despite the potential threat of an onslaught on Court policy and personnel, a decision to call a parliament was taken early in 1692. The surviving sources give little indication as to the nature of the deliberations which preceded this decision. However, the Court cannot have been unaware of the threat to the maintenance of the English interest in Ireland if the administration showed that it was not prepared to trust those on whom it relied for the government of the country, particularly at local level, and whose continued preparedness to remain in Ireland was the only ultimate guarantee of a continuing English strategic presence. Furthermore, an Irish parliament, however restive it might be, could enact no legislation hostile to Court policies or interests; the restrictions on

11. Simms, *Williamite Confiscation, passim.*
12. *H.M.C. Portland,* iii, 479-81, [James Bonnell] to Robert Harley, Nov. 1691.
13. *C.S.P. Dom.,* 1691-2, p. 357, Nottingham to the lords justices, 5 July 1692; *ibid.,* p. 380, Sydney to the King, 22 July 1692.

legislative initiatives imposed by Poynings' Law saw to that. A memorandum of advice to the King, drawn up in 1690, put the matter succinctly: to present a government bill to the Irish parliament 'was no more in effect than referring it to yourself, since by the constitution of the government the acts made must be first approved here [Westminster], before they can be admitted or debated there'.[14] Sooner or later one such measure would have to be a money bill, since the hereditary revenue voted by Charles II's parliament could not be expected to meet all the future demands of the government.

It took nine months to put together a legislative programme. The cumbersome requirements of Poynings' Law were complicated by the King's absence on the continent and the Queen's unwillingness to take major decisions on her own. Added to this was the reluctance of government officials in Dublin to hasten the day when parliament must meet, a reluctance combined with a serious problem of overwork and complicated by differences of opinion between Whitehall and Dublin over the content and form of particular bills.[15] The process got under way in January 1692 when the secretary of state, the earl of Nottingham, instructed the lords justices in Dublin to draw up lists of measures necessary for the settlement of Ireland.[16] It had not been completed when parliament assembled the following October. Indeed, of the ten bills eventually laid before parliament only three were ready to be presented at the start of the session. The bulk of the government's legislative programme was only put together after the new lord lieutenant, Viscount Sydney, arrived at the end of August and it was not ready for despatch to England in accordance with the provisions of Poynings' Law until 29 September, six days before parliament was due to assemble. The net result of this delay was that the majority of government bills were not presented to parliament until 24 October or later.

14. *C.S.P. Dom.*, 1691-2, p. 66. Although this is included in the Calendar for 1691, internal evidence makes it clear that is was written in 1690. The same is true of another memorandum (*ibid.*, pp 67-71), where the Irish parliament is referred to in similar terms as having 'only a negative voice, a power of rejecting or refusing'.
15. At a later stage I hope to publish an analysis of the drafting procedures in both Dublin and Whitehall prior to the 1692 parliament.
16. *C.S.P. Dom.*, 1691-2, p. 103, Nottingham to the lords justices, 16 Jan. 1692; *ibid.*, pp 111-12, same to Chief Justice Reynell, 26 Jan. 1692.

Land, defence and supply were the three main concerns of the Court's legislative programme. Of these the land question was the most difficult to incorporate into a legislative settlement. To keep its policy intact the Court had to find a formula which would give coherence to contradictory interests, on the one hand preserving the King's promises to the Catholics, while on the other avoiding any provocation to his Protestant followers. The Court's attempt to provide a flexible settlement was enshrined in a bill for confirming the Acts of Settlement and Explanation. The purpose of the confirmatory bill was to deal with the post-war land problem within the overall context of the Restoration settlement of 1662 and 1665. It was destined not to reach the statute book.[17]

The land settlement, whatever form it might take or whatever interests it might be intended to satisfy, would be of purely academic interest if the military resources to support the state were insufficient, undisciplined or unpopular. James II's Catholic subjects had learned that lesson to their cost in 1690, when the legislation of the Jacobite parliament was negatived by the defeat of James II's forces on the battlefield. The administration was anxious, therefore, both to regulate the legal position of the army in Ireland and to provide for a militia by mutiny and militia acts respectively.[18] In both cases there were contemporary English precedents which might be adapted to Irish circumstances though the measures contemplated for Ireland turned out to be but pale imitations.[19]

While the purpose of the Militia Bill was strategic, the significance of the Mutiny Bill was greater than its military application might suggest. The main function of any mutiny bill was to provide for a code of discipline within the army and to protect civilians from military plunder, a particularly explosive issue in Williamite Ireland. Historians, however, have generally interpreted the English mutiny acts passed in the years following the Glorious

17. *C.S.P. Dom.*, 1691-2, p. 362, Nottingham to the lords justices, 21 July 1692; *ibid.*, 1695 and Addenda, pp 190-2, the lords justices and Privy Council of Ireland to [the lords of the Council], 21 July 1692; *ibid.*, 1691-2, pp 394-5, [R. Yard] to Sir Joseph Williamson, 2 Aug. 1692.
18. *C.S.P. Dom.*, 1691-2, p. 129, heads of acts received from the lords justices of Ireland, with remarks thereon, 6 Feb. 1692; *ibid.*, 1695 and Addenda, pp 198-99, Sydney to Nottingham, 3 Sept. 1692.
19. *An Account of the Sessions of Parliament in Ireland, 1692* (London, 1693), pp 21-22.

Revolution as having a wider significance than their title would suggest. It has generally been argued that the time limit of one year placed on their duration suggested an acceptance of the principle enshrined in the Bill of Rights requiring annual parliamentary approval for a standing army.[20] In 1692, when a mutiny bill was prepared for Ireland, it fell far short of what had been enacted in England. While the drafts of the original bill do not survive, an opposition pamphleteer claimed subsequently that it contained 'not one fifth part' of the English act. In particular it was alleged that those sections of the English Mutiny Act which dealt with 'the good of the subject and the kingdom in general', especially that part obliging officers to 'orderly quarters, faithful payment of the soldiers and to just and true musters', were omitted and, what was even worse, the duration of the Irish bill was to be three years and not one.[21] In other words, the Court sponsored an Irish mutiny bill but used the Poynings' Law procedure to prepare an emasculated version of the English statute. In any event the bill was also to be defeated in the Commons on the last day of the session.[22]

The lord lieutenant's request for the granting of supply at the opening of parliament, the subsequent disputes over the money bills, and the emphasis which Sydney placed on the money bill issue at the prorogation, have misled historians into thinking that supply was initially high on the Court's list of priorities for the first session of the parliament.[23] The fact of the matter is that the Court had no intention of seeking supplies in this first session. It was Sydney himself, after his arrival in Ireland, who decided that circumstances were favourable to a request for money. Indeed, it was his view that the requirements of government made it a virtual

20. The traditional view has been challenged by Jennifer Carter in 'The Revolution and the Constitution', *Britain after the Glorious Revolution, 1689-1714* ed. Geoffrey Holmes (London, 1969), p. 44.
21. *Account of the Sessions*, pp 22-4.
22. *C.J.I.*, ii, 34.
23. W. E. H. Lecky considered that this was the only reason why the parliament was convened — Lecky, i, 440. The same view was held by Kiernan, *Financial Administration*, p. 106. J. A. Froude, *The English in Ireland in the Eighteenth Century* (3 vols., London, 1872-4), i, 225, and J. T. Gilbert, *An Account of the Parliament House, Dublin* (Dublin, 1896), p. 10, saw it as one of the reasons for summoning a parliament.

necessity, for without some increase in revenue it would be impossible to administer the country effectively. But it was Sydney's own initiative:

> I hope I shall not be blamed for endeavouring to get some money for Their Majesties of the parliament here, though I do it without their order.[24]

Three money bills were prepared at the Dublin Council board in September and were despatched to London along with the other bills at the end of September.[25] It seems never to have occurred to Sydney or the Council that the Commons might seek more power in financial affairs than merely the right to endorse or veto a bill prepared at the Privy Council. From the Court's point of view, of course, this was the undoubted value of the safeguards provided by Poynings' Law.

The competence of the English parliament to legislate for Ireland did not become a serious issue in Protestant Ireland until the end of the decade; nevertheless, the Court was not unaware of the imperial dimension in 1692. While preparing the legislative programme the law officers in London were watchful that no bill should be presented to the Irish parliament which implied a lack of legal authority or binding force in any of the statutes which the English parliament had enacted for Ireland since the accession of William and Mary. A draft bill for 'derogating the old oaths of supremacy and uniformity and appointing new ones' was an important casualty of the lawyers' scrutiny. It was argued that the enactment of such a measure by the Irish legislature would be tantamount to suggesting that the English statute of 1691, which specifically dealt with Ireland, required re-enactment in Dublin to be effective, or, at the least, unassailable. For this reason, the draft bill was abandoned and others were modified. All of which underlines the immense usefulness of the Poynings' Law procedures for the administration, for not only were the Court's land, defence and revenue policies enshrined in the bills to be laid before parlia-

24. *C.S.P. Dom.*, 1695 and Addenda, p. 203, Sydney to Nottingham, 18 Sept. 1692. J. C. Beckett, in *The Making of Modern Ireland, 1603-1923* (London, 1966), p. 183, has indicated that money was not originally expected from the opening session.
25. *C.S.P. Dom.*, 1695 and Addenda, pp 107-8, Sydney to Nottingham, 19 Sept. 1692.

ment but the administration could also ensure that the English parliament remained the ultimate legislative authority.[26]

The Court's assiduous attention to legislative detail was not matched by any corresponding political forethought. The lord lieutenant, Sydney, was certainly aware of the potential for discontent and his despatches to London from the time of his arrival in Dublin at the end of August showed that he realised that there was a need for some politic adroitness in handling the Privy Council. He claimed much later to have consulted during the period of preparation those who later led the parliamentary opposition, particularly to the government's money bills, and that in the weeks before parliament it was they who urged him to seek money in the first place.[27] They may have deliberately misled him, or he may not have been capable of comprehending the political atmosphere. The fact of the matter is that his only serious concern before parliament met was the danger of an eruption of anti-Catholic feeling. Generally he exuded optimism.[28]

It may be that Sydney was too isolated from the mainstream of political comment and discussion, surrounded by Privy Councillors whom he wrongly saw as a microcosm of the political nation. Certainly it is curious that he did not advert to the possibility of a major investigation into the allegations of official corruption which were widespread. Indeed, on the occasions when he mentioned the dangerous question of the administration of the revenue and the forfeited estates, it seemed as if he feared opposition more from those whose malpractices might be uncovered by a government commission of enquiry, which he was planning to inaugurate after the prorogation, than from the probings of members of the committee of grievances in the House of Commons.[29]

Sydney was not a happy choice as viceroy. Rightly or wrongly, he himself was not untainted in the public eye by the allegations of corruption or self-advancement. His Achilles' heel

26. *H.M.C. Finch*, iv, 53-55, 67-8, 216, Nottingham to William Blathwayt, 1, 12 Apr., 10 June 1692; *C.S.P. Dom.*, 1695 and Addenda, pp 190-2, the lords justices and Privy Council of Ireland to [the lords of the Council], 21 July 1692.
27. *C.S.P. Dom.*, 1695 and Addenda, pp 217-18, Sydney to Nottingham, 6 Nov. 1792.
28. *Ibid.*, p. 205, Sydney to Nottingham, 28 Sept. 1692.
29. *Ibid.*, p. 203, Sydney to Nottingham, 18 Sept. 1692.

was his personal holdings of forfeited estates. Early in 1692 a bill was debated in the English Commons which contained a clause directing Sydney to surrender his Irish estates in exchange for others.[30]   Though it never became law it can have done little to increase his prestige as viceroy-designate. His critics added to the list of his shortcomings.   According to William King, bishop of Derry, reports were spread abroad that Sydney sold places, indulged papists and favoured Dissenters, a combination of sins unlikely to be forgiven or overlooked by the political nation in Williamite Ireland.[31]   In this respect his earlier association with the government of Ireland – he was a lord justice in 1690 when the main lines of the unpopular land and religious policies were being laid out – was a most unpromising apprenticeship for those who hoped to see a radical shift away from the pragmatic policies pursued by William's government since 1690. Although a good Whig – he was after all one of the leading conspirators who persuaded William of Orange to invade England – his influence after the Revolution rested more on his personal friendship with the King than on any political following of his own or on any proven diplomatic skills.[32]

Apart from the viceroy, the two most important office-holders in Dublin were the lord chancellor, Sir Charles Porter, and the vice-treasurer, Lord Coningsby.   In the political context of 1692 both men were political liabilities. Coningsby had been one of the lords justices since September 1690 and Porter had joined the commission in December of the same year. In consequence both men were associated in the public mind with the policies and corruption of the Irish administration. They had both signed the Articles of Limerick in October 1691 and had upheld the terms of the Articles throughout the following year.[33] While Coningsby's political outlook was Whig, Porter was a Tory in politics and he had served James II as lord chancellor of Ireland until his removal

---

30.   Simms, *Williamite Confiscation*, p. 85.
31.   T.C.D., Lyons Mss., 264a. This document is in the form of notes for an extended letter or pamphlet on the parliament of 1692. However, no expansion of these notes in letter or any other form appears to be extant.
32.   G. N. Clark, *The Later Stuarts, 1660-1714* (Oxford, 1934), p. 175. On appointing Sydney secretary of state in England in 1690, King William is reputed to have remarked, 'he will do till I find a fit man; and he will be quite willing to resign when I find such a man' (quoted in *The Dictionary of National Biography, sub* Sydney).
33.   J. G. Simms, *Jacobite Ireland, 1685-91* (London, 1969), pp 258-65.

from that office at Tyrconnell's suggestion in 1687.[34] It was from these men that Sydney took over the management of affairs in September 1692, although both of them, as major office-holders, remained at the centre of power under the new lord lieutenant. So Sydney not only inherited the unpopularity of the lords justices and administration but continued to rely on their services as well.

Sydney's political awakening began on the day parliament assembled. On that very evening he heard that Sir Francis Brewster, soon to emerge as one of the key opposition leaders, was organizing political cabals and was likely to cause trouble for reasons that had as much to do with English politics as with Irish grievances.[35] The next day the lord lieutenant was bemoaning the lack of bills to keep parliament occupied, a rather surprising complaint from one who had despatched the main part of his legislative proposals to London only six days earlier.[36] Nevertheless, Sydney was forecasting accurately what the Commons would do with time on their hands and plenty to complain about. In the days which followed, the political atmosphere, particularly in the Commons, intensified to such an extent that within a fortnight Sydney was telling Nottingham that they had 'begun like a company of madmen'.[37]

Despite the fact that most members were parliamentary novices in 1692, in the opening days of the session both Houses did all the things an English parliament in the seventeenth century might have been expected to do. A large majority of the Commons were too young to have sat in final sessions of Charles II's parliament twenty-six years earlier, though there were about thirty veterans from that parliament as well as other members, like the Speaker, who were simultaneously members of the English parliament as well. By and large, however, members of the 1692 parliament had no previous parliamentary experience and so *ad hoc* committees were established in the early days of the session to cope with a variety of procedural difficulties. In the Commons these search committees were usually composed of lawyers, whose professional training enabled them to appreciate the significance of the parliamentary records. Naturally the perusal of these records frequently

34.   *Ibid.,* pp 33, 185-9.
35.   *C.S.P. Dom.,* 1695 and Addenda, p. 209, Sydney to Nottingham, 6 Oct. 1692.
36.   *Ibid.,* pp 208-9.
37.   *Ibid.,* p. 213, Sydney to Nottingham, 17 Oct. 1692.

brought a committee back to the parliaments of 1613, 1634 and 1640. Such excursions into the parliamentary past must have had an important educative effect on those engaged in the search, bringing to their notice earlier controversies and claims as well as the more routine ordering of the House's business.[38]

Apart from these *ad hoc* committees, the traditional standing committees, of elections and privileges, grievances, religion and trade, were established at the outset.[39] It was the Commons' committee of grievances in particular which played a crucial part in undermining the policies and the authority of the Court through its investigations into the allegations of malpractice in the administration of the revenue and of the forfeited estates.

While the meeting of parliament provided an opportunity for the airing of grievances, it is unlikely that the political onslaught directed against the Court could have been so well focused without the sustained efforts of certain members with an ability to dominate and manipulate a majority in the Commons. The sources are too slight to build up a comprehensive view of the personnel of the opposition, but it is possible to gain a reasonably accurate picture of the main participants from the recurrence of certain names among those chosen to serve on committees and also from the anxious accounts which Sydney sent to London. Two groups of opposition leaders are identifiable: on the one hand those whom Sydney called 'English troublemakers', and on the other a small group of discontented lawyers.

Not all the lawyers in the Commons were enemies to the Court, but a hard core of five or six caused Sydney considerable anxiety. On the occasion when he complained that the Commons were behaving 'like a company of madmen', he went on to castigate those lawyers who were dominating the proceedings of the House and doing 'what they please, and they are certainly the greatest enemies to the King in the kingdom'.[40] In his retrospective notes

38. Bishop Anthony Dopping of Meath published the 'Modus Tenendi Parliamenta in Hibernia' and, more relevantly perhaps, Scobell's procedural handbook, shortly before parliament convened: Anthony [Dopping], Lord Bishop of Meath, *Modus Tenendi Parliamenta in Hibernia ... To which is Added the Rules and Customs of the House Gathered out of the Journal Books from the Time of Edward the Sixth*, by H. S. E. C. P. (Dublin, [1692]).
39. *C.J.I.*, ii, 12-13.
40. *C.S.P. Dom.*, 1695 and Addenda, p. 213, Sydney to Nottingham, 17 Oct. 1692.

on the 1692 parliament Bishop King supported Sydney's strictures with the comment that members had paid too much attention to the 'harangues of lawyers'.[41] It is true that the sort of constitutional claims which the Commons made must have had the professional expertise of lawyers to frame them and to find arguments and precedents to support them. However, professional *esprit de corps* will not suffice to explain the motivations of the lawyer politicians.

Thwarted ambition lay behind the political stance of at least some of these lawyers. John Osborne, the prime serjeant, is perhaps the most important example. A member of practically all the Commons committees, it was he whom Sydney largely blamed for the upheavals in the Commons.[42] The fact that Osborne, as prime serjeant, was a lesser office-holder does not make his opposition unusual. Indeed his very position as prime serjeant may have been in itself an understandable reason for his bitterness. At one stage he had seemed a likely candidate for the chief justiceship of the common pleas but his candidacy had collapsed before ratification, very likely because of his attempts in 1690 to discredit those Protestants who had remained in Ireland under James II's government.[43] In 1692 his preferment prospects were bleak, since the post of prime serjeant was usually a stepping-stone to judicial appointment, not a substitute for the chief justiceship of the common pleas.[44] It was poorly paid. When Sydney dismissed Osborne as prime serjeant in November, he had some difficulty in finding a successor, so meagre was the financial reward.[45]

41. T.C.D., Lyons Mss., 264a. I wish to thank the Board of Trinity College Dublin, for permission to quote from Mss. in the college library.
42. *C.S.P. Dom.,* 1695 and Addenda, p. 215, Sydney to Nottingham, 22 Oct. 1692.
43. F. E. Ball, *The Judges in Ireland, 1221-1921* (2 vols., New York, 1927), ii, 8. Osborne's attitude had been made clear in 1690, when he sought, through a motion in chancery, to have all Protestants who had acted in any civil employment in Ireland under Kind James charged with high treason. A copy of the motion is in N.L.I., Ms. 2,055.
44. The office of prime serjeant was peculiar to Ireland (see Beckett, *Making of Modern Ireland*, p. 189). Alan Brodrick, the third serjeant, was also one of the troublesome lawyers in 1692. See below, n. 101.
45. *C.S.P. Dom.,* 1695 and Addenda, p. 222, Sydney to Nottingham, 13 Dec. 1692. In this letter Sydney remarked, 'I believe you will find it difficult to persuade a man who is good for anything to come hither for that employment, which is only worth £30 a year, besides his practice'.

The so-called 'English troublemakers' posed a more serious threat to the survival of Sydney's administration in the long run. They concentrated on the mismanagement of the forfeited estates, an issue much used by the Country opposition in the English parliament in the same period.[46] The three whom Sydney named specifically were James Hamilton, James Sloane and Sir Francis Brewster.[47] To say that these men were 'English' troublemakers, sent over from England, is not to say that they had no connections with Ireland and were found seats simply to cause trouble. In fact each of them was a substantial landowner in Ireland and a member of a Protestant settler family. Hamilton and Sloane were related to each other, while Brewster was a considerable landowner in Kerry.[48] They were 'English' troublemakers in the sense that they had strong connections with the English Country opposition, and so their opposition to Sydney's administration had as much to do with the wider issues of English politics as with the more specific grievances of Protestant Ireland. When Sydney reported to Nottingham that Brewster was making unfavourable remarks in Dublin about the secretary of state, the latter did not seem particularly surprised and had clearly anticipated an extension of English political battles into Ireland.[49] Events were to bear out these fears. The correspondence of Robert Harley shows that one of the most formidable members of the English Country party was being kept informed of events in Dublin, and both Brewster and Sloane in the following February presented statements to the English parliament detailing alleged abuses in Ireland.[50]

Court and Country are probably the most useful terms for describing the political divisions in the Irish parliament of 1692. A few years later the distinction between Whig and Tory became

46. Simms, *Williamite Confiscation*, pp 82-95; Dennis Rubini, *Court and Country, 1688-1702* (London, 1967), pp 157-68.
47. *C.S.P. Dom.*, 1695 and Addenda, pp 209, 215, Sydney to Nottingham, 6, 22 Oct. 1692. Sydney writes of 'Mr Hambleton', but it is clear from other sources that he is referring to James Hamilton.
48. Both the Sloanes and the Hamiltons originated in Ayrshire and settled in Ulster in the early seventeenth century. For the Hamiltons see M. Perceval-Maxwell, *The Scottish Migration to Ulster in the Reign of James I* (London, 1973), *passim*; for the Sloanes and their connections, E. St John Brooks, *Sir Hans Sloane: The Great Collector and his Circle* (London, 1954), pp 24-5. There is an entry on Sir Francis Brewster in the *D.N.B.*
49. *C.S.P. Dom.*, 1691-2, p. 480, Nottingham to Sydney, 14 Oct. 1692.
50. *H.M.C. Portland*, iii, *passim; Commons' Journals*, x, 826-33.

more significant but this was not so in the rudimentary atmosphere of 1692. At its simplest the Court and Country division was a distinction between those who held office and those who did not. It was the very term which Bishop King's friend and correspondent, George Tollet, used when writing from London a fortnight after the session opened.[51] He had learned from Dublin that there was a fear of the Irish parliament 'dividing into a Court and Country party'. This does not imply two rigid groups facing each other in organized combat; rather it suggests those who supported the Court and its policies for reasons of profit or principle, as opposed to the uncommitted but generally dissatisfied members who were prepared to follow in the footsteps of those who best articulated their grievances. What is remarkable about the politics of 1692 is the apparent universality of Country sentiments in the Commons, evidenced by the failure of the Court to challenge divisions on fundamental issues on the floor of the House. While a notable fallacy among historians in the past was their failure to realize that 'parliament' and the 'Commons' were made up of individuals and rarely responded as a single unit with a single mind on any issue, in the Dublin parliament of 1692 the Commons came remarkably close to unanimity on a large number of issues.

From the start of the session it was clear that the Commons were not merely emulating the procedures of the English parliament but were doing so in a determined effort to tip the scales of political power in favour of the Protestant nation and away from the stifling control of the executive. Sydney witnessed events uncomprehendingly and wrote somewhat hysterically to London that the Commons 'talk of freeing themselves from the yoke of England, of taking away Poynings' Law, of making an address to have a habeas corpus bill and twenty other extravagant discourses have been amongst them'.[52] In fact this was not separatist feeling but a welling-up of Country sentiment, a phenomenon that is fully explicable once it is remembered that Ireland had been governed exclusively by the executive for almost twenty-six years, and that those years had seen the Protestant nation at best forced to concede some of the gains of the 1650s and at worst, and latterly, facing complete annihilation. Experience had shown that executive government alone was no guarantee of Protestant security; indeed,

51. T.C.D., Lyons Mss., 240, George Tollet to Bishop King, 18 Oct. 1692.
52. *C.S.P. Dom.*, 1695 and Addenda, p. 213, Sydney to Nottingham, 17 Oct. 1692.

quite the reverse. So the fundamental constitutional aim in 1692 was to restore to the Protestant political nation the power and influence it had not enjoyed in the government of Ireland since 1666. Parliament was to be both the instrument of this restoration and the guarantee of its future preservation. With this end in view the leaders of parliamentary opinion led a successful attack on the Court's legislative programme and substituted a rival one of their own; they formulated constitutional claims designed to give the Commons a genuine control of the supply; above all, they successfully orchestrated a concerted attack on Court policy and personnel. It amounted to a formidable assertion of parliamentary authoity.

This rejection of virtually two thirds of the meticulously prepared government bills amounted to a full-scale repudiation of Court policy. In all, ten bills were presented during the session, three at the beginning and the remaining seven between 24 October and the beginning of November. Of the four which passed through all stages to the royal assent, three were uncontentious and the fourth, a money bill, falls into a special category and requires separate treatment.[53] The six other bills represented the main strands of government policy and none of these reached the statute book.

The intense hostility of the political nation to the Court's policies on land and towards Roman Catholics, issues closely linked in any case, lay behind the rejection of the Bill for confirming the Acts of Settlement and Explanation and the Bill declaring void the Attainders and other Acts of the Jacobite parliament of 1689.[54] This latter measure made provision for the burning by the common hangman of the official records of the 1689 parliament. As such it might have been expected to be a popular bill in the assertively Protestant mood of 1692. It was rejected, however, because in the words of an opposition pamphleteer, 'the House found it for Their Majesties' service and the honour of the Protestants of Ireland to preserve the records of the Irish barbarity'.[55] Very likely this is a reiteration of an argument used in the Commons against giving the bill a second reading. In Protestant eyes the legislation of 1689 was

53. The following acts were passed in 1692: (1) an Act of Recognition (2) an Act for Encouragement of Protestant Strangers (3) an Act for an Additional Duty of Excise upon Beer, Ale and other Liquors (4) an Act for taking Affidavits in the Country.
54. *Account of the Sessions,* pp 12-13.
55. *Ibid.,* p. 13.

documentary proof of the Catholic and Jacobite objectives and the
Attainder Bill was a virtual Protestant roll of honour. Similarly, the
rejection of the government measure for confirming the Restoration
settlement was posthumously justified on the grounds that it actually put at risk the security of Protestant landowners, a reasonable enough argument in the light of the changes that had occurred
since 1665 and within the confines of the Restoration settlement.

The explanations given *post factum* for the rejection of these
government measures might seem to be no more than rationaliza-
tions, but it would be unwise not to credit them with considerable
significance in gaining the defeat of the bills. Popular fears ran
deep in the Protestant nation, for it seemed that government policy
would lead in time to another Catholic resurgence. James Bonnell,
secretary to the forfeiture commissioners, expressed these forebod-
ings when he wrote to a friend in the middle of October that there
was 'no prospect of the Irish interest weakening or popery losing
ground' and that Irish Protestants were like the colonists in New
England, 'among the natives of whom they are always in danger'.[56]

No single issue was of greater significance in the minds of
Irish Protestants than the security of their estates. They might
share with the political nation in England a whole set of aversions
and prejudices, from revenue corruption to the dangers of arbitrary
government, but the land question, linked as it was to the Catholic
threat, was a problem peculiar to Ireland and one which added to
the Country opposition there a dimension which its English counterpart lacked. Events in 1641 and more recently in 1689 had
underlined the hazardous nature of the Protestant presence in
Ireland. It was no time for the government to attempt a policy of
balancing Protestant and Catholic interests.

The principles which informed English Country sentiment
were basic to the rejection of the Militia and Mutiny Bills. Here
were measures whose ostensible purposes were obviously welcome
but which had been drawn up in such a way as to underline the
'second-class citizen' status of the King's subjects in Ireland. The
Irish Militia Bill, it was argued, gave too much power to the
executive, excluded specific provisions of the English act and
showed little regard for the realities of Irish life in the counties,
where the militia must be raised.[57] Naturally there was an anxiety

56.   T.C.D., Ms. 1.6.13 (transcripts of Strype letters in Cambridge University
Library), fos. 189-90, James Bonnell to Rev. John Strype, 18 Oct. 1692.
57.   *Account of the Sessions*, p. 21.

to demonstrate that in rejecting this bill the Commons were not acting out of a comprehensive desire to thwart the government at every turn, and so a committee was appointed to draft the heads of a more acceptable militia bill, a task which had not been completed at the prorogation.[58]

The Mutiny Bill was lost in similar circumstances. Like the Militia Bill, its provisions fell far short of its English equivalents. Whereas the duration of an English mutiny act was one year, the Irish bill was to last three years. In addition many of the clauses which appeared annually in the English acts were studiously omitted from the Irish version.[59] It is reasonable to argue that the rejection of both these measures was tantamount to an assertion that the Englishman in Ireland was in no sense an inferior Englishman, exempt from the benefits of living in England itself and forced to accept the dictates of what was widely seen as a corrupt and wrong-headed administration.

But it was not enough to reject the Court's legislative programme. Even before the bulk of the government bills were returned from London, the Commons endorsed the proposals of a select committee suggesting an alternative selection of bills.[60] In the main these consisted of existing English statutes which might be adapted to Irish circumstances and re-enacted by the Dublin parliament. Some of the suggested measures were essentially utilitarian, designed to speed up the administration of justice or to provide for the maintenance of roads or the protection of woods. Others, however, were clearly intended to provide for the English in Ireland such legal safeguards of the subject's rights as were already enshrined in English statute law. Chief among these was the suggestion that the English Habeas Corpus Act of 1679 be re-enacted in Ireland, a suggestion which caused Sydney some alarm.[61] But the Commons were not acting irresponsibly and ignoring Irish conditions, for they recommended that a proviso be added to the proposed bill, limiting its application to Protestants.[62] In other words it was not an undiscriminating attempt to confer the blessings of English liberty on all and sundry, rather it was the liberty of the

58. *C.J.I.,* ii, 30.
59. *Account of the Sessions,* pp 22-4.
60. *C.J.I.,* ii, 19-20.
61. *C.S.P. Dom.*, 1695 and Addenda, p. 213, Sydney to Nottingham, 17 Oct. 1692.
62. *C.J.I.*, ii, 19.

Protestant subject that was at issue. Liberty and security were synonymous in post-Revolution Ireland.

At first sight there seems something pedantic about the proposal that the English Act abolishing Star Chamber, passed in 1641, should be re-enacted in Ireland. Admittedly the court of Castle Chamber, the Irish equivalent, had never been formally abolished by statute law nor had the other prerogative courts in the provinces. Nevertheless, Castle Chamber had ceased to function in 1641 and the provincial prerogative courts had disappeared with the abolition of the presidencies in 1672.[63] Why, then, bother to enact a statute which would have no practical effect? The answer may well lie not in the main intention of the 1641 act but in the specific controls it placed on the King and Privy Council, particularly on their authority 'to examine or draw into question, determine or dispose of the lands, tenements, hereditaments, goods or chattels of any of the subjects of this kingdom; that the same ought to be tried and determined in the ordinary courts of justice and by the ordinary course of the law'. If such a clause were included in an Irish act an effective stop would be applied to the current proceedings of the Dublin Privy Council in adjudicating the land claims arising both from the Articles of Limerick and the post-war forfeitures.[64] So, far from being a somewhat academic attempt to bring Ireland into line with constitutional change in England, the suggested re-enactment of the 1641 act would have inhibited the government from carrying out its post-war land policy and deprived the Irish Privy Council of one of its more significant roles.

But it was one thing for parliament-men to propose alternative bills to those prepared by the government; it was quite another matter to see those bills through the conciliar and parliamentary processes and into the statute book. Since Poynings' Law, particularly from Strafford's time, placed formidable obstacles in the way of any parliamentary initiative, the second stage in the opposition's three-pronged attack on the administration centred on the question of parliament's control of supply and, in particular, the drafting of money bills, the key to political power at a time when the hereditary revenue was no longer adequate to meet all the expenses of government.[65] Therefore, when the two Money Bills prepared at

63. See Liam Irwin, 'The Lord Presidency of Munster 1625-72' (Nat. Univ. Ireland M.A. thesis 1976).
64. Simms, *Williamite Confiscation,* pp 46-7 and *passim.*
65. Kiernan, *Financial Administration,* p. 114 and *passim.*

Sydney's behest were returned from London and laid before parliament, the opposition leaders persuaded the Commons to make a stand on principle and to assert that it was the House's 'sole right' to decide the 'ways and means' of raising money and also to prepare the heads of bills for raising supply. Having passed these heady motions, the Commons then threw out one of the Money Bills on the grounds that they had had no part in preparing its heads, but the other bill was allowed to proceed through all its stages because of the 'exigencies' of affairs.[66]

The significance of these parliamentary claims was considerable. Their effect would be to shift the legislative and political initiative in Ireland from the executive to parliament, leaving the Council with only its more formal functions in the preparation of money bills and, in the course of time, whatever other measures a parliamentary majority might press for. In claiming the right to initiate the heads of money bills the Commons were not infringing on the provisions of Poynings' Law, for they were not, technically, claiming the right to initiate and prepare the actual bills themselves. This approach ensured that the principle of parliamentary control of taxation was vindicated while the legal bounds of the Irish constitution were not encroached upon. It could hardly be said that it was an evasion of Poynings' Law. The spirit of that law, the intention of its legislators, bears little or no relation to the circumstances of the 1690s. The changing uses of Poynings' Law between 1495 and 1692 showed that the letter of the law was what mattered.[67] Even in Charles II's Irish parliament the practice of the Commons drawing up heads of bills, including money bills, was becoming an accepted procedure.[68] What was new in 1692 was that the Commons had voted it their 'sole right' both to decide the 'ways and means' of raising money and to initiate the heads of money bills. In England claims of this sort by the Commons were directed against the House of Lords.[69] In Ireland they were intended primarily to diminish the role and the power of the Privy Council.

The rejection of one of the Money Bills, together with the constitutional claims which the financial question had sparked off,

66. *C.J.I.*, ii, 28.
67. Dr Aidan Clarke has shown how Strafford used Poynings' Law to the government's advantage: Clarke, *'Hist. Poynings' Law.'*
68. Fergus M. O'Donoghue, 'Parliament in Ireland under Charles II' (Nat. Univ. Ire. M.A. thesis 1970), p. 99.
69. Carter, *'The Revolution and the Constitution'*, p. 49.

caused Sydney much embarrassment. After all, it was the lord lieutenant himself who had recommended the preparation of money bills after he had assessed the financial needs of the government and adjudged the political climate to be favourable. At the prorogation on 3 November he lectured the Commons on the course the session had taken, telling them that they had 'not answered the ends for which they were called together', and declared unequivocally that the Commons did not have a sole right to initiate financial legislation, a stand on principle which must have surprised some of his audience, who would not have been unaware of the fact that he had been prepared to compromise on the sole right issue in the hope of salvaging the Money Bills. With the session at an end, however, he was anxious to put the record straight lest future sessions of the parliament might raise the issue again. He ordered that a written protest be entered in the journals of both Houses.[70] Parallels with earlier times are discernible. It was reminiscent of events in 1635, and more especially of 1640 when Wentworth had reminded parliament of their limited powers as legislators under Poynings' Law.[71] Parliament-men were not the only inheritors of precedent.

Paradoxically, the Commons' vote on the sole right issue provided Sydney with a useful smoke-screen behind which to hide the more immediate and pressing need for prorogation on 3 November, the course which the enquiries of the committee of grievances was taking into allegations of corruption and embezzlement in the management of the revenue and the forfeited estates. This was the most damaging aspect of the opposition's tripartite attack on the administration's men and measures in October 1692. Since the early days of the session the committee had been building up their case against those who were reputed to have diverted public funds to their own private uses. After an enquiry spread over three weeks the evidence assembled by the committee pointed to a former commissioner of the revenue, William Culliford, as having misappropriated public funds and the revenue from the forfeited estates. Others, too, were reputed to be implicated, and by the end of October it was said that the only consideration holding back some members of the Commons from assenting to the naming of names was 'the greater characters they bore'.[72] By 3 November charges had been formulated against Culliford on grounds of for-

---

70. *C.J.I.*, ii, 35-6; *Account of the Sessions*, p. 26. It seems that Sydney modified part of his speech before having it printed.
71. Clarke, *'Hist. Poynings' Law'*, 212-13.
72. *C.J.I.*, ii, 16-17, 20, 27; *Account of the Sessions*, p. 18.

feiture embezzlements and these were to be discussed on the following day, but the prorogation forestalled this. Within the very hour of Sydney's arrival at the Lords for the prorogation ceremony the Commons were about to consider another report on the forfeited estates which 'represented discoveries of very great consequence, drawn from the accounts relating to the forfeited Irish estates both real and personal'.[73]

Bishop King commented with delicate irony that the lord lieutenant by his abrupt prorogation had given occasion of criticism to those who suspected him of siding with corrupt officers. Others put it less delicately. The opposition pamphlet, the *Account of the Sessions*, spoke of those 'who dreaded the proceedings of the House, [and who] were to the misfortune of this nation, in so great credit with His Excellency'.[74] Some two weeks after the prorogation Robert Harley indicated how it was being interpreted, indeed how it was to be used, by the Country opposition in England:

> Lord Coningsby came yesterday to the House. It is whispered that had the parliament sat a day longer in Ireland, he would have been impeached or voted an enemy to the public, but the viceroy, his friend, prorogued them.[75]

Three months later the value to the English opposition of Sydney's *debacle* in Ireland became fully apparent.

Meanwhile Sydney had some explaining to do. In a letter to Nottingham he made no mention of the revenue or forfeiture investigations, not even as a contributory factor, in his decision to prorogue parliament so abruptly. Instead he reiterated his stand on the Money Bill question. He explained away his delay of nearly a week after the Commons' votes on the 'sole right' before proroguing parliament with the rather artificial excuse that he was waiting for the votes to be printed.[76] In spite of his public and private explanations it seems clear that the reasons for the precipitate prorogation should be sought in his concern to avoid the con-

73. *Account of the Sessions*, p. 24.
74. T.C.D., Lyons Mss., 264a; *Account of the Sessions*, p. 27.
75. *H.M.C. Portland*, iii, 507, Robert Harley to Sir Edward Harley, 17 Nov. 1692. Coningsby sat for Leominster in the English House of Commons.
76. *C.S.P. Dom.*, 1695 and Addenda, p. 218, Sydney to Nottingham, 6 Nov. 1692.

sequences of the Commons' enquiries. His only weapon was to send them home.

The prorogation ended the session but it did not put an end to the political crisis. Not wishing to let matters rest, indeed realizing the full potential of the circumstances surrounding the abrupt end to the session, the opposition leaders decided to carry the argument to the English mainland. Four members, obviously those who intended to conduct the debate on the forfeiture abuses, petitioned Sydney for permission to go to England 'to solicit for the Protestant and English interest' of Ireland.[77] To this request Sydney, not surprisingly, took considerable exception, commenting that if the petitioners wished to send agents to England to ask the King's pardon 'for the factious and riotous assemblies which have been made in this town since the prorogation', they would be doing well.

Sydney seems to have lost all sense of political reality in the atmosphere of political turmoil which prevailed in Dublin after the prorogation. He first contemplated prosecuting the petitioners — for what is not clear — and then decided to dismiss John Osborne from his position as prime serjeant.[78] Sydney allowed the atmosphere of animosity to percolate through his court to such an extent that one of the opposition leaders came close to a physical confrontation with members of the lord lieutenant's retinue. [79]

If the ministry in England was already concerned at the extent of the political onslaught on the Irish administration in the Dublin parliament, it became increasingly concerned at the consequences of Sydney's impolitic behaviour after the prorogation. In mid-November James Sloane arrived in London and immediately started to vilify the Dublin administration, in particular the treatment he had personally received at Sydney's court.[80] So concerned was the secretary of state that he wrote to Sydney what amounted to a

77. On 9 November Sydney reported to Nottingham: 'the gentlemen who intended to do mischief are very angry at it [the prorogation] and have had seditious meetings to consider what they were to do. At last they brought me the enclosed petition' (*C.S.P. Dom.,* 1695 and Addenda, pp 218-19). The petitioners were Sir Robert King, Sir Arthur Rawdon, Sir Arthur Langford and Francis Annesley.
78. *C.S.P. Dom.,* 1695 and Addenda, p. 219, lord lieutenant and Privy Council to Nottingham, 9 Nov. 1692.
79. *Account of the Sessions,* p. 27.
80. P.R.O. of Ireland, Wyche Mss., fo. 61, [W. Ball] to [Sir Cyril Wyche], 15 Nov. 1692.

thinly veiled rebuke. While the King approved of what the viceroy had said to the petitioners, there was no need to prosecute them; indeed he should send for them again and 'require them to acquaint you with such matters as they can justly complain of'.[81] It was clearly appreciated in Whitehall that, if the administration in Dublin was to survive, it would be as well for the lord lieutenant to admit that there was cause for discontent on a wide range of issues.

By November Nottingham must have pondered on the wisdom of appointing Sydney in the first place. In fairness to the lord lieutenant, of course, his position was an invidious one, particularly after the prorogation. It was natural that he should wish to take a strong line with those who had wrecked the parliamentary session; it was proper that he should attempt to thwart their future endeavours to embarrass his government. Had he left the opposition leaders unchecked or unrebuked he would have failed in his own esteem as a firm and capable viceroy. But he should not have forsaken politics nor should he have confused bluster with firmness.

In February 1693 Sydney made a belated effort to shift the area of hostile debate on to safer ground by resurrecting the Money Bill issue. He decided to seek the opinion of the Irish judges on the Commons' claims to have a sole right to initiate the heads of money bills.[82] The judiciary might be relied upon to present an opinion which would harmonize with his own narrow interpretation of Poynings' Law.[83]

Sydney was not disappointed by the judges' findings. In a lengthy review of law and precedent they confirmed his stand on Poynings' Law. They found that the Commons did not have a sole right, though they allowed that parliament did possess a veto on any bill they disliked and so the subject need not be governed by an unpopular law.[84]

Sydney readily concurred in their conclusions. Indeed, as a particular mark of favour, he knighted those judges not already

81. *C.S.P. Dom.*, 1691-2, p. 512, Nottingham to Sydney, 26 Nov. 1692.
82. *Ibid.*, 1693, p. 28, warrant by the lord lieutenant and Privy Council, 6 Feb. 1693.
83. Judges held their appointments during pleasure.
84. City of Dublin Public Libraries, Pearse Street, Ms. 39 (Gilbert coll.), opinion of the judges, 1693.

possessed of a knighthood, a reward for services which somewhat diminished the impartiality of their findings in the public eye and left the lord lieutenant himself open to further criticism.[85] He was unerringly insensitive to the political implications of his own behaviour.

The judges' opinion neither silenced Sydney's critics on the sole right issue nor even succeeded in narrowing the area of grievance to that issue alone.[86] Throughout the winter his opponents were single-mindedly pursuing their objectives, the overthrow of his administration and a radical change in government policy. The friends of the Dublin government warned of what was happening. John Richards, dean of Ardfert, wrote to Sydney's chief secretary, Sir Cyril Wyche, from London on 8 January:

> I suppose you have long ere this heard the noise into Ireland lately made here by Sloane, Brewster, and two or three more insignificant fops about the prorogation of the Irish parliament. When I came to town all places rung ding dong of it, and that His Excellency encouraged the papists only and had disobliged all the Protestants of Ireland.[87]

But nothing could be done to prevent the affairs of Ireland becoming a major issue at Westminster in the early spring of 1693.

Both Houses of the English parliament began their enquiry into the state of Ireland at the end of February. Ten witnesses gave evidence to the Lords and five to the Commons, four of the latter witnesses being also members of the Irish Commons.[88] Their statements, which were entered in the journals of both Houses, were a comprehensive indictment of government in Ireland since 1690. Most of the witnesses, with some differences of emphasis,

---

85. *C.S.P. Dom.,* 1693, p. 35, concurrence of the lord lieutenant and Privy Council, 14 Feb. 1693; T.C.D., Lyons Mss., 264a. Bishop King criticized Sydney for 'knighting the judges next day as supposed for giving their opinion against the parliament'.
86. *C.S.P. Dom.,* 1693, p. 38, Sydney to Nottingham, 20 Feb. 1693.
87. P.R.O. Ire., Wyche Mss., fo. 65.
88. *Lords' Journals,* xv, 247-71, *passim; Commons' Jnls.,* x, 826-33; *The Parliamentary Diary of Narcissus Luttrell 1691-1693* ed. Henry Horwitz (Oxford, 1972), pp 438-43. The following gave evidence to the Lords: Sir William Gore, Sir John Magill, Sir Francis Blundell, Sir Francis Brewster, the countess of Ardglass, Colonel Frederick Hamilton, James Sloane, Francis

covered the same ground: the abuses in the quartering of soldiers, the alleged corruption in the management of the revenue and the forfeited estates, and the dangerously conciliatory policy towards Catholics. Blame for these grievances was laid unhesitatingly at the door of the Dublin administration and virtually all the deponents set them in a context of arbitrary government where the Commons were prevented from putting right what had gone wrong and where the very future of parliament in Ireland was in doubt. With such evidence before it, the Country party leaders persuaded the Commons to present an address to the King asking for the removal of the great abuses and mismanagement in the affairs of Ireland.[89]

It was now clear both to Sydney and his opponents that the English parliament's censure of the Irish government made the survival of his administration improbable. Just two weeks after the English Commons presented their address to William and Mary, Sydney told Nottingham of the impact it was having in Dublin: 'the proceedings of the parliament in England have made some of our Members here very insolent'.[90] Before the English parliament's enquiries Sydney thought it just possible to hold a second session, but with the English censure on record he realised that it was highly unlikely that he could meet the Irish parliament again with any degree of success. By May he was counselling even more strongly against another session. Indeed he warned Nottingham that there was a distinct danger that the Irish judges might be impeached because of their findings on the sole right issue if the present Irish parliament was allowed to meet again.[91] Eventually, in June, the King ordered a dissolution, by then an inevitable decision, the only surprise being that he had waited so long. Sydney was recalled at the same time.[92]

Whether the dissolution was absolutely necessary or whether the appointment or a new viceroy would have been sufficient to produce a more peaceful second session is debatable. James Bonnell, no friend of Sydney's, did not have any doubts:

Annesley, Colonel Fitzgerald and John Pulteney. The five witnesses before the Commons were Sir Francis Brewster, Sir William Gore, Sir John Magill, James Sloane and David Cairnes. Cairnes was not a member of the 1692 Irish parliament.

89.   *Commons' Jnls.*, x, 833.
90.   *C.S.P. Dom.*, 1693, p. 69, Sydney to Nottingham, 17 Mar. 1693.
91.   *Ibid.*, p. 121, Sydney to Nottingham, 5 May 1693.
92.   *Ibid.*, p. 179, Nottingham to Sydney, 13 June 1693; *ibid.*, p. 187, warrant to Sydney to dissolve the Irish parliament, 20 June 1693.

We know not whether our new government will call a parliament: this last is now dissolved by Lord Sydney; being just upon his going he had no mind to let it be seen that this parliament would have agreed with other governors as I hope and doubt not it would.[93]

This was by no means the whole truth. If the appointment of a new lord lieutenant was to produce a more harmonious relationship between Dublin Castle and parliament, it would have to be accompanied by new departures in government policy and personnel, and that was something which neither King William nor his ministers were prepared to contemplate in 1693. Two years would have to pass before they were.

Sydney was replaced in June 1693 by three lords justices, Lord Capel, Sir Cyril Wyche and William Duncombe. Sir Charles Porter, to his own annoyance and Sydney's regret, was left out of the new commission, though he remained lord chancellor.[94] The new lords justices were clearly intended to provide that blend of opinion which would help to heal the discontent and factionalism which had led to Sydney's downfall. On the one hand, Capel's Whig credentials made him an acceptable choice to those who had complained of government policy in 1692 in relation to land and religion and who had tried to make the Irish parliament an effective political forum.[95] On the other hand, both Wyche and Duncombe were moderate men. Wyche, a learned man with an interest in science, had of course been chief secretary to Sydney and was quite high in the viceroy's estimation.[96] Duncombe, too, had a reputation for moderation in his attitude towards Catholics[97] and both

93. T.C.D., Ms. 1.6.31 (Strype transcripts), fo. 196, Bonnell to Strype, 26 June 1693.
94. *C.S.P. Dom.*, 1693, pp 147-8, Sydney to Nottingham, 22 May 1693.
95. *Bishop Burnet's History of His Own Time* ed. M. J. R[outh] (2nd edn., 6 vols., Oxford, 1823), iii, 245; J. H. Plumb, *The Growth of Political Stability in England 1675-1725* (Harmondsworth, 1969), pp 59, 61-2 n. 41, 135-6. Capel had been one of the most vigorous supporters of the Exclusion Bill in 1680 and a recognized advocate of the privileges of parliament in England in the reign of Charles II.
96. *C.S.P. Dom.*, 1693, p. 192, Sydney to Nottingham, 24 June 1693. Sydney wrote of Sir Cyril Wyche and Lord Chancellor Porter, 'there are no better than these two in this country'. Of Wyche, specifically, he considered that he would serve 'faithfully and with success'. The *D.N.B.* has an entry on Wyche.
97. There is a very brief sketch of Duncombe's career in *The Diary of John Evelyn* ed. E. S. De Beer (6 vols., Oxford, 1955), v, 150 n.

men were inclined to favour those of moderate opinion when it came to promotions or appointments.[98]

However, the next eighteen months witnessed the gradual erosion of Duncombe's and Wyche's authority and Capel's growing ascendancy. Of course this was not unconnected with the control of the English ministry by the Whig Junto. Nevertheless, there were Irish reasons too for the emergence of Capel as the dominant figure. Throughout 1694 he made himself appear indispensable to the successful government of Ireland. From the time he became a lord justice he consistently struck an optimistic note when reporting to London on the possibilities of an Irish parliament.[99] All that was needed, he implied, was a change in government policy, adroit and politic handling of the local political leaders, and a willingness to concede to parliament a *de facto* initiative in legislation without reneging in principle.[100]

Capel came into his own in May 1695 with his appointment as lord deputy. He could now bring to fruition his careful cultivation of the Protestant gentry over the preceding eighteen months and look forward with some confidence to the meeting of a new parliament in the following August. Two of the main exponents of the sole right in 1692 were brought into his administration. Robert Rochfort was appointed attorney-general and Alan Brodrick, who had been dismissed from the post of third serjeant by Sydney, became solicitor-general.[101] Similarly Sir Robert King, one of those

98. When the diocese of Dublin fell vacant in November 1693, the lords justices were unable to agree on the most suitable candidate for the succession. Wyche and Duncombe recommended Bishop William Moreton of Kildare, a man of moderate opinions, who had gained his place on the Privy Council when Bishop Dopping was suspended for his inflammatory attack on the Catholics in 1691. Capel, on the other hand, recommended either Dopping or Archbishop Vesey of Tuam (*C.S.P. Dom.*, 1693, pp 400, 405).
99. *H.M.C. Buccleuch and Queensberry*, ii, 99-101, [Capel] to [Secretary Trenchard], 14 July 1694.
100. *Ibid.*, p. 209, Capel to Shrewsbury, 31 July 1695. Capel apologized to Shrewsbury for his delay in writing, which was 'caused by a little journey I took, to run for a plate, the better to discourse with the gentlemen of the country'.
101. Both Brodrick and Rochfort had been advocates of the 'sole right' in 1692 (B.L., Add. Mss. 9, 715, fos. 60-67). Rochfort, indeed, was alleged by Brodrick, in a letter written over a decade later, to have been 'the person who first started the question ... and in express words added the offensive word

who had petitioned Sydney in November 1692, was recommended for a place on the Privy Council.[102] It was clear by the time parliament met that Capel's careful setting-up of a Court party was going to pay considerable dividends. It was in sharp contrast with Sydney's failure to prepare the political ground in 1692. Capel realized that if parliament was to have a role in the government of Ireland — and financial necessity made this increasingly likely — then parliament would have to be managed. Sydney's failure in 1692 had taught that lesson.

Money bills caused little controversy in 1695. This was due to Capel's readiness to compromise. What he did was to present the Commons with an Excise Bill designed to bring in a nominal revenue.[103] When this bill had been passed with only a few objections from the remnant of the sole right faction, he left it to the Commons to decide how much money they wished to raise and the ways and means of raising it.[104] They were then free to initiate the heads of the Money Bills for the really substantial amount. The net result was that Capel obtained a large supply without any constitutional wrangles between government and parliament and could even claim that he had not given way on the issue of principle.

The heads of bills procedure became increasingly accepted henceforth as a legitimate means of giving the Irish parliament a legislative initiative of sorts within the constraints of Poynings' Law. The experience of 1692 had shown that without such a compromise solution the Irish parliament could not be relied upon to fulfil its legislative functions.[105]

The Poynings' Law procedure had unduly influenced the government into believing that an Irish parliament had little positive function and might be depended upon to give ready

sole to the question, for it originally run thus, that it was the right of the commons to frame money bills' (Surrey R.O., Guildford Muniment Room, Midleton Mss., ii, fo. 98ᵛ, Alan Brodrick to St John Brodrick, 5 June 1703). I am indebted to Dr David Hayton for this reference.

102. *H.M.C. Buccleuch and Queensberry*. ii, 161, Capel to Shrewsbury, 15 Nov. 1694. He was subsequently appointed (*C.S.P. Dom.*, 1695 and Addenda, p. 339).

103. It was intended to bring in only £7,000.

104. *C.J.I.*, ii, 52, 55; *H.M.C. Buccleuch and Queensberry*, ii, 203, Capel to Shrewsbury, 6 Sept. 1695.

105. Four financial measures were enacted into law in 1695.

endorsement to government bills. It was an error of judgement on the part of Sydney and Nottingham to appear to allow so narrow a function to an Irish parliament, particularly in the absence of any attempt to form a cohesive Court policy. It was all the more disastrous at a time of deep political unrest and disquiet at the course government policy was taking. When Sydney complained that the parliament 'had not answered the ends for which they were called together', he put his finger on the nub of the problem. He was complaining, in fact, that the parliament had not been an instrument of government policy. He had failed to realize that Poynings' Law, far from ensuring a legislature resigned to its own impotence, might have the opposite effect of making members all the more determined to use whatever means were at their disposal to advance their objectives. The Commons were not prepared to be a mere ratifying body.

The lesson of 1692 was that the members of the Irish House of Commons wanted a parliament which would have some control over the executive and some influence on the course of events; in other words, they sought a parliamentary constitution. When he preached before them on 23 October 1692, their chaplain, Dr Edward Walkington, spoke eloquently of the constitution:

> For we have all the blessings of other governments, without any of their mischiefs, or inconveniences: the kingly power securing us from the insolency of faction; and the authority of our representatives in parliament securing us from the encroachments of an arbitrary prerogative, which makes our lives, our liberties, our estates and our religion too, our own; so fully our own, that they can't be touched, but pursuant to those laws to which we ourselves have given our consents.[106]

Walkington, of course, was not describing the Irish constitution. The parliamentary constitution which he lauded had never existed in Ireland in any real sense. At the time he spoke parliament was only three weeks old, its predecessor dissolved twenty-six years before. In effect he was articulating, with Whig rhetoric, the aspirations of his congregation. While these desires could never be fully realized, nevertheless within the narrow limits of the Irish constitution the *debacle* of 1692 led in time to the establishment of

106. Edward Walkinton [*sic*], *A Sermon Preached Octob. 23, 1692 in St. Andrew's Church, Dublin, before the House of Commons* (Dublin, 1692), pp 9-10.

a permanent and reasonably effective place for parliament in the domestic government of Ireland. A start in this direction was made in 1695, the year in which Walkington became bishop of Down and Connor on the recommendation of Lord Deputy Capel.[107]

107. *C.S.P. Dom.*, 1694-5, p. 480.

THE BEGINNINGS OF THE 'UNDERTAKER SYSTEM'

David Hayton

The establishment of the Irish parliament as an indispensable institution of government in the years after the Glorious Revolution meant that political activity in Ireland thenceforth took place within a parliamentary context. Thus the central political problem of the first half of the century — the achievement of cohesion between the English-appointed executive and the Anglo-Irish governing class — has to be viewed in parliamentary terms, political cohesion being achieved largely through successful parliamentary management. As we have already seen, ministers and parliament-men started off in 1692 quite out of step, but it was not long before a solution to the problem of management had been found which ensured that the government would receive regular grants of supply and at the same time be safe from a repetition of the squalls which had capsized Lord Sydney's administration.[1] The solution was for the task of managing the Irish parliament to be given over to Irish politicians — men who were known as 'undertakers', because they 'undertook' to provide the government with a majority in the Commons, in return for a voice in policy-making and a substantial share of the official patronage for themselves and their dependants. The so-called 'undertaker system' subsisted until the 1770s: its emergence, in the period immediately after the Glorious Revolution, is the subject which will be discussed here.

The early eighteenth century is a period in Irish history about which remarkably little has been written. Political history, in particular, has suffered neglect, and many basic questions concerning the post-Revolution Irish parliament have yet to be asked, let alone answered. Any discussion of parliamentary management in this period must therefore be in the nature of a preliminary report. There is, however, a prevailing orthodoxy of a sort, which will have to be considered and revised. It occurs in general histories, and runs as follows. To begin with, it is alleged, parliamentary management was included among the duties of the lord lieutenant, who used his powers of persuasion and patronage to built up a Court party under his own leadership. This arrangement is supposed to have lasted until 1724, when the failure of the Irish government to quieten the agitation against Wood's Halfpence prompted the English ministers

1. J. C. Beckett, *The Making of Modern Ireland, 1603-1923* (2nd edn., London, 1971), pp 152-3.

to look for another method of coping with the fractious Irish parliament. The outcome of their search was a new 'system' by which the responsibility for management was transferred from the lord lieutenant to 'undertakers'. Thus the 'undertaker system' is seen as having been the fruit of a reform devised and imposed from without.

This view assumes a change in English government policy, but there is no evidence, either in official correspondence or in private papers, that the employment of 'undertakers' was advocated from Westminster.[2] In fact it is possible to account for their appearance without resorting to unfounded suspicions about English policy, and this paper will set out an alternative interpretation. By taking a longer perspective, and investigating the political history of Ireland in the period before the Wood's Halfpence dispute, we can see that throughout the early eighteenth century parliamentary management was of necessity always in the hands of 'undertakers' of one kind or another; that between 1715 and 1725 a subtle change took place in the type of 'undertaker system' which existed; and that this change was engendered by conditions and events in Ireland. Special attention will be paid to the way in which Members of the Irish parliament organized themselves into parties and power-groups, since an important cause of the change in the system of management after 1715 was a shift in the pattern of parliamentary allegiances.

2

It is important to remember that in early eighteenth-century Ireland parliamentary management consisted very largely in controlling the House of Commons. The Commons had more power than the House of Lords because of the way in which legislation was carried out. The previous essay showed how in order to circumvent the constitutional requirement that bills be framed by the government and presented to the Irish parliament for acceptance or rejection as they stood, with no possibility of amendment, it became a convention for 'heads of bills' to be drafted by the Irish parliament and forwarded to the government for approval; after the 'heads' had been so approved and, if necessary, amended by the Irish and English

2. The correspondence between Dublin Castle and the English government for the years 1723-5 is to be found in the Public Record Office (S.P. 63/380-386; 67/7-8). Of the leaders of the English ministry, Walpole's papers are in the Cholmondeley (Houghton) Mss. in Cambridge University Library; Newcastle's in the Newcastle Mss. in the British Library (Add. Mss. 32, 686-7): I was unable to inspect Townshend's papers, which are apparently in the Townshend Mss. at Raynham Hall, Norfolk.

Privy Councils, they were embodied into bills and returned. The significance of this procedure, as far as the relative importance of Lords and Commons was concerned, lay in the fact that the heads were only discussed by one of the two Houses, whereas fully-fledged bills had to be passed by both. In most cases it was the Commons who brought forward heads, and it was always the Commons who initiated the legislation granting a supply. Since it was rare for parliament to reject a money bill outright, an opposition usually concentrated its energies on trying to ensure that the amount of money voted in taxes was less than the government required. The crucial stage in the passage of a money bill came when the heads were debated. For the lord lieutenant these proceedings in the Commons constituted the nub of the whole parliamentary campaign. In contrast, the members of the House of Lords spent much of their time in arguing over comparatively trivial matters: questions of procedure, private bills and such like. One chief secretary admitted to an English secretary of state, 'I never trouble you with what the House of Lords do, because in truth they have hardly any business before them'.[3] The upper House was also more easily controlled. Bishops often allowed their opinions to be influenced by hopes of preferment, and the temporal peers were generally too penurious to be independent. In Anne's reign alone we hear of Lord Inchiquin with his lands and fortune 'absolutely encumbered'; the earl of Roscommon 'utterly dependent' on his pension from the crown; and Lord Blayney petitioning parliament for relief.[4] The viceroy did not need to spend much effort in order to put together a working majority in the Lords; it was inevitable that his interest and involvement would be with the vitally necessary and more arduous task of managing the Commons, and it was there that 'undertakers' appeared.

It has hitherto been accepted that before the mid-1720s the viceroy took a leading part in the management of the Commons. There seems to be some support for this view in contemporary correspondence, where the government party in parliament is sometimes referred to as 'the lord lieutenant's friends', and where there are reports of the viceroy being involved in the day to day business of drumming up votes. In fact, a collage assembled from these snippets of evidence would give a distorted representation of his role. The term 'lord lieutenant's friends' was a means of denoting

3. P.R.O., S.P. 63/365, fo. 101, Edward Southwell to Sir Charles Hedges, 1 Mar. 1705.
4. P.R.O.N.I., D.638/25/2 (De Ross Mss.), Inchiquin to Coningsby, 3 Mar. 1709; P.R,O., S.P. 63/370/105; *C.J.I.*, ii, appendix, p. xxxviii.

the supporters of the ministry; it did not necessarily imply a parliamentary grouping attached to the viceroy personally. As for the viceroy soliciting votes himself, it cannot be denied that 'good words, burgundy and closeting' were features of his routine, but such activities did no more than supplement the work of the managers in the Commons. In emergencies the lord lieutenant would intensify his exertions, intervening almost as a *deus ex machina*. Thus Lord Wharton, at a critical stage of his viceroyalty, 'addressed himself to all sorts of men ... with unspeakable application' in order to baffle the cocksure leaders of the opposition. For the rest of the time the viceroy would rely on his 'friends and well-wishers' (as they were styled in Wharton's case) to conduct the parliamentary battle for him.[5]

The viceroy always had to employ Irish politicians to take charge of business in the Commons. He could not of course attend meetings of the House himself and the members of his household staff, the secretaries and aides-de-camp, were too inexperienced to be able to deputize successfully. This was true even of the chief secretary, who at best might be able to act with the managers as a junior partner but who was rarely a dominant figure. During the session of 1715-16 Charles Delafaye, one of the two chief secretaries in attendance upon Lords Justices Grafton and Galway, wrote of the parliamentary campaign that 'we were forced to meet every night with the chief of our friends to provide against the next day's battle.' The significant part of the quotation is the phrase 'with the chief of our friends': three days before, Delafaye had acknowledged that William Conolly, Speaker of the House of Commons, was the person 'to whose single interest the King is more obliged than to all Ireland besides for the good we have had this session'.[6] Furthermore, it was customary for both the viceroy and his chief secretary to be strangers to Ireland, unfamiliar with the talents and dispositions of members of the Irish parliament and lacking the 'interest' which derived from frequent personal contact. And it was difficult for a lord lieutenant to improve his acquaintance with the kingdom when he did not reside there permanently. As Professor Beckett has put it, 'coming over, as he did, only for sessions of parliament, he lacked both the knowledge and the personal connections which he would have needed if he were to manage the House himself'.[7]

5.   *The Letters of Joseph Addison* ed. Walter Graham (Oxford, 1941), p. 134, Addison to Halifax, 7 May 1709; *ibid.*, p. 177, Addison to Godolphin, 12 Aug. 1709.
6.   P.R.O., S.P. 63/373/336, Delafaye to [Stanhope?], 17 Dec. 1715; *ibid.*, 63/373/306, same to [same?] , 14 Dec. 1715.
7.   Beckett, *Making of Modern Ireland,* p. 190.

By employing Irish politicians to manage the Commons the lord lieutenant did not inevitably jeopardize his own authority. He might have been able to keep the Court party in stricter subordination had it not been for the type of manager he was forced to employ. Few of the leading men in the Commons were government supporters out of conviction, and prepared to occupy a position of subservience. Instead they were hard-headed jobbers, principally concerned to advance their own careers and get the better of their rivals. When opposition to the government seemed politically advantageous they did not hesitate to oppose. Examples abound of high-ranking officials making trouble for the crown in parliament, from the prime serjeant, John Osborne, in 1692, to Lord Chancellor Midleton and his followers three decades later. The independence of these politicians was bolstered by the fact that their parliamentary influence stemmed from a variety of sources and not simply from office. Support came from kinsmen, friends and admirers, and from members whose attachment was paid for with other currency than viceregal favour, such as the provision of seats in parliament. Community of principle carried weight with back-benchers, sometimes overriding all other considerations and turning the skilful orator into a man of influence. The viceroy, therefore, had to treat with political magnates who might be almost as powerful out of office as they were in. Even the greatest weapon in the administration's armoury, its patronage, often served to enhance the personal authority of the politicians.

In the early eighteenth century the Irish government received comparatively little political interest from the fund of places and pensions at its disposal. In practice much of its patronage was expropriated. The lord lieutenant had to let his managers have a say in the bestowal of offices: if their recommendations were ignored they might threaten a withdrawal of services, something that a government was seldom willing to precipitate. The effect was that a successful candidate was likely to regard his advancement as being due to the interposition of his patron rather than the spontaneous benevolence of the viceroy. In the case of appointments in the revenue service, administrative organization combined with political necessity to weaken the authority of the lord lieutenant. The Irish politicians who sat on the revenue commission took orders from the English treasury, not from Dublin Castle: although they always listened politely to whatever the lord lieutenant had to say, they were not compelled to obey him and often found a reason to avoid accepting his suggestions. Not surprisingly, many office-holders saw their primary obligation as being to patron rather than employer, and any politician who quarrelled with the viceroy could count on a good many of his followers accompanying him into opposition whether or not they held office. A mass defection of placemen in 1709 moved one visitor to Dublin to comment: 'upon the whole, from what I have been able to make of the people here, they are all politicians and deeply engaged on one side or the other, though the men of interest seem much superior in number to the men of conscience.'[8] The Court party in the Commons always contained only a minority of staunch 'King's friends'. In correspondence prior to the 1720s such men are rarely if ever mentioned as constituting a separate interest in the House, and later, when they are spoken of more frequently, they appear as but one element in a large confederation. The lord lieutenant relied on his managers not just to provide expertise and leadership, but actually to ensure a majority for his administration.

The relationship between viceroy and managers, therefore, could not be that of master and servants. Because of their strength the managers were courted, and one of the first duties of any viceroy on his arrival in Dublin would be to seek their advice. Counsel was taken throughout the parliamentary session, and Grafton, for one, was said to have established a semi-permanent 'secret council'.[9] In this way the managers could influence viceregal policy: in 1717 the nomination of lords justices was allegedly determined during a lengthy *tete-a-tete* between the duke of Bolton and one of the leading politicians.[10] The possession of power and influence, however, would not by itself qualify these men for the title of 'undertakers'. The word 'undertaker' has a precise meaning in the context of the eighteenth-century Irish parliament, that is one who 'undertook' to secure the successful passage of government business in return for concessions. What must be looked for is evidence of some sort of contract entered into by the lord lieutenant and the leaders of the Court party.

The principal difficulty in identifying the parliamentary managers of the early eighteenth century as 'undertakers' is that the expression was seldom used. Politicians were wary of employing it themselves or of giving a pretext for others to use it of them, for to

8.   N.L.I., Wicklow Mss. (P.C. 226-7), Charles Robins to [Hugh] Howard, 13 Aug. 1709. I am indebted for this reference to Dr A. P. W. Malcomson.
9.   Sir Richard G. A. Levinge, *Jottings of the Levinge Family* (Dublin, 1877), pp 65-66, Sir Richard Levinge to Edward Southwell, 17 Oct. 1721.
10.   P.R.O., S.P. 63/375/214, William Conolly to Charles Delafaye, 3 Nov. 1717.

have had the reputation of being 'undertakers' would have done them considerable harm. Among members of parliament there was a strong suspicion that 'undertakers' were only needed to assist a legislative programme that was unlikely to succeed on its own merits. In 1714 a gang of 'malecontents' fomented opposition to the Court by spreading a rumour that the government's managers had 'undertaken for a land tax', a measure which was deeply disliked by the gentry.[11] In any case, the gentlemen who sat in the Commons resented the assumption being made that their support could be reckoned on and even promised in advance. Although it was true that votes were manipulated and used in political barter, the fiction of independence had to be kept up. When Lord Sunderland wished to sound out his managers on some legislative proposals he was informed by his go-between in Dublin that 'it is not easy to get men to say what parliament will do, or to get them to give an opinion, for there is such jealousy of undertakers that the very suspicion may hurt themselves as well as disappoint the business'.[12] We cannot expect to find much evidence of bargains being struck between viceroys and their managers when the latter were so reluctant to see the terms of agreements committed to paper.

Nevertheless, when the practical relationship between the two sides is examined, it becomes clear that there always existed some sort of contract. The viceroy fulfilled his obligation by endorsing requests for patronage and making concessions in matters of policy, and in return the managers backed his administration in parliament, despite the fact that this could easily involve them in work they did not relish. An episode from the parliamentary session of 1707 illustrates the nature of the relationship. The leaders of the opposi-

11. Midleton Mss. (when inspected, in the custody of Simon Meade, Pen y lan, Meifod, Powys), iii, fos. 205-6, [Alan Brodrick] to [Thomas Brodrick], 14 Dec. 1714. (I am grateful to the earl of Midleton for permission to consult and refer to these papers, which have now been deposited in the Surrey R.O., Guildford Muniment Room.) Country gentlemen in England were equally suspicious of 'undertakers'. As a Gloucestershire squire, Sir Richard Cocks, recalled in 1700, in a speech intended for the English parliament, 'I have heard gent[lemen] deservedly speak against undertaking for parliaments ...'. (Bod., Ms. Eng. hist. b. 209, fo. 84.)
12. Blenheim Mss. (when inspected, in the ownership of the duke of Marlborough, Blenheim Palace, Woodstock, Oxon.), F. I. −23, Tyrawley to [Sunderland], 12 Mar. 1714-15. (Acknowledgement is made to the duke of Marlborough for permission to use material from the Blenheim archives.) See also William Coxe, *Memoirs of the Life and Administration of Sir Robert Walpole* ... (3 vols., London, 1798), ii, 400-402, Lord Midleton to Thomas Brodrick, 7 Nov. 1724.

tion had been brought over to support the new lord lieutenant, Pembroke, by the appointment of one of their number as attorney-general. They were placed in a dilemma when Pembroke requested that the supply voted by the Commons should be for a period of two years, something his new managers had consistently opposed in the past, on the grounds that a one-year grant was necessary to safeguard what in their view was the fundamental right of Irishmen to have annual sessions of their own parliament. The managers knew full well that a *volte-face* would be unpopular with their supporters, and tried to persuade the viceroy to alter the terms of his request. Eventually a compromise was reached by which money was voted for a year and three quarters. During the negotiations outside observers realized that what was being offered was an 'undertaking'. The participants in the bargaining may have avoided the expression, but others did not share their delicacy of feeling. It was said at one point by an opponent that the managers 'undertook for a year and a half', while to a similarly disapproving eye their final proposal had the disagreeable appearance of an ultimatum: 'three politicos were sent ... with a resolution not to give the duty to support the government but for a year and three quarters ... and in that case they offer to close with the government'.13

In two other episodes, which are both well documented, the aims of the negotiations and the nature of the offers and stipulations made are quite explicit. Opposition politicians are revealed as treating with the government and presenting demands for office and power as the price of their support. Before the session of November-December 1713 the lord lieutenant, Shrewsbury, entered into discussions with one of the leaders of the opposition, Alan Brodrick. Brodrick made it a basic condition that Shrewsbury change his Irish ministry. In particular he urged the removal of the lord chancellor, Sir Constantine Phipps, the champion of the party on whose support the administration relied. This was a demand which the viceroy could not grant, and the talks lapsed.14 After the parliamentary session had taken place, and the ministry's forces in the Commons had suffered defeat after defeat, culminating in the refusal of the House to vote a supply for the period after Christmas 1713, contact was renewed. Early in the following year Shrewsbury invited the leading opponents of his administration — 'the chief managers of

13. N.L.I., Ms. 2,472 (Ormonde Mss.), pp 243-44, [Archbishop John Vesey] to Major Theodore Vesey, 22 July 1707; B.L., Add. Mss. 9,715, fos. 174-5, Anderson Saunders to [Edward Southwell], 10 July 1707.
14. Midleton Mss., ii, fo. 125, [Alan Brodrick] to Thomas Brodrick, 11 Oct. 1713.

the Commons', as they were described – to Dublin Castle. He began the conference by paying tribute to the 'discernment' and 'interest' of his guests, and then asked them if they were willing to 'proceed with temper in carrying on the public business and the supply'. Their answer was that, until the Queen removed Phipps from office, they would stay in opposition. As one of them remarked, 'my Lord Chancellor's continuing to be in that station' was 'such a grievance, as was intolerable', and so long as he remained there no vote of supply could be expected.[15] This was exactly what happened: the chancellor kept his place; the composition of the ministry did not alter; and the opposition continued to oppose.

In the other episode, already referred to in the previous essay, the demands of the would-be managers were conceded and an 'undertaking' was made. When Lord Deputy Capel received a set of terms from the opposition in 1694 his response was to accept the offer, conditions and all: his government badly needed a grant of money from parliament; the then opposition leaders seemed powerful enough to be able to guarantee the fulfilment of any promises they made; and they were the allies of his own party colleagues in England. The demands were expressed in a letter from one of these opposition politicians to the lord deputy, in which the writer announced that he had canvassed many members of parliament concerning the forthcoming session and declared:

> If I have any credit with your Lordship, give me leave to pledge it, that your Lordship will find our party as entire as ever men were, and every one of them as faithful to the King's interest and as truly devoted to your Lordship's service, as ever were yet known in this or any other kingdom.

At the same time he laid down conditions:

> I dare answer for it, they will not fail your expectation. But they are desirous of having the previous things done before the

15. P.R.O.N.I., T.254/I.K./1/11 (Abercorn Mss.), Abercorn to [Edward Southwell], 5 Jan. 1714. It is worth noting that even here, with the viceroy making an appeal for support and the politicians laying down conditions, the verbal proprieties were observed, Shrewsbury taking care to say that 'he knew very well that in such assemblies [*i.e.* parliament] no wise man would undertake for more than himself'. His guests, on the other hand, 'could not forbear wresting some of the expressions, to have an opportunity of carping at the unreasonableness, of putting them upon being undertakers'. I wish to thank the duke of Abercorn for permission to quote from his family papers.

meeting of a parliament, which I mentioned to your lordship ...[16]

What the 'things' were is clear from Capel's own subsequent
correspondence. He wrote to the English government proposing a
ministerial reshuffle in Ireland, which would have admitted to power
several members of the parliamentary opposition. Most of the
changes he recommended were carried out, and when parliament met
the former opposition gave the lord deputy their support.[17] Even at
this early stage, in the second session of the Irish parliament after
the Revolution, 'undertakers' were already at work.

3

In order to understand how the 'undertakers' of the early
eighteenth century differed in their situation from the likes of
Speaker Boyle and the Ponsonbys, it is necessary to know something
of the 'political structure' of the Irish House of Commons; what it
was like in the reigns of King William and Queen Anne, and how it
changed thereafter. This subject is so large that a separate paper
would be required in order to do it justice, but for the immediate
purpose of this essay a rough sketch will suffice. Broadly speaking,
there evolved in the two decades after the Revolution a system of
political organization in Ireland similar to that in England, with
parliament divided into two warring parties, the Whigs and the
Tories. This development reached maturity in the second half of the
reign of Queen Anne, when the struggle between the two parties sub-
merged all other considerations and distinctions. With the accession
of George I the duel was over; the Whigs triumphant. The Tories
were under an anathema at court, because of their party's association
with the cause of the Stuart Pretender, and most men assumed that
there would never again be a Tory ministry in England or Ireland.
Consequently the Tory party, and with it the party system as a
whole, in Ireland began to disintegrate. By 1727, and the beginning
of the next reign, the Irish House of Commons had come to bear an
appearance similar to that of the English House of Commons of the
early 1760s as described by Sir Lewis Namier. Gone were the armies

16. *H.M.C. Buccleuch and Queensberry*, ii, 110-111, [St John] Brodrick to
Capel, 5 Aug. 1694.
17. *Ibid.,* 159-61, Capel to Shrewsbury, 15 Nov. [1694]. See also *H.M.C.
Downshire*, i, 492-3, [Sir Charles Porter] to Sir William Trumbull, 3 July 1695;
Bishop Burnet's History of His Own Time ed. M. J. R[outh] (2nd edn., 6 vols.,
London, 1823), iv, 184-5.

of Whigs and Tories, to be replaced by a nest of smaller factions, some centred on individual politicians or political families, with a group of 'King's friends' more numerous than before and a body of independent-minded 'patriots' who were always to be found in opposition.

The key to the changing pattern of parliamentary politics is the concept of 'party'. At its simplest the story is of the rise, temporary ascendancy and decline of 'party' as a force in political life. Like much else in eighteenth-century Ireland, the party division was imported from England, where the terms 'Whig' and 'Tory' had been in use ever since the Exclusion crisis to indicate the two sides in parliament. The English parties were divided on fundamentals, holding opposing views on the constitution and the function of government. Tories envisaged an alliance between church and crown, enforcing obedience to both and denying the subject any right to resist, a right which the Whigs in contrast upheld, whether it was exercised in defence of civil or religious liberty. In practice the conflict between the two philosophies was fought out over two issues: the extent to which Protestant Dissenters were to be allowed freedom of worship and access to political power; and whether Tory principles of Non-resistance and Passive Obedience were truly compatible with the 'Glorious Revolution' which had been effected by King William. When Irishmen started to call themselves Whigs and Tories, they inherited the principles of their English counterparts, and also the issues over which the clash of principles had crystallized. Because of circumstances peculiar to Ireland, the debate about Non-resistance and Passive Obedience began later there than in England. Irish Protestants were well aware that their estates, and, it was felt, their very lives, depended upon the maintenance of the Revolution settlement, and they were loth to call that settlement into doubt. The furthest that most Irish Tories would go was, as one M.P. expressed it in a Commons debate, to admit that the Revolution had been necessary but to hope that no similar feat of resistance would ever be called for in the future.[18] Nonetheless, there was a difference between the two parties from the beginning in their attitude to the Revolution. The Whigs, as the more earnest Williamites, pressed for the severest penalties to be exacted from the Catholics, who in their view constituted a vast Jacobite 'fifth column'. Tories felt this vengeful spirit to be improper, and did what they could to prevent the passing of the more savagely oppressive provisions of the Penal Laws.

18.   P.R.O., S.P. 63/367, fo. 264, newsletter, 10 Nov. 1711.

The Beginnings of the 'Undertaker System'

During King William's reign the three issues on which there were distinctive Whig and Tory positions, that is the legislative treatment of Protestant Dissenters, the validity of the Revolution and the necessity for penal laws against Catholics and Catholicism, were from time to time relegated to the background by the issues raised in debates between 'Court' and 'Country' parties in parliament. As was also the case in England, the Country party in Ireland was an opposition group which sought to embarrass the administration and gain popularity by raising grievances and appealing to the patriotism of back-bench M.P.s. In the programme of the Irish Country party was blended suspicion of the executive (a characteristic 'Country' attitude) and Irish patriotism, the latter manifested in a concern for the economic welfare of the kingdom and a determination to defend the rights of the Irish parliament. In 1692 the opposition had claimed that the Irish House of Commons had a 'sole right' to initiate money bills, and during the next few years this became one of the most widely discussed issues in Irish politics. Then in 1698 a proposal in the English parliament for an act to limit the export of Irish woollens awakened fears of economic exploitation by the mother country and sparked off further agitation. Preoccupations of this kind encouraged the use of terms like 'Court' and 'Country' rather than 'Whig' and 'Tory' to denote the two sides in parliament, but if we look closely we can see that the division of the Commons into Whigs and Tories was already effective.

In the 1690s front-bench politicians in the Irish parliament were banded into two factions, and those factions were always on opposite sides. When one group moved into office the other moved out. The men who had been opposition agitators in 1692 gradually took over the ministry from 1694 onwards and their enemies, who had previously been spokesmen for the Court, went into opposition. For a brief period during the transition both groups had representatives in high office, and then the battle in the Commons was not so much between government and opposition as between the two factions within the government. These groups were closely connected with the parties in England – the 'sole right men' of 1692 were allied to the English Whigs while the other side intrigued with the Tories – and the issues they debated were some of them 'party' issues. The 'sole right men' were the more vehement enemies of popery, and they inveighed against government ministers for having betrayed the Protestant interest by concluding the over generous Treaty of Limerick. In 1695 they were still denouncing their opponents as Jacobites and favourers of papists.[19] The 'sole right

19. Surrey R.O., Somers Mss., F/13, [Capel] to [Shrewsbury], 7 Oct. 1695.

43

men' also included in their ranks men sympathetic to the claims of Protestant Dissenters for a legally-based toleration, and this became another point at issue.[20] We can say that in William's reign there was an incipient two-party system, only partially cut across by the antithesis of 'Court' and 'Country'. A list of members of the parliament of 1695, marked in a contemporary hand and in a manner so as to indicate political allegiance, presents a picture of the House of Commons divided broadly into Whigs and Tories. Of those who were re-elected at the start of the next reign over two thirds were to retain their previous 'party' affiliation.[21]

Under Queen Anne the element of 'Court' against 'Country' vanished from the Irish political scene. The first instance that I have found of the use of the terms 'Whig' and 'Tory' to refer to parties in the Irish parliament dates from the first session of the new reign, that of 1703-4.[22] Even then it was more common for the two sides to be labelled 'the Court' and 'the Country party'. The opposition still presented themselves as patriots, complaining about the condition of the Irish economy and protesting at the damage being done by English legislation. However, a change in the framework of parliamentary debate was imminent. The imposition in 1704 of an obligatory sacramental test to be taken by all holders of crown and municipal office raised to prominence the question of Protestant Dissenters and their place in the state. The flood of Scots presbyterians into Ulster in the 1690s had alarmed the predominantly Anglican squirearchy, and some churchmen were even apprehensive of a presbyterian *coup d'etat*. Tories praised 'the Test' as an important and much needed bulwark against the apparent expansionism of the presbyterians in the north, and busied themselves in looking for ways in which to strengthen the defences further. The recall in the same year of the Convocation of the Church of Ireland provided an additional platform for Tory views. Parsons now took to politics in defence of the church, exploiting pulpit, press and Convocation to

20. J. S. Reid, *History of the Presbyterian Church in Ireland* ed. W. D. Killen (3 vols., Belfast, 1867), ii, 444-456; John McBride to William Hamilton, 7 Sept. 1695, quoted in Sir J. Hamilton, *The Hamilton Manuscripts* ... ed. T. K. Lowry (Belfast, 1867), p. 152; Bod., Ms Ballard 6, fo. 77, Bishop Thomas Lindsay to Arthur Charlett, 8 Dec. 1698.
21. T.C.D., Ms. 1179, pp 37-9. Comparison can be made with party allegiances in Anne's reign by studying the parliamentary lists which survive from the years 1706-13 (see note 23).
22. B.L., Add. Mss. 9,712, fo. 51, Robert Echlin to [Edward] Southwell, 23 Nov. 1703.

attack the twin targets of Presbyterianism and Whiggery. In due course some immoderately partisan clergymen began to expound the High Tory doctrines of Non-resistance, Passive Obedience and Hereditary Right, and for the first time the Revolution and 'Revolution principles' became issues in Irish politics. By 1707 debates in the Irish parliament had taken the form of a running battle between two parties, who referred to themselves respectively as 'the church party' and 'the honest gentlemen' ('honest' in the sense of not being Jacobites) and who were known to each other and to everyone else as Tories and Whigs. Eight lists of members of the House of Commons which survive from the period 1706-1713, and which give an indication of voting behaviour, show how profoundly important was the party division in Irish politics at this time.[23] It was next to impossible for a member of parliament to avoid being attached to one party or the other, and very difficult to change sides once party allegiance had been established. A professional civil servant, Joshua Dawson, who had followed a pattern of party political neutrality in serving every administration since 1700, Whig or Tory, as under-secretary, joined in the Tory government's energetic and partisan campaign in the general election of 1713, contesting County Londonderry against a leading Whig, and as a result was dismissed from his post when the Whigs came to power in the following year.[24]

The 'rage of party' had only a short life in Ireland, and after Anne's death the political dichotomy soon dissolved. Tories had become identified too closely with the Jacobites to count any longer as serious candidates for power: the defection to the Stuart camp of the former chieftain of the Irish Tory party, the duke of Ormonde, was an especially bad blow. Although the Tories did not suffer catastrophic losses in the Irish general election of 1715, despondency soon assailed them and in the ensuing session of parliament they were beaten down by the relentless pressure of the Whigs. After a few months only a handful of Tories were at their posts in the Commons to defend members of the previous administration from charges of 'arbitrary behaviour' and disloyalty to the house of Hanover.[25] Tory politicians, anxious to be considered again for

23. Details of the present whereabouts of these lists, and of the information which they yield, can be found in the appendix to D. W. Hayton, 'Ireland and the English Ministers, 1707-16' (Oxford Univ. D. Phil. thesis 1975). Chapters 4 and 5 of this thesis contain a fuller discussion of the phenomenon of 'party' politics in Ireland in the reign of Queen Anne.
24. Lecky, i, 314.
25. *C.J.I.*, iii, 66, 102.

government appointments, began to desert their comrades and before long many had gone over to the Whigs. The diehards remained in opposition. The Tory party may have lasted as a separate entity until at least 1727, for in that year Lord Anglesey addressed a gathering of Tories on the subject of their future political strategy,[26] but what was left was a rump. Since 1714 there had been a steady decline in the number of those who professed themselves 'churchmen' in politics. If an issue arose such as a projected repeal of the Test, which could be taken as involving the interests of the Church of Ireland, Tories would be expected to come together and make a show of strength.[27] Such issues did not often arise, however, for the Whig ministers usually took care not to appear to threaten the interests of the church. Since the government also refused to allow the Irish Convocation to meet, the hot-blooded clerics who had done so much to raise the political temperature in Anne's reign were left with little to clamour against and less opportunity to make themselves heard when they did raise their voices.

With the collapse of the Tory party inside and outside parliament, and the virtual disappearance of Toryism as a live force in Irish politics, political debate and parliamentary manoeuvring came to be conducted once again on a theme of 'Court' against 'Country'. The issues which came most readily to hand for the opposition were the standard complaints of the 'Country party': the pitiful state of the Irish economy and the imperilled rights of the Irish parliament, in particular the right of the Irish House of Lords to act as the final court of appeal for cases within Ireland, a claim which was disputed by the British House of Lords and legislated against in the notorious 'Sixth of George the First'. In fact, the title of 'Country party' was the only one which this new opposition could adopt, since its members included both Tories and Whigs. The Irish Whigs had been squabbling amongst themselves even before George I had landed in England, and in the Irish parliamentary session of 1715-16 a section of the party, which resented the way the spoils of victory had been parcelled out, flirted with opposition in the hope of bringing

26. P.R.O.N.I., T.1774 (Tickell Mss.), [Thomas Tickell] to Carteret, 23 June 1727. See also *Letters Written by His Excellency, Hugh Boulter, D.D., Lord Primate of All Ireland* ... (2 vols., Dublin, 1770), i, 139, Boulter to Carteret, 29 June 1727; P.R.O.N.I., D.562/92 (Foster/Massereene Mss.), Bishop Theophilus Bolton to [Carteret], 16 July 1728.
27. In 1719 Speaker Conolly listed seventy-three Tories, presumably those likely to oppose the projected repeal of the Test (P.R.O.N.I., T.2825/A/1/1B [Conolly Mss.]).

about a redistribution.[28] In succeeding years the opposition remained a coalition of Tories and discontented Whigs, and in order to maintain unity its leaders by and large avoided taking their stand on questions which would have revived memories of the days of 'party' strife.

In Anne's reign the conflict of Whigs and Tories had tended to swamp all other considerations governing political behaviour. Ties of kinship or patronage, for example, might count for little against the pull of party. With the disintegration of the two-party system these other factors became more important. Principle no longer exercised the most powerful influence overall on men's conduct: the Court and Country parties of the reigns of George I and George II seem primarily to have been associations of men bound together in pursuit of power, place and profit rather than believers in a common ideology. The front-bench politicians did not support Court or Country out of a commitment to principles of loyalism or Irish patriotism: they were quite happy to take office when the opportunity offered, and to withdraw their loyalty if that became necessary. Some of the rank and file were staunch 'courtiers' or 'patriots', but they represented only a part of the whole. The others followed their patrons or leaders, in or out of office. A common attitude was that expressed by one back-bencher, who wrote to a Country party leader in 1731 and wished him 'everything you desire to strengthen your interest, which I am satisfied, let it go by what denomination it will, Country or Court, is and must be designed and intended for the good of this kingdom.'[29] The main components of the Court and Country parties were 'connections', groups of members attached to individual politicians, patrons or heads of families: Archbishop Boulter of Armagh referred in 1729 to 'the several clans' which made up the Court side, and which had to be kept together, while in the previous year another member of the government had written of the necessity of having a man of enough influence in charge of the Court party, otherwise 'people will either wander as sheep without a shepherd, or will get into factions that may render the administration here uneasy'.[30] The pattern of parliamentary politics had

28. Midleton Mss., iii, fo. 205, [Alan Brodrick] to [Thomas Brodrick], 14 Dec. 1714; B.L., Add. Mss. 47,088, fo. 60, Charles Dering to Lord Perceval, 1 June 1716.
29. P.R.O.N.I., D.2707/A/1/2/86 (Shannon Mss.), Jonathan Bruce to Henry Boyle, 9 Nov. 1731.
30. *Letters Written by ... Hugh Boulter ...*, i, 265, Boulter to Newcastle, 23 Oct. 1729; P.R.O.N.I., T.2534/2, Marmaduke Coghill to [Edward Southwell], 13 June 1728.

become almost kaleidoscopic, with new combinations forming and dissolving in the space of a session. It was a far cry from the days of Whig and Tory party strife when the young Members elected to parliament for the first time in 1727 could decide '(for the good of their country) to act in a body ... distinguished by the name of Toopees, which is not more than a particular kind of foretop which they have to their wigs, which they fancy denotes youth and smartness'.[31]

4

One of the most important effects produced by this change in 'political structure' on the government's method of parliamentary management was simply to decrease the number of managers or 'undertakers' involved. The Whig and Tory parties had each been directed by a caucus of politicians, and any negotiations with the viceroy were conducted by the leadership as a whole. Shrewsbury had to summon eight of the Whig managers to the Castle in 1714, while in 1707 Pembroke invited seven Tories for discussions in order to find out the party's views. The replacement of the Whig and Tory parties by smaller factions narrowed the circle of political leadership and, from witnessing a war between two large armies, the Irish parliament became the battle-ground of *condottieri*. Instead of having to parley with each party's general staff, the viceroy could now negotiate with a few magnates. There were two or three principal managers at the most to see that the government's business was transacted, and usually one of them was pre-eminent. The existence of this presiding individual was the most notable characteristic of the 'undertaker system' of the mid-eighteenth century, and it had appeared before the end of George I's reign. In 1728, when the head of the Court party was forced by ill health to retire from politics, it was reported that the government's forces fell into disarray, 'the people who had served under him, not caring immediately to list under a new leader'.[32] The practice of having one politician permanently in charge of the Court party was in part a consequence of the emergence of a political world in which personality and personal relationships counted for more than issues. It was also the result of a number of developments after 1714 which concentrated political power in the hands of one man. This man proved so successful as a parliamentary 'undertaker' that when he disappeared from the scene

31. N.L.I., Ms. 8,802/11, Edward Cooke to Lord [————], 22 Feb. 1728.
32. P.R.O., S.P. 63/391/236, Thomas Clutterbuck to Charles Delafaye, 20 Nov. 1729.

the government's only thought was to find someone to take his place.

The politician whose career marks the inception of a new 'system' of management was William Conolly. Like his eventual successor, Henry Boyle, Conolly possessed considerable personal influence in the Commons, where his wealth and interest guaranteed him 'numerous dependants'.[33] He achieved pre-eminence as a parliamentary manager through holding three important offices, which had never before been held simultaneously by one man. From 1715 Conolly was Speaker of the Irish House of Commons, a lord justice (in the absence of the lord lieutenant) and 'first' commissioner of the revenue. The Speakership enabled him to influence the proceedings of the Commons, and it made his goodwill vitally necessary to the government. If the occupant of the Chair favoured the interests of the ministry he could make things go well; if not, there was certain to be trouble. The office of lord justice was coveted for the prestige it conferred: it carried no patronage of its own (although the lords justices were consulted by the English government before the appointment of new judges and bishops), but Conolly's nomination served to show that he retained the trust of the ministry. The 'first' commissionership of the revenue was in a way the most important post of the three, providing Conolly with a source of patronage which he was able to use much as he liked. Just how valuable this patronage was as an engine of political power can be deduced from the fact that the revenue service was the fastest-growing department of state in Ireland, with several hundred officers in its employ (the majority of whom were appointed by the revenue commissioners themselves) and an expenditure on salaries alone of almost £50,000 a year.[34]

The concentration of these offices in Conolly's hands owed something to chance. Certainly, good fortune helped bring him the opportunity of the Chair. Before 1714 he had been one among several prominent Whigs in the Commons, but by the time the first Hanoverian parliament met the other Whig party leaders had all left the Commons, through being ennobled or being appointed as judges. Conolly was then the obvious choice to be Speaker, and his only rivals for leadership in the Commons were younger men, like St John Brodrick, the son of the lord chancellor. Brodrick quickly proved that he could be effective as a trouble-maker, but by the time he had

33. P.R.O.N.I., T.2774 (Tickell Mss.), [Thomas Tickell] to Carteret, 23 June 1727.
34. Hayton, 'Ireland and the English Ministers', pp 51-3.

gained enough experience to be considered as a potential government manager Conolly was firmly established in that role. Conolly became the first Speaker to act as a lord justice as a consequence of his rivalry with Lord Chancellor Midleton, which, as we shall see, was a feature of Irish politics from 1715 until 1725. Conolly had been included by the government on the commission of lords justices after the parliamentary session of 1715-16, to demonstrate that he was held in as high regard as the chancellor, and it became essential to keep him there to prevent it being thought that he had lost favour. It was partly by accident, too, that he was able to make more of his position as 'first commissioner' of the revenue than had his predecessor, Thomas Keightley. Keightley had not been a man of much political weight and had been 'first' commissioner in name only. Conolly, as one of the foremost men in parliament, was better able to overawe his colleagues; added to which, he was of a hardworking disposition while the other commissioners were for the most part absentees. His long-suffering wife once complained that 'he is every day at least six hours at the Custom House ... I wish some of the commissioners were ordered to their business, for I think it is hard he should always have the labouring ...'. Finally, the wholesale dismissal of Tory officers from the revenue service after Queen Anne's death gave the new Whig commissioners more vacancies to fill than they would otherwise have had, and temporarily increased the amount of patronage at their disposal.[35]

Conolly established his position as the leading government manager in the Commons as early as 1715, but he had to wait until 1725 before he became the principal and unrivalled 'undertaker'. This was because of the continued presence in the government of Lord Midleton, formerly Alan Brodrick, a Whig politician who had been raised to the office of lord chancellor of Ireland in 1714. Midleton resented Conolly's advancement, and for the next ten years the two men were engaged in a prolonged struggle for power. Conolly's strategy was to ingratiate himself with the government at all times, even when his opponent was in favour; Midleton's appears to have been to make as much mischief as possible, with the assistance in the House of Commons of his son St John, who, he claimed, was a wild young man beyond parental control.[36] Midleton

35.   Christ Church, Oxford, Wake Mss., xii, Bishop John Evans to Archbishop William Wake, 20 May [1718]; P.R.O., S.P. 63/391/71, Mrs K. Conolly to [Charles Delafaye], 17 June 1729; N.L.I., Ms. 16,007, p. 10, Sunderland to the Irish revenue commissioners, 28 July 1715.
36.   P.R.O., S.P. 63/375/204-5, Conolly to Charles Delafaye, 3 Oct. 1717; West Suffolk R.O., 423/881 (Grafton Mss.), Grafton to Walpole, 23 Sept. 1723.

kept his place for so long because of the English ministers' reluctance to divide the Irish Whigs any further by dismissing him, and because there was uncertainty as to which of the two rivals, Conolly or Midleton himself, had the larger following in parliament. Grafton, viceroy from 1720 onwards and a man whose initial dislike of Midleton grew into detestation, found his demands for the chancellor's removal frustrated by the caution of his ministerial colleagues. In the spring of 1721 Grafton had a 'conference' with 'two of the chief ministers', at which was aired 'their proposal of continuing [the] lord chancellor, grounded upon difficulties of finding a successor and the disturbances the threat might give to the measures in parliament'. At this time even Conolly agreed. Although Midleton's remaining in office might be taken as a sign 'that his merit is so great that he could not be removed, nor could the King's affairs be carried on without him', the Speaker resigned himself to it: 'that and more', he wrote, 'must be borne.'[37] Even after Midleton had been actively involved in the agitation against Wood's Halfpence, Walpole was not prepared to take the step of getting rid of the chancellor. He replaced Grafton with Lord Carteret and left it up to the new chief governor of Ireland to decide, remarking to Newcastle that Carteret would have to 'take his party betwixt the two great men there'.[38] After taking stock, the viceroy plumped for Conolly, and Midleton was at last forced out of office.

Although the creation of the 'system' operated by Conolly had been unplanned, the ministers became aware of its advantages, and when the Speaker was forced to retire from public life in 1728, they tried to keep power and influence in one pair of hands. Unfortunately, there was no-one in Conolly's party who had nearly as much 'interest' in the Commons, or managerial expertise, so a compromise was reached by which two 'undertakers' were employed, Sir Ralph Gore and Marmaduke Coghill. Gore was the senior partner, succeeding Conolly as Speaker and as leader of the Court party. He would not agree to become first commissioner of the revenue, preferring to retain the more lucrative office of chancellor of the exchequer, so Conolly's place on the revenue board went to the second-in-command, Coghill.[39] Their partnership was reasonably successful, but Gore died in 1732 and a new manager had then to be sought

37. P.R.O.N.I., T.2825/A/1/17 (Conolly Mss.), Conolly to Grafton, 11 May 1721.
38. B.L., Add. Mss. 32,687, fos: 54-55, Walpole to [Newcastle], 1 Sept. 1724.
39. *Letters Written by ... Hugh Boulter ...*, i, 267, Boulter to Newcastle, 30 Oct. 1729.

from outside the Court party. Coghill's influence by itself was insufficient and no-one among his lieutenants was capable of taking the place of Gore. The government was forced to turn to the leader of the opposition, Henry Boyle, who like Conolly was a skilful parliamentarian and a man with an extensive personal 'interest' in the Commons. Boyle's election as Speaker was supported from the Castle, and eventually he was installed in the two offices which Conolly had enjoyed, those of lord justice and first commissioner of the revenue. He was first appointed as Gore's successor at the exchequer, but soon switched offices with Coghill, to the benefit of the administration.[40]

The other important difference between this 'system' of management and the one which had prevailed before was that the viceroy now had more freedom of manoeuvre. In the earlier period, when political allegiances were hard and fast, the lord lieutenant had a very limited choice as to whom he engaged as his parliamentary managers. There were only two groups of politicians to choose from; it was impossible to create a 'mixed' ministry and extraordinarily difficult even to detach one or two politicians from their friends. The two viceroys who did try to form 'mixed' administrations, Pembroke (in 1707) and Shrewsbury (in 1713) were completely unsuccessful. When the lord lieutenant was himself a partisan, and known to be a Whig or a Tory, he had no choice at all in the overall composition of his ministry. Lord Wharton, a notorious Whig, came over to Ireland in 1709 to find an Irish ministry that was still almost wholly Tory in complexion. Although he did nothing at first to alter the administration, the Tories opposed him to a man and the Whigs stood by him, thus forcing a change in the ministry regardless of the wishes or actions of the viceroy.[41] When Wharton was replaced in 1710 by Ormonde, a Tory, Irish politicians immediately assumed that the ministry would return to its old party colouring and accordingly the Tories once again became the Court party while the Whigs went back into opposition, many of them still holding office.[42] The fact that the viceroy had no choice as to which party was enlisted under the Court's banner seriously restricted his freedom in deciding upon policy. There was considerable pressure on him to follow the logic of party conflict and bow to the

40.   B.L., Add. Mss. 21,123, fo. 96, Coghill to [Edward Southwell], 25 Feb. 1735.
41.   B.L., Add. Mss. 47,025, fo. 121, Sir John Perceval to Edward Southwell, 26 May 1709; Blenheim Mss., C.I. -23, Wharton to [Sunderland], 20 June 1709.
42.   T.C.D., Ms. 2531, p. 322, Archbishop King to [Edward Southwell], 13 Mar. 1711.

demands and prejudices of his managers — to pursue their enemies and to endorse measures which would benefit their friends: for example, Whig ministries produced legislation to penalize Catholics, while Tory ministries gave more of their attention to restricting the activities of Dissenters; and as regards government patronage, it became more and more difficult to keep in office men who adhered to the other party — every swing of the pendulum after 1700, from Whig to Tory, to Whig, back to Tory and finally to Whig again, was accompanied by a purge of office-holders progressively more extensive, until in 1714 and 1715 almost every Tory placeman was turned out.[43]

After the two-party system had broken down, the lord lieutenant was somewhat more happily placed. He had a little more say in choosing his parliamentary managers, and thus more freedom in making policy. In the House of Commons more members were 'King's friends' first and foremost, a fact which naturally strengthened the government's hand. Moreover, the appointment of two Englishmen, Hugh Boulter in 1724 and Richard West in 1725, to the great offices of primate and lord chancellor respectively, meant that the viceroy could thenceforth have the assistance of two loyal and expert advisers stationed permanently in Ireland. West died after only a year and a half in office, but his replacement was another Englishman, Thomas Wyndham. As a result of these various changes the balance in the relationship between the lord lieutenant and his parliamentary managers was weighted less heavily in favour of the latter. Government policy in general was no longer prescribed by political parties, and on the specific question of patronage the viceroy found himself more often able to act according to his own wishes or to please persons other than his supporters in parliament.

The viceroy was still at a disadvantage, however, and the parliamentary session of 1733-4 provides evidence of the practical limitations on his power. The lord lieutenant, Dorset, having backed Henry Boyle's election to the Chair, proceeded to withhold his confidence from the new Speaker. Dorset apparently preferred the company and advice of politicians of the second rank, and may well have tried to play off Boyle and his lesser rivals against one another. The Speaker was moved to protest at 'my lord lieutenant's private and reserved behaviour, his not communicating his pleasure to any, and keeping those who are most ready to serve him at a distance

---

43.   Hayton, 'Ireland and the English Ministers', chapter 9.

from his councils'.[44] The scheme, if such it was, did not work. Boyle was strong enough to cause difficulties for the government if he felt resentment, and in any case members of parliament had to be certain of the direction of Court favour before they could be expected to vote as the viceroy desired. A straight forward approach was necessary; it was no good giving countenance simultaneously to rival politicians and representatives of distinct and even opposing factions. After enduring the vexations and disappointments of a troublesome session Dorset changed course. Henceforth Boyle was to be supported fully: he was made a lord justice; his requests for patronage were given viceregal endorsement; it was obvious to all that he was the chief 'undertaker'.

5

To sum up. The inherent weaknesses of the viceroyalty made the employment of parliamentary managers necessary throughout the early eighteenth century. These managers were always 'undertakers', although they disliked the word and tried to prevent its use. With the break-up of the Whig and Tory parties after the death of Queen Anne the 'undertaker system' changed its character, becoming virtually a monarchy instead of an oligarchy. William Conolly set a pattern in his career as a parliamentary manager, and paved the way for the more protracted ascendancy of Henry Boyle. In this new context the lord lieutenant was better placed in dealing with his managers than he had been before, but he still could not establish a dominance. The 'undertakers' remained as they had always been: powerful, independent men, whose expectations and desires a viceroy slighted at his peril.[45]

44. Chatsworth Mss. (Chatsworth House, Derbyshire), Henry Boyle to Burlington, 17 Aug. 1731 (this reference was communicated to me by Dr A. P. W. Malcomson); *H.M.C. Egmont Diary*, i, 450, 462-3; ii, 2; *H.M.C. Stopford-Sackville*, i, 149, Dorset to George Dodington, 10 Jan. 1734. I wish to thank His Grace the duke of Devonshire and the Trustees of the Chatsworth Settlement for permission to refer to material in the Chatsworth Mss.
45. It is a pleasure for me to acknowledge a debt of gratitude to the Academic Council of the Queen's University of Belfast for electing me in 1973 to a Junior Fellowship at the Institute of Irish Studies, Queen's University, and thereby enabling to be completed the research on which this paper is based. I am also grateful to Professor J. C. Beckett and Professor Edith M. Johnston for commenting upon drafts: I alone, however, am responsible for any errors of fact or interpretation which may be discovered in the finished product.

THE MONEY BILL DISPUTE OF 1753

Declan O'Donovan

The Money Bill dispute of 1753 was the centrepiece of a struggle between the Castle administration and a party in the House of Commons led by the Speaker, Henry Boyle. The Castle had its allies also in the Commons and these were made up of the Ponsonby faction presided over by Henry Boyle's old rival, the earl of Bessborough; the adherents of the primate, George Stone; and a number of 'respectable' members, who automatically supported government. On its side, Henry Boyle's group was composed of his own faction, that of the earl of Kildare and that of the Gores, led by the highly capable but crypto-Catholic prime serjeant, Anthony Malone, with important financial assistance from the teller of the exchequer, Nathaniel Clements. Both Malone and Clements had married into the Gore family. In addition, the party was supported — and to an extent radicalized — by the 'Country' or 'patriot' members, whose natural position was one of antipathy to government and to the English interest in Ireland. In 1753 they were represented in the party leadership by Thomas Carter, the master of the rolls, an experienced and skilful political organizer and parliamentarian, and by the temperamental Lord Kildare. Although only a handful in the Commons, the 'patriots' had the strong backing in opposition of middle- and lower-class Protestants, and especially of the presbyterians. It was this element which prodded Henry Boyle and his colleagues into open opposition, and provided popular support for the constitutional objections of Carter and Malone, who managed financial business in the Commons, and of Sir Richard Cox, a maverick member of Boyle's faction who was the party's pamphlet spokesman. That Boyle's party became known in 1753 as the 'patriot party' is a tribute to the strong views and persistence of its 'patriot' supporters; but it is also due to the deliberate attempt of the Castle to crush the party's influence in public affairs. Were it not for these two factors, Henry Boyle would scarcely have lent his weight to the Money Bill opposition, and without his participation the opposition forces would certainly not have succeeded.

The struggle between Henry Boyle's party and the Castle had its roots in the appointment of the ambitious George Stone as archbishop of Armagh in March 1747 and it ended with Henry Boyle's success in excluding Stone from political affairs as part of a settlement with the marquess of Hartington, who was sent to Ireland in 1755 to negotiate with the opposition and so calm the country prior to the European war against the French, which was then

C

imminent. This re-examination of the Money Bill dispute will be principally concerned with the parliamentary session of 1753, with the debate on the bill and with the circumstances under which it was rejected by the House of Commons. It will be shown that the Castle's tactics were based on the assumption that Henry Boyle would never oppose the Money Bill, or that if he did, he and his party would be destroyed by order of the King and the British ministry. The former assumption was shared by the lord lieutenant, the duke of Dorset, and his son and chief secretary, Lord George Sackville; the latter was more in the mind of the primate, who saw an opportunity in the Money Bill question to confirm his power in Ireland and his influence in London. It will also be shown that the debate on the Money Bill was technically quite evenly balanced, but that it inevitably raised wider constitutional questions with important consequences: and finally, that economic conditions were an important background element to the dispute. In conclusion it will be suggested that the dispute provided a focus and accelerator for gathering patriotic sentiments, which were to culminate in the establishment of legislative independence in 1782. First, however, we must examine the background to the dispute: the role of the 'undertakers' in Irish political management and the question of the Money Bill itself.

2

The Irish administration needed support in the House of Commons to ensure the safe passage of supplies and other legislation, and not least to ward off attacks by the 'Country' members or by ambitious or disappointed politicians. In an age when party groupings were loose, there were no automatic government or opposition benches, but in return for a share in favour, influence and the management of public business, party leaders in the House would 'undertake' to support government during the parliamentary session. Such leaders could not themselves provide a majority of the 300 members, but they brought with them a hard core of support to which most members would adhere. As important as their degree of support was the acumen, speaking ability or managing skill of these leaders. In fact, there was no difference of function between the Irish parliamentary chiefs and their British counterparts. But, it has come to be believed that by the 1750s these 'undertakers' had taken the Castle's management of Irish politics entirely into their own hands. The origin of this belief can traced directly to Archbishop Stone, and to a pamphlet, *Letter to the Duke of Bedford*, published by Stone's protege, E. S. Pery, in 1757. The first recorded exposition of the theory is in a letter Stone wrote to the duke of Newcastle in March 1752, after the Castle had suffered a defeat at Henry Boyle's

hands in the House of Commons;[1] and in the next three years the
primate pressed his views in a series of letters to Newcastle and to
his own brother Andrew Stone, who was Newcastle's secretary and
confidant. The primate's object was to smash the considerable
influence of the Speaker's party, and to counter the ministry's
worries about this policy he presented the image of an anti-English
clique, long grown used to a controlling role in Irish politics. Stone
exaggerated, but there was enough truth in the view to make it
plausible to later observers, even though the nomenclature he used,
'undertakers', was not current in this period. However, Stone's
views had much less weight with contemporary British and Irish
opinion, nor were they particularly influential with the King or the
British ministry.

3

The term money bill is a little loose, as it could apply to any
bill authorising the raising or expenditure of money for the King's
service.[2] The principal money bill, or supply bill as it was more
exactly called, was a bill continuing the Commons' grant of 'additional duties' on alcohol, tobacco and other goods. This vote was
designed to make up the deficiency of income accruing from the
royal 'hereditary' revenue, an amalgam of common law levying
rights and parliamentary taxes granted *in perpetuum*. The yield

1.   B.L., Add. Mss. 32,726, fo. 213, George Stone to Newcastle, 3 Mar. 1752.
This is the first item of correspondence published by C. Litton Falkiner in
'Correspondence of Archbishop Stone and the Duke of Newcastle', *E.H.R.*,
xx (1905).
2.   The account given here relies on T. J. Kiernan, *History of the Financial
Administration of Ireland to 1817* (London, 1930), chapter 4, and on the
following pamphlets: *A Short Account of H.M. Hereditary Revenue and Private
Estate in the Kingdom of Ireland* (Dublin, 1754); *Considerations on the late
Bill for Payment of the Remainder of the National Debt ...* (Dublin, 1754);
*The Proceeding of the Honourable House of Commons of Ireland, in Rejecting
the Altered Money-Bill on December 17, 1753, Vindicated ...* (Dublin, 1754);
Remarks on a Pamphlet Intitled Considerations ... (Dublin, 1754). The first two
pamphlets were pro-Castle, the second being written by a noted lawyer,
Christopher Robinson; the latter two were 'patriot', written respectively by Sir
Richard Cox and William Bruce. *Considerations* argued that the bill 'could not
with propriety be called a *money bill* ... that title should be restrained to those
bills which grant money to the Crown' (p. 20); Richard Rigby thought the bill
'absurdly called' (*Correspondence of John, Fourth Duke of Bedford ...* ed. Lord
John Russell [3 vols., London, 1842-6], ii, 142, Rigby to Bedford, 25 Dec.
1753). *The Proceeding*, however, saw these criticisms as pointless since the bill
directed the application of money and contained nothing else (p. 35).

of these duties depended on the prosperity of the country and the efficiency of collection, but between the years of rebellion, 1715 and 1745, the income of the Irish treasury was not sufficient to meet government expenses. The Jacobite threat panicked the Irish Commons into giving George I *carte blanche* to defend the kingdom. In effect, the only way to raise the necessary money was to borrow. The national debt which thus began was increased in subsequent years to meet exchequer deficits as a matter of course. Special money bills, called loan bills, were passed to authorize borrowing and to raise duties to meet the interest of the debt. These bills specifically appropriated possible surpluses to the discharge of part of the debt itself. The appropriated money was carefully distinguished from the general fund and was not disbursed by government warrant. However, there was never any distinction drawn between the unappropriated money voted by the parliament in additional duties, and the much more considerable hereditary revenue. The two different kinds of treasury income formed a general fund for the financing of government and the King's servants drew on the money without distinguishing which source of income they were drawing from. For its part, parliament had the recognised right of calling government officials to task for the management of the general fund, and the Commons likewise made no attempt to distinguish between the two sources.

This parliamentary right was guarded jealously. It was practised as a matter of principle but also as a means of influencing public policy and winning political power, although parliament's most effective sanction was its ability to wreck government financing by simply refusing to vote supplies. The Commons were quick to oppose any attempt to diminish their powers. The Irish House of Commons had in fact acquired the right to initiate all money bills except the supply bill drawn up by the Irish Privy Council as a cause for calling a new parliament, thus setting a customary limit to the force of the act of Philip and Mary stipulating that bills might originate in the Privy Council as well as in parliament.[3]

3. Strictly speaking, bills leaving the Irish parliament were merely 'heads of bills', and only when approved by the Irish Privy Council did they become bills. By the mid-century, however, it would have been unthinkable for the Irish Council to have interfered with the heads of a money bill. Indeed, in regard to any disliked bill, Dublin Castle preferred to try to have it dropped or amended in parliament, or at the English Council board, rather than risk hostility in the Irish House of Commons by taking action in the Irish Council; nor was it usual for the Council to initiate bills formally itself, though the connection between Irish parliamentary leaders and the Council — they were customarily members — made the real situation more fluid. For evidence of the declining role of the

In 1749, however, and again in 1751 and 1753, the Commons were presented with an unusual situation. There was a surplus rather than a deficit in the treasury and the issue arose of whether King or Commons had the ownership of this extra money which had been produced by the more prosperous economic conditions and by improvements in revenue collection. Except in 1749, the issue was formally brought forward by the lord lieutenant in his speech from the throne at the beginning of the parliamentary session and was immediately taken up by the Commons in their address of thanks to the King on each occasion. The dispute concerned the legal right to the disposal of the surplus. Government claimed the right to be entirely in the crown and argued therefore that the King's previous consent was necessary for the use of the money; 'patriot' M.P.s claimed that the right did not lie *solely* in the crown. The Commons did *not* claim the *exclusive* right to dispose of the money; only that they had an independent right to its disposal; and far from opposing the application of some of the surplus to the national debt, country gentlemen were fervently in favour of this course of action.

When we speak, therefore, of the Money Bill of 1753 we mean the bill to apply the surplus in the treasury, and not the supply bill normally understood to be 'the Money Bill', which in fact passed the Commons as usual in December 1753 and became law. Speaker Boyle and his friends were not out to deny the government money necessary for its continued operation.

4

In 1753 there were other factors at work besides the arguments of principle and the personality clashes. First, a general and widespread resentment of the government had taken hold. The proceedings of the House of Commons were the subject of intense interest. One important matter was the consideration of the petitions of Francis Caulfeild against William Brownlow for the Armagh election, and of Frederick Trench and Richard Eyre against the return of Charles Daly and Robert French for Galway, which occupied the committee of privileges and elections full-time. Their report on the Armagh election was finally presented on 10 December. The Castle had won the vote in committee by four but the final verdict in

Council in legislation see P.R.O.N.I., D.2707/A/1/6/3A, B (Shannon Mss.), the Irish lords justices to Bedford (lord lieutenant), 23 Nov. 1760: 'since the sitting of parliaments have become more regular, the framing of bills originally in the Council has become less and less frequent and has been for many years past almost totally disused, unless on the occasion of a calling of a new parliament...'.

favour of its candidate, Brownlow, was the narrowest possible in a huge House, 120-119. As a result, the 'patriot' petitions against the Galway election were given up. The Armagh result was particularly important because it concerned Primate Stone in his own bailiwick. Fully realizing this, he had given every assistance to Brownlow. The primate had not expected to win the vote and the Court side had had some luck. Stone was quick to make use of his good fortune and wrote to his brother: 'it will seem very strange that an election should be carried chiefly by my personal interest in the country; and that a question wherein His Majesty's dignity is so immediately concerned should be lost.'4

The implication of this remark was of course that certain examples should be made, an objective made all the more necessary because of the promises offered in canvassing. The under-secretary, Thomas Waite, explained to Sir Robert Wilmot, his opposite number in London: 'our friends will look for satisfaction ... they have a right to expect security and protection.' This could not be ensured 'whilst men and measures remain as they now are and have been for twenty years past'. Lord George, however, was less confident of the merit of fighting the Armagh election and argued merely that the Castle had to involve itself in this private matter in order to save the Money Bill.5 The doubtfulness of this proposition must have been apparent to Wilmot and others in Whitehall, because the letters from Sackville and Waite were uniform on one point, that the Speaker would not oppose the Money Bill despite the pressure being exerted by Malone and Kildare. Had it not been for the election result, it is possible that this judgment would have been proved right. But as Sackville himself was quick to note, Boyle's defeat over the Armagh election was the first he had met with in twenty years.6 Given that the Irish Speakership was an active office and that control of the issue of contested elections in the Commons was one of the great buttresses of its political influence, Boyle had now reached the stage where his immediate objective must be to defeat his opponents whatever the larger consequences.

Up to this point, the Speaker had balanced very deliberate restraint with popular policies. For instance, on the question of imposing a tax on Irish absentees, which Kildare had pressed, Boyle,

4.   B.L., Add. Mss. 32,733, fo. 445, Stone to Andrew Stone, 15 Dec. 1753.
5.   Derby Borough Library, Catton collection (Ireland): photocopies in P.R.O.N.I., T.3019, Waite to Wilmot, 11 Dec. 1753; *ibid*., Sackville to Wilmot, 11 Dec. 1753.
6.   *Ibid*., Sackville to Wilmot, 11 Dec. 1753. Stone's letters to Newcastle were more inclined to contemplate the Speaker's opposition to the Money Bill: see his letter of 17 Nov. 1753 (B.L., Add. Mss. 32,733, fo. 266).

although allowing the issue to warm up, eventually used it to display his willingness to cooperate with the Castle. With his and Malone's assistance the matter was dropped in November. He balanced this conduct by taking up the popular position against a proposal to build a new Liffey bridge.

As the crisis of the Money Bill approached, the Speaker and his closest advisers were in a defensive tangle: how to show their power and recover their position without causing a confrontation with England; how to maintain the vital distinction between opposition to persons or private measures and opposition to the King or government measures; how to retain popular support without being forced into dangerous waters; and how to guard what they considered the legitimate rights of the Commons without rejecting the Money Bill. To see how the Speaker's party faced the issue of the Money Bill, we must now turn to the financial proceedings of the House.

The first step in the granting of additional duties was the investigation by the committee of supply into the treasury accounts. When the committee found that the hereditary revenue would not meet expenses for the next two years, the House would resolve to meet the deficiency stated in the committee's report. A detailed examination of accounts then followed by the public accounts committee.[7] The supply committee was a committee of the whole House and it was followed by a similarly constituted committee of ways and means. In 1753, the chairmanship of these committees was resumed by the master of the rolls, Thomas Carter, who had been absent, through illness, in 1751, and had been represented in both capacities by Prime Serjeant Malone. The supply report was received on 8 November and the report on ways and means two days later. The small committee then appointed to draw up heads of money legislation was evenly divided: Carter, Malone and John Gore for the patriots; Attorney-general Flood, Solicitor-general Tisdall and John Bourke (the Speaker's son-in-law but a revenue commissioner through Stone's favour), for the Castle. The committee immediately split on the preamble and as a result the heads presented by Carter on 13 November omitted any reference to the authority for applying the surplus. After a full debate on the following day, the heads were accepted without amendment, an event which can only mean that the patriots were not aggressively seeking to force the issue. They

7. The public accounts were referred to the committee of accounts after the agreement to grant a supply. Its report, presented about a month after the start of the session, was then formally referred to the committee of supply. John Bourke seems to have had principal charge of the examination of public accounts in this period.

61

were in fact prepared to accept a situation in which neither their claim nor the Crown's would be explicitly recognized. The House in its discussions on the 10th had been principally occupied with the dropping of the tax on the salaries and pensions of absentees, a question taken up by Kildare's relative, Thomas Pakenham, who proposed that the resolutions of the ways and means report should be re-committed. This was opposed by Sackville, who had the support of Anthony Malone, and 'others of the Speaker's friends'. In his letter to Pelham on the 11th, Sackville expressed no apprehension about the Money Bill.[8]

When the heads of the Money Bill were presented to the Castle on 15 November, the administration professed to be taken by surprise, to be outraged by the behaviour of the Speaker and his friends and to expect that the previous consent of the King to the disposal of the surplus would, as a matter of course, be inserted. There was to be no compromise.[9] The Speaker, the master of the rolls and the prime serjeant (who was considered the leading culprit) were all 'immovable'. Of the letters to Whitehall, only Sackville's mentioned that Boyle and Carter had expressed the hope that 'His Majesty would not insist upon words being inserted which must create such a general uneasiness in the minds of the people'. Stone as usual went further than the others and represented the affair as a desperate attempt to assuage Lord Kildare and to whip up popular support. The primate repeated his urging of dismissals and a tougher general policy to combat rising 'undertaker' power. In this he was joined for the first time by Dorset and Sackville who, however, were less frank and less pressing. The bill was allowed to go through unopposed because, they said, of unpreparedness and because initial action by Whitehall rather than the Castle would strengthen their position.

This turn in affairs was decisive. Three days later the patriots won their first major success of the session with the help of Nathaniel Clements, the teller of the exchequer. Stone wrote a further letter declaring that 'if some new model is not effected it will be in vain to attempt the support of English government longer'.[10] Newcastle's reply to the previous letters announced that the King was very angry and doubted not 'but Your Grace and all His Majesty's principal

8.   P.R.O.N.I., T.2863/1/59 (Henry Pelham Mss.) Sackville to Pelham, 11 Nov. 1753.
9.   *H.M.C. Stopford-Sackville*, i, 202-3, Sackville to Pelham, 15 Nov. 1753; B.L., Add. Mss. 32,733, fo. 299, Dorset to Newcastle, 16 Nov. 1753; *ibid.*, fo. 266, Stone to Newcastle, 17 Nov. 1753. Lord Chief Justice Singleton wrote to Granville supporting Stone: see *ibid.*, fo. 293, Newcastle to Dorset, 22 Nov. 1753.
10.   B.L., Add. Mss. 32,733, fo. 289, Stone to Newcastle, 21 Nov. 1753.

servants will use your utmost endeavours to get all the bills passed upon their return to Ireland'. Privately, Newcastle said that dismissals would be agreed to.[11] Newcastle went further after the expulsion of the surveyor-general, Arthur Jones Nevill, for mal-administration, and the defection of Clements, both of which alarmed the ministry. 'His Majesty was greatly surprised to see the lengths which the gentlemen in opposition were going.' And Newcastle made the very accurate observation: 'nothing could be so fortunate for the duke of Dorset as their opposition upon a point of prerogative in which they were sure of the King of the English nation.' The Castle was urged to stick to public points, to avoid personalities and to submit a list of possible replacements, since it was believed in England that 'Lord George Sackville has not one single man of character and ability to support him in the House of Commons'.[12]

Newcastle's opinions clearly belonged at St James's as much as they did at Whitehall, and Stone was alarmed. Acknowledging receipt of the Money Bills he confessed himself uneasy,

> That Your Grace should think these disorders to have been in any degree owing to our misconduct. Indeed, my lord, the cause of them is of much longer growth and lies much deeper. The constitutional dependency upon England is the object upon which the prime serjeant's eye is constantly fixed.[13]

The English Privy Council's letter inserting previous consent was made known to the opposition and soon copies of it were being circulated around the city. The lord lieutenant called a meeting of government servants for 15 December, and as a further gesture neither the primate nor the chief secretary attended. That, how-ever, was as far as it went. Dorset merely intoned the Privy Council letter, and formally called on His Majesty's servants in the House 'to use their utmost influence in their respective stations to support the just prerogative of the crown'. Clearly there was to be no possibility of compromise. 'When His Grace had finished', re-ported Stone, 'after a silence of a few minutes the Speaker rose first and others retired after him without a word being spoken.'[14] Sackville who had retained 'great hopes' of the Speaker until the day before this meeting, was genuinely shocked.[15]

11. *Ibid.*, fo. 293, Newcastle to Dorset, 22 Nov. 1753.
12. *Ibid.*, fo. 345, Newcastle to Stone, 30 Nov. 1753.
13. *Ibid.*, fo. 369, Stone to Newcastle, 6 Dec. 1753.
14. *Ibid.*, fo. 445, Stone to Andrew Stone, 15 Dec. 1753.
15. P.R.O.N.I., T.3019 (Wilmot Mss.), Sackville to Wilmot, 15 Dec. 1753.

On the previous day, the money bills had been returned to the House and a committee had been appointed to compare these with the transmiss. The changes were reported on the 15th and the House resolved to go into committee on the following Monday, 17 December. On that day the debate began at two in the afternoon and continued until about midnight, when the vote was taken and the worst fears of the Castle were realized. The bill to apply part of the treasury surplus to the discharge of the national debt was rejected as, thanks to Sir Edward Poynings, it could not be partially amended. One of the more fiery patriots warned that, should the English alterations stand, the money might disappear anywhere, even to Hanover! 'Lord George Sackville answered him with a good deal of emotion.' A supporter of the Castle warned that the fate of the House of Lords might also befall the Commons. He was referring to the claim of the Irish Lords to be the final judges of their peers, a claim which had occasioned the notorious 'Sixth of George the First'. When the patriot majority of 122-117 was declared the mob went mad: 'bonfires, riot and noise the whole night. Lord George Sackville was obliged to leave his chair before the House and through a backdoor from the coffee-room retire through by-streets to the Castle in a common vehicle.' The next day Sackville wrote an angry, making-the-best-of-it letter to Henry Pelham in which he discovered that he too shared the primate's 'undertaker' theories.[16]

Parliament continued to sit for the remainder of the week, busying itself with the bill to require restitution from Surveyor Nevill. On 22 December the lord lieutenant gave his assent to three bills, including the Supply Bill (the money bill proper). The Speaker made his usual speech in reply and passed up the opportunity to renew the attack. The House then adjourned for the Christmas recess.

Aware that his viceroyalty was seriously threatened, Dorset took the initiative and dispatched his second secretary, Robert Maxwell, to London with a long business letter.[17] Dorset's reasoning was not adopted entirely from Stone, who wrote a letter to his brother (intended to be seen by Newcastle), claiming

16. R.I.A., Ms. 12.R.9 (Charlemont Mss.), no. 28, Thomas Adderley to Charlemont, 29 Dec. 1753; P.R.O.N.I., T.3019, Sackville to Wilmot, 18 Dec. 1753; P.R.O.N.I., T.2541/IA1/2/176 (Abercorn Mss.), Rev. George Bracegirdle to Abercorn, 18 Dec. 1753; B.L., Add. Mss. 35,592, fo. 234, William Yorke to Hardwicke, 26 Dec. 1753; P.R.O.N.I., T.2863/1/62 (Henry Pelham Mss.), Sackville to Pelham, 18 Dec. 1783.
17. B.L., Add. Mss. 32,733, fo. 503, Dorset to Newcastle, 21 Dec. 1753.

that all his warnings and analyses had been more than justified and sharpening his campaign against Malone. As for Nathaniel Clements, it was 'utterly impossible to go on while he continue[d] in that office [teller of the exchequer]'. With optimism still flying high, Stone made just the kind of rash, definite promise that George II so admired: 'if these gentlemen or some of them are removed there is no doubt of having a large majority before next session: and the example would keep things quiet for many years.' Finally, he offered to present his case personally in London, a suggestion which was ignored.[18]

Stone's inclination to go to London may have been inspired by the highly publicized embassy of the earl of Kildare. 'It is not a measure', wrote Bishop Synge of Elphin, 'either concerted or approved of. But if Wilful will do it, he cannot be controlled.'[19] There was an element of farce in the journey. Kildare was reported to have left on the 22nd, but did not do so, owing, he said, to deliberate obstruction by the authorities, who were determined to give Maxwell a head start. According to Waite, he then bid fourteen guineas for a vessel to make the passage but was outdone by Wynne, the Castle messenger, who bid sixteen.[20] He eventually sailed on the 30th having been delayed by foul weather. The ministry nervously wondered what the combustible earl would attempt. His arrival was constantly watched for, and a great deal of thought was given to what should be said to him, whether the King should receive him, and if so under what circumstances.[21]

The problem was largely solved by the King and by Henry Fox, Kildare's brother-in-law. George refused to see Kildare; and Fox, of whom Hardwicke had unworthy suspicions, put his brother-in-law under wraps when he did arrive on 6 January. Fox persuaded Kildare to have a round of diplomatic outings with the ministers and forego

18.   *Ibid.*, fo. 541, Stone to Andrew Stone, 24 Dec. 1753.
19.   P.R.O.N.I., Mic. 147/9 (Roden Mss.), xvii, 108-9, Bishop Edward Synge to Lord Limerick, 25 Dec. 1753.
20.   P.R.O.N.I., T.3019, Waite to Wilmot, 29 Dec. 1753; *ibid.*, Sackville to Wilmot, 23 Dec. 1753; B.L., Add. Mss. 32,733, fo. 604, Andrew Stone to Newcastle, 30 Dec. 1753; *ibid.*, fo. 594, John Roberts (Pelham's secretary) to Newcastle, 29 Dec. 1753; B.L., Add. Mss. 32,734, fo. 3, Hardwicke to Newcastle, 1 Jan. 1754 — Hardwicke wondered what instructions Kildare had, and added tartly 'for they must be more Irish than I suppose all of them to be, if they would send such an ambassador a second time without any precise instructions'.
21.   B.L., Add. Mss. 32,734, fos. 21, 23, Pelham to Newcastle, 7, 8 Jan. 1754; *ibid.*, fos. 25, 57, Hardwicke to Newcastle, 8, 20 Jan. 1754; P.R.O.N.I., T.2760/24 (Sackville Mss.), Holdernesse to Dorset, 12 Jan. 1754.

a great scene with the King.[22] The earl's missionary zeal, held back in Dublin and cooled by frost and floods on the road from Chester, was safely aborted at Holland House. Nevertheless, 'reliable reports' reached the Irish newspapers and Kildare's enthusiastic supporters were fed with suitably heroic accounts of the visit.[23]

The appalling winter weather which had frustrated Kildare also delayed the arrival of the English ministry's deliberations on the defeat, which were sent to Dublin on 28 December. They arrived twelve days later. A public letter from the southern secretary, Lord Holdernesse, announced that a select cabinet had considered Dorset's letter. It was the King's pleasure that parliament should not sit again that session, that Thomas Carter, Anthony Malone, Michael O'Brien Dilkes (the quarter-master-general and barrack-master-general, who was also the Speaker's half-brother) and Bellingham Boyle (another relative of the Speaker) should be stripped of their employments and pensions. Carter was, in addition, to be removed from the Privy Council. Full information was required about the state of the Commons.[24] The tone was peremptory, and Bishop Synge as 'a plain man', allowed himself 'to wonder a little why such a letter was wrote'. He told Lord Limerick: 'I own the style choked me. Except for four years it has not been much in use since the Revolution.'[25]

We have some idea of the options the ministry considered from a document dated 10 December in the Wilmot papers.[26] This is a plan of instructions for Lord George Sackville and is marked 'not sent'. It indicates that Whitehall was considering a shortening of the session if the bill were passed by a small majority, and a dissolution if it were defeated. The Castle was to present a detailed report of election prospects with particular reference to office-holders. This plan may have been a private one of Wilmot's, or it may have been intended as a piece of paper which Lord George could use in his canvassing. In any event the idea of a dissolution could not have been seriously considered. A general election in early 1754 could only have proved disastrous for the Castle. The private letter from Newcastle which accompanied the formal instructions of Holder-

22. B.L., Add. Mss. 32,734, fo. 57, Hardwicke to Newcastle, 20 Jan. 1754.
23. *Universal Advertiser,* 10, 15 Jan. 1754; *Pue's Occurrences,* 17 Jan. 1754; *Belfast Newsletter,* 15 Jan. 1754.
24. P.R.O.N.I., T.2760/20, Holdernesse to Dorset, 28 Dec. 1753.
25. P.R.O.N.I., Mic. 147/9 (Roden Mss.), xvii, 114, Bishop Edward Synge to Lord Limerick, 24 Jan. 1754. Presumably, he meant the Tory ministry of the four last years of Queen Anne's reign.
26. P.R.O.N.I., T.3019.

nesse took an entirely different line.[27] Dorset was to consider 'how well meaning persons who have been misled may be brought back to a proper submission to His Majesty's authority'. Newcastle clearly believed that there were many of these and that Henry Boyle was one of them. The Castle was to pay special attention to the vital importance of being supported by 'persons of credit and ability' and again Newcastle indicated he had doubts that such persons existed on the government side. Finally, he warned that influential opinion in England believed that the opposition was due to personality clashes.

The answering of this disturbing missive was a subject of argument at the Castle. Dorset knew his fellow duke rather better than did his son or the primate. He saw that his conduct of the lord lieutenancy was now itself an issue and that he was being asked, in words that bespoke the King's wishes, to guarantee future quiet. The newspapers were confidently predicting a new viceroy: Chesterfield, Granville, Holdernesse, Bedford and Albemarle were all mentioned in turn. Richard Rigby thought it would be Granville, who as Carteret had been sent over to settle matters at the time of the Wood's Halfpence crisis in 1724, but related that Holdernesse was so confident of being sent to Dublin that he was hawking positions in his retinue.[28] The belief expressed by Bishop Synge that 'those at the helm begin to blame each other and on one side charge ill success to too sanguine conduct on the other', was certainly accurate.[29]

On the night of 13 January 1754, Dorset, Sackville, Stone and Lord Chancellor Newport met at the Castle to discuss the line to be taken. That there was disagreement is evident from the letters that were subsequently sent to England.[30] Dorset's long, evasive letter must have infuriated the primate. It was a mass of contradictions. He accepted entirely Newcastle's hint that 'these attempts

27. B.L., Add. Mss. 32,733, fo. 582, Newcastle to Dorset, 28 Dec. 1753.
28. *Bedford Corresp.*, ii, 142, Rigby to Bedford, 25 Dec. 1753. The possibility of appointing a lord deputy may also have been under consideration: see B.L., Add. Mss. 32,995, fo. 58, an undated paper included in a collection of documents described as brought by Maxwell or relating to his visit.
29. P.R.O.N.I., Mic. 147/9, xvii, 108-9, Bishop Edward Synge to Lord Limerick, 25 Dec. 1753.
30. B.L., Add. Mss. 32,734, fos. 35-47, Dorset to Newcastle, 14 Jan. 1754; *ibid.*, fo. 49, Stone to Newcastle, 14 Jan. 1754; *H.M.C. Stopford-Sackville*, i, 204-5, Sackville to Pelham, 14 Jan. 1754. Newport thought it prudent not to write, much to Hardwicke's annoyance: see B.L., Add. Mss. 32,734, fo. 57, Hardwicke to Newcastle, 20 Jan. 1754.

(though in appearance upon great public points) had their rise in private pique and resentment'. He also promised to hold the primate and Lord George in check. He repeated Stone's line on the undertakers but not with enthusiasm: he was 'sensible enough' of attempts to keep the lord lieutenant 'under a sort of subjection' but had in his previous viceroyalty gone along with this so long as 'due respect' was paid to the King and His Majesty's business was carried on. He followed Stone in placing most of the blame, as Hardwicke had thought of doing, on the safely papist shoulders of Anthony Malone. Having declared on 16 November that he had received assurances at the start of the session and that he was 'greatly surprised' to find the issue of the King's previous consent revived,[31] Dorset now informed Newcastle that the attack on the Money Bill 'was of early determination and denounced to me with peremptoriness by the Speaker, Mr Carter and Mr Malone at the beginning of the session'. Finally, although he gave very full details of the various forces in the Commons, he was not to be lured into the sort of promises and guarantees which he now felt the primate had given too frequently and too readily:

> I shall scarcely be able at once to give His Majesty that entire satisfaction in particulars which I may collect from a general view of things and from a moral certainty of the effects those measures will have which His Majesty is determined shall be pursued.

George II, unfortunately, could recognise a 'moral certainty' a mile off and was in no danger of confusing it with a guarantee!

This was a letter to be shown to the King, and Stone therefore took counter-measures. His purpose in writing, he said, was to supply material circumstances omitted in the letter or 'softened by the caution and reserve incidental to letters drawn for the perusal of more than one person'. He denounced the leanings towards accommodation and leniency and particularly lamented the lord lieutenant's omission of any mention of Clements, who had succeeded in softening Dorset. Stone defended himself vigorously against the charges of ambition and private vendettas in which Dorset was now inclined to concur. Then, to emphasize the seriousness of his disagreement, he advised the King in terms of profuse devotion and ardent self-sacrifice not to renew his appointment as a lord justice.

31. B.L., Add. Mss. 32,733, fo. 259, Dorset to Newcastle, 16 Nov. 1753.

Sackville's letter to Pelham was distrait and not very much to
the point, his main purpose being to show himself a man of
moderation, but a previous letter to Claudius Amyand at the
treasury was much sharper, and expressed either a different mood
or less guarded feelings.[32] Sackville's defence had been undertaken
by Stone, who agreed that the chief secretary had been 'the occasion of disputes which would not have happened if he had not been
in office, or some of equal capacity ... [but] the fatigue he [had]
undergone [had] been very great and the success very promising'.

Dorset's letter was very much approved but Newcastle said he
never saw the King 'more really pleased with a letter' than with
Stone's.[33]   There were no more warnings or recriminations.
Dorset was to attempt negotiations with the Speaker, Cox was to be
dismissed from his post as collector of Cork, but with Clements,
who had friends at Whitehall, Newcastle came to a full stall: the
King was not disposed to consider his dismissal.

On 5 February, with the ministry's approval, Dorset prorogued
the Irish parliament.[34] Another piece of unfinished business was
cleared up early in March when the money designated in the rejected bill for the discharge of part of the national debt was withdrawn from the treasury by King's Letter and applied to that
purpose. The Castle and the ministry both felt that this action was
'a clear vindication of His Majesty's rights'.[35]   This was not
strictly true, as the patriots had not argued that the King had no
right to apply the surplus but only that the Commons had a right to
apply it without previous consent.[36] The loosening of the treasury
purse-strings was a considerable relief to the run-down credit
system and to the money supply, although it did not come in time
to save the bank of Dillon and Ferrall. Because no loan duties
had been passed, the creditors of the national debt had not had
their interest paid. They were now belatedly reimbursed.

32. B.L., Add. Mss. 32,733, fo. 555, Sackville to Amyand, 25 Dec. 1753;
see also his letters to Wilmot of 18 Dec. 1753 and 20 Jan. 1754 (P.R.O.N.I.,
T.3019).
33. B.L., Add. Mss. 32,734, fo. 71, Newcastle to Dorset, 24 Jan. 1754; *ibid.*,
fo. 77, same to Stone, 24 Jan. 1754.
34. Ironically, one of the bills lost was a bill to improve the efficiency of the
revenue collection and to eliminate revenue frauds. It was re-introduced by
Hartington in the next session and passed as 29 Geo. II, c.3.
35. B.L., Add. Mss. 32,734, fo. 122, Dorset to Newcastle, 5 Feb. 1754.
36. A point particularly stressed in John Leland's *The Case Fairly Stated ...*
(Dublin, 1754).

5

In an attempt to weaken patriot support Sackville had the text of the lost Money Bill printed and, together with a pamphlet in its favour commissioned from a well-known lawyer, Christopher Robinson, it was distributed throughout the country by the post office.[37] It was the first of the considered arguments published on either side and precipitated a discussion in print which generally reached a high standard and provides essential material for an examination of the serious issues which were thought to be involved. Robinson's pamphlet was succeeded by a spate of further efforts, most of them brought out by semi-professional writers and enterprising publishers attracted by the huge interest in the controversy.

The purpose of the government pamphlets was to show that 'if the bill had passed into a law, it would not have vested any new power in the crown over the money which now is or hereafter may be in the treasury of this kingdom'.[38] They proved first of all on the basis of law and precedent that the King had an incontestable right to dispose of all unappropriated money in the treasury and to apply any surplus to whatever purpose. The leaders of the patriots accepted this, but as an attempt to allay popular fears it was counter-productive. To show Irish Whigs that they had been living under such an unchecked executive ever since the Revolution was no way to win support for the Castle.

Since it was their aim to demonstrate that the attempt of the Commons to apply the surplus was unjustified, the government's writers then argued that unappropriated revenue was at the *sole* disposition of the crown. Robinson's *Considerations* avoided saying that such money was the property of the crown, but argued that it was granted in trust by parliament for public services. This was not, however, the line followed by Henry Pelham's advisers,[39] or by the author of other government pamphlets encouraged perhaps by Stone. The anonymous author of *Some Observations Relative to the Late Bill* confessed himself very sorry to be under the necessity of pointing out the feeble nature of the constitution of the kingdom

37. Robinson, *Considerations on the Late Bill ... .* See *H.M.C. Stopford-Sackville*, i, 204, Sackville to Pelham, 14 Jan. 1754, and the *Universal Advertiser*, 2 Feb. 1754.
38. Robinson *Considerations ...*, pp 4-5.
39. P.R.O.N.I., T.1863/1/70, 89-93 (Henry Pelham Mss.),

and asserted that the hereditary revenue was indisputably the King's own estate.[40] Another writer spelt out the consequence of this and said that the King was under no obligation to spend his own money in Ireland.[41] The point of this was that the surplus was due principally to the increased yield of the hereditary revenue, which in any case produced something over two thirds of the unappropriated money in the treasury. Robinson's approach was more accurate as well as more diplomatic, since the hereditary revenue voted to the crown in Tudor and Stuart times, though vested inalienably in the monarch and his heirs, was nevertheless granted to defray the expenses of the public services.

The patriot reply, led by Sir Richard Cox, brought out this point and remarked further that the perpetual grants were not made 'without much murmuring and a struggle'.[42] In reply to the writer of *A Short Account*, Cox's *Proceedings* quoted the English act 2 William III, c. 2, which stipulated that quit rents, *etc.* belonging to the crown of Ireland were inalienable and should be used always to defray the expenses of the Irish government.

As far as Cox was concerned, the government arguments about the provenance of the surplus were irrelevant. He was able to show that the additional duties were voted to make up the deficiency in the hereditary revenue; that they were never allowed to be taken for granted; that the accounts were called for to discover the amount of money needed to meet expenses (it was a standing order of the House of Commons that no supplies might be voted until the committee of accounts had presented its report); and in short that the additional duties were not a permanent element in the executive's coffers. In consequence, if a surplus materialized which was less than the total amount granted in additional duties, the Commons had an independent right to apply it to public service, particularly since the object of the present application, the national debt, had been raised and serviced by parliamentary grants.

The government's counter-argument was that both the statutory hereditary revenue and the additional duties had been granted generally, without precise instructions, and that the crown was, therefore, entitled to disburse the money for whatever purpose it

40.   *Some Observations Relative to the Late Bill for Paying off the Residue of the National Debt of Ireland* ... (Dublin, 1754). See also *An Answer to Part of a Pamphlet Entitled the Proceedings* ... (Dublin, 1754).
41.   *A Short Account of H.M. Hereditary Revenue* ... .
42.   [Cox], *The Proceeding of the Honourable House of Commons of Ireland* ..., p. 26.

considered appropriate. A surplus could not be taken back by the Commons without the King's previous consent. This position was watertight unless the patriots could show that in practice the Commons had been permitted to exercise some rights over redundancies. This Cox was able to do for the time of Queen Anne.[43] For the intervening period, however, he had to rely on a flimsy interpretation. There were no surpluses on unappropriated revenue and consequently there were no precedents.

When the first surplus appeared in 1749 the committee of public accounts discussed the matter and it was resolved to apply a portion to the reduction of the national debt. Although Cox claimed that there was no argument about the Commons' proceedings in this way and that their right was readily acknowledged, this was not so.[44] When the intentions of the Speaker, Malone and Carter became clear, the viceroy, Harrington, was taken by surprise. As we have seen, there was little time between the report of the committee of accounts and the introduction of the supply bills, and Harrington was therefore faced with the choice of allowing the bill to go through (as Dorset was to do in 1751 and 1753), opposing the heads of the bill or coming to terms. He was in no position to oppose, being unpopular in Dublin on account of his persecution of Charles Lucas and depending on the Speaker's friends for support in that affair. Accordingly, he agreed to accept the formula that the surplus should be applied 'agreeably to Your Majesty's most gracious intentions in discharge of part of the aforesaid national debt'.[45] He was well aware, however, of the dubiousness of the compromise and wrote anxious letters to the ministers explaining his difficulties, assuring them that 'His Majesty would have the whole merit of the thing', and that everyone understood the application as being 'a grace and favour from the crown'. He hoped his conduct would be approved but if it was not, he asked that he should be disavowed rather than bring the government into difficulties.[46] In 1754, the Castle propagandists asked every 'impartial reader' whether he did not consider that the word 'intentions' was

43. *Ibid.*, pp 62-5. See also a letter on Robinson's *Considerations* in the *Universal Advertiser* of 21 Feb. 1754; and Bruce's *Remarks on a Pamphlet Entitled Considerations ... .*
44. [Cox], *The Proceeding ...,* pp 7-8. Kiernan does not seem to have taken account of the evidence in the State Papers and was misled by Cox (Kiernan, *Financial Administration,* p. 151).
45. 23 Geo. II, c. 2.
46. P.R.O., S.P., 63/411, Harrington to Bedford, 31 Oct. 1749; P.R.O.N.I., T.2863/1/31, same to Pelham, 1 Nov. 1749; P.R.O., S.P. 63/411, same to Bedford, 17 Nov. 1749.

just as good as the word 'consent', a proposition with which the impartial reader could hardly have agreed. A sounder move was Harrington's direction to the attorney-general, who was considered to speak for the crown in the Commons, to introduce the motion. However, the incumbent, St. George Caulfeild, does not seem to have indicated that previous consent had been given[47] and so, although the crown's partnership in the application was fully acknowledged, it was the implicit recognition of the partnership of parliament that assuaged the anxiety of Malone and Cox.

From 1749 government pamphleteers hurried on to 1751, where they were on very firm ground indeed. The surplus was repeated but the government this time took a determined initiative. The words 'gracious consent' were used in Dorset's speech from the throne, in reference to a further reduction in the national debt. The Commons took up the challenge in their address and substituted the words 'gracious recommendation' which in their view respected both royal and parliamentary rights. These words were also inserted in the heads, which were not opposed but were altered in England and then safely passed through the Commons on reintroduction. The Castle considered this a clear precedent, which it was, although the Speaker's feelings were indicated when he spoke noncommittally at the ceremony of royal assent of 'this provision' and more pointedly remarked on the House's desire to cooperate with the administration.[48] Cox's explanation for the retreat was that the Commons were already heavily engaged in the investigation of the barracks, which was to result in the censure of Surveyor Nevill, and that there was no wish to exacerbate relations further. The Commons believed that its honour and rights had been at least partly saved by their address to the King. Cox, nevertheless, disapproved of the weakness: 'expedients in politics are dangerous things.'[49]

The explanation offered, though awkward, was probably truthful. In 1751 the Speaker did not much relish the idea of a full-blooded set-to. Moreover, times were good, popular feeling had not yet been aroused and a determined effort to reject the bill would have been even more hazardous than it was in 1753 when, as we

47. The Court pamphlets did not claim that he did. Cox said that in any case the attorney-general normally moved such resolutions and added that during the debate Malone had openly declared previous consent unnecessary ([Cox], *The Proceeding,* pp 9-10).
48. *C.J.I.,* v, 205.
49. [Cox], *The Proceeding,* p. 20.

have seen, the Castle was surprised at the lengths to which the Speaker and his friends were prepared to go.

The laurels of the pamphlet debate were with Cox, who was well versed in parliamentary lore and possessed an acute grasp of essentials. His *Proceeding* was heavily influential, and many respected its arguments who were contemptuous of the behaviour of the Speaker's party.

6

The political fury of 1753 was closely linked to the difficult economic conditions that succeeded the fair years of the late '40s and very early '50s, just as opposition to the Money Bill in 1737 had been motivated partly by slumping prices and a sharp recession in the linen trade, and as the earlier opposition to Wood's Halfpence had been sharpened by economic depression. Such evidence as is available points to the Irish country gentry being in severely straitened circumstances at this time. Take, for example, William Hamilton, M.P. for Strabane, who wrote in 1750 to the earl of Abercorn's agent apologizing for 'being so long in arrears', and referring to the 'long confusion' in his affairs. Another, better documented case is that of Sir Edward O'Brien. Consistently in arrears with interest on large debts incurred in the early '40s, he was being pressed to settle his accounts, and, having tried with varying success to sell off parts of his estate, which in any case was heavily mortgaged, he sought in the drastic tightening of 1754 to raise in England what he could not obtain in Ireland — credit, the lifeblood of his class.[50] To be well with a sound banker, or better still with Nathaniel Clements at the treasury, was a great asset; and the financial importance of Clements in particular became a vital issue in the struggle between the Speaker's party and the Castle in 1754-5.

What were the particular economic difficulties of 1753? The harvest of 1752 had been poor and the following winter severe, resulting in a steep rise in food prices.[51] In the area around Strabane, for example, oatmeal, the staple diet of the poor for most of the year, cost 10d. a peck in February 1753, an increase of 3½d.

50.   P.R.O.N.I., T.2541/IA1/2/26 (Abercorn Mss.), William Hamilton to John Colhoun, 14 Sept. 1750; *The Inchiquin Manuscripts* ed. J. Ainsworth (Dublin, 1961), pp 159-64.
51.   P.R.O.N.I., T.2541/IA1/2/143, John Colhoun to Abercorn, 2 Feb. 1753. Colhoun sent Abercorn regular details of prices: see P.R.O.N.I., T.2541/IA1/2/ 112, 139, 143, 151, 165; T.2541/3.

on the previous year. Grain prices increased further during the summer of 1753 and then an early, hard winter set in, keeping grain prices very high. In February 1754 it cost even more to buy oatmeal than in the previous year. Complaints about high prices were frequent in the Dublin newspapers, especially in the *Universal Advertiser*, an avowedly 'patriot' journal.[52] The clamour raised in the summer of 1753 and increasing in the winter of 1753-4 thus coincided with deteriorating economic conditions for the urban poor.

For the country gentlemen the problem was livestock not grain. Charles O'Hara commented:

> The merchants had slaughtered so much upon speculation last year and exported so much bad beef that they had not only overstocked foreign markets but had also revived the imputation of unfair traders. Beef, therefore, sells low this year.[53]

This applied to mutton too, and another difficulty for men living in sheep-farming areas was that the previous winter had made for poor quality mutton and wool. The demand for wool was low in England, which had sufficient home supplies, and this also helped to force Irish prices down.

There was also trouble in the politically influential linen industry. Charles O'Hara reported that 'the northern factors had sent their linen to market at such immoderate prices that many of them remained unsold'. However, it was not simply a matter of poor marketing in Ireland: 'the duty being taken off the foreign yarn has deprived us of any demands from England so that commodity is low.'[54] In April 1753 the prices of cloth and yarn were 'a little fallen and by December were falling steadily. Early in the following year they had 'greatly fallen'.[55] The Linen Board had not been keeping pace with the massive expansion of the industry;

---

52. *Belfast Newsletter*, 28 May 1754; *Universal Advertiser*, 6 July 1754. A writer in *Faulkner's Dublin Journal*, 26 June 1753, complained: 'the poverty and distress among many home and room keepers of Dublin upon account of the excessive dearness of provisions and high house rents are incredible'. He said that many people had been obliged to sell clothes and furniture.
53. P.R.O.N.I., T.2812/19/1 (O'Hara Mss.), Charles O'Hara, 'A survey of the Economic Development of Co. Sligo in the 18th Century', p. 16.
54. *Ibid.*, p. 17.
55. P.R.O.N.I., T.2541/IA1/2/151, John Colhoun to Abercorn, 24 Apr. 1753; T.2541/IA1/3/7, same to same, 24 Feb. 1754; T.2541/IA1/2/175, Nathaniel Nisbitt (agent at Lifford) to same, 8 Dec. 1753.

its records and administration were in a mess; members carried their political animosities into linen affairs and the Linen Bill of 1752, which had been altered in England, was widely thought to have exacerbated the situation.[56]

With prices generally falling and trade contracting, it is not surprising that many merchants who had ridden the credit boom and over-stretched their resources should have now gone under. Even as the arguments for and against the Money Bill were swinging to and fro in the House of Commons, businesses were closing in Dublin and elsewhere. One private correspondent wrote:

> Never was so many bankrupts known. There is such a rot among the dealers that many who were esteemed opulent have been lately obliged to shut up and money is so scarce all over this kingdom that the bankers will not at any rate discount their own bills if they have but a single day to run, and houses and lands are upon the decline.[57]

Opposition in the House of Commons sharpened when gentlemen were stung by the absence of November rents, by the unavailability of credit and by the high prices of all provisions and services in a city which was usually expensive enough during parliament winter. M.P.s hardly needed the encouragement of the hard-pressed merchants, linen-makers and populace.

By February 1754, bankruptcies were coming thick and fast, the demands on the money supply were acute and, in the absence of help from England where credit was also low, the banking system came close to collapse. On 6 March the Dublin bank of Dillon and Ferrall suspended payments. A general failure was only prevented by prompt action by the treasury on the Castle's instructions and by agreements among leading bankers, merchants and private persons to accept bills on the other banks.[58] The agreements were

56. 'We must have a linen bill next session or we are undone', wrote Bishop Edward Synge to Lord Limerick on 25 May 1753 (P.R.O.N.I., Mic. 147/9, xvii, 88-9). Synge wrote fourteen other letters on linen affairs to Lord Limerick in 1753 and early 1754 (*ibid.*, 90-123, *passim*).
57. P.R.O.N.I., D.619/21/B/112 (Anglesey Mss.), James Rooney to Sir Nicholas Bayly, 4 Dec. 1753.
58. The Castle played a positive role in arranging the agreements and having them published. Lord George had been over-optimistic about the economic situation (see P.R.O.N.I., T.3019 [Wilmot Mss.], Sackville to Wilmot, 11 Feb. 1754 and Clements to Wilmot, 12 Mar. 1754). Clements gave the bank of Wilcox and Dawson £6,000 cash to stave off collapse and helped other banks by paying demands on the treasury in cash rather than by bills on the banks.

published in the newspapers. A credit crisis in Galway was dealt with in the same way.

The exchange rates with English currency, which was itself declining, were unfavourable, usually a reliable index of economic malaise. In 1748-9, the exchange rate hovered at par (8$^{1}/_{3}$%). Indeed, Nathaniel Clements was allowing the King's mistress, Lady Yarmouth, exchange rates of well below par.[59] In October 1753, a time of year when the outflow of exports usually caused lower exchange rates, the rate charged by the Dublin banker, Henry Mitchell, to the earl of Abercorn was 9½%, which compared with 8¼% in September 1748, 8½% in December 1749, 8$^{1}/_{3}$% in September 1751, 8¾% in October 1752, and 8½% in September 1755.[60]

This hidden debilitation resurrected some half-buried prejudices. There was a strong feeling that Ireland was being imposed upon by England. There were grumbles about English restrictions on Irish trade; about English imports; absentee landlords; English pensioners, and officers on the Irish establishment; the excepting of major English pensions and salaries from tax; and about a general management of Ireland in England's interest. Newspapers reported a number of attacks on ladies wearing fine imported materials. There were proclamations against unlawful and riotous assemblies and against the destruction of foreign manufactures. The *Universal Advertiser* carried complaints, such as that on 14 November 1753, alleging huge imports of silks, embroideries, toys, wines, foods, 'nay even their linen' by 'some gentlemen and ladies of the first fashion and distinction' who were even suspected of paying no duty on their luxuries.

This attack may have been aimed at the residents of the Castle, who were given to displays of extravagance. The bishop of Derry remarked, not entirely favourably:

The duke of Dorset has had the most shining assemblies that were ever seen in Ireland, everyone endeavouring to outdo another in equipage and grandeur.

The *Dublin Courant* reported on 21 December 1751 that Dorset's voyage down Dame Street to Parliament House was made 'in a new and elegant built coach, lately brought from Paris'. The royal birthday was celebrated with enormous pomp and ceremony in

59. T.C.D., Clements ledger, 1749 (Lough Rynn Mss.), p. 183.
60. P.R.O.N.I., T.2541/IA1/2/164, 29, 93 and 137, and /IA1/3/103.

1751 and 1753. The illuminations were 'the most extraordinary that has ever been seen', and the 'dress and equipage was superior to anything shown on the like occasion'.[61] The expense of making Dublin Castle fit for the arrival of the lord lieutenant and his retinue seems to have been much greater for Dorset than for any of his immediate predecessors, and rebuilding and refurbishing at the Castle continued throughout his viceroyalty.[62] The ostentation of the Sackvilles did not help them in 1753.

The fears aroused by the economic depression and the resentment caused by the tax and coinage reforms, the altered Linen Bill, the salary rises for judges and soldiers,[63] the aggressively English character of the government, its uninhibited canvassing of parliamentary support and its defence of Arthur Jones Nevill, were all concentrated in the single issue of the Money Bill. The treasury surplus was absolutely necessary to boost the money supply. But how was the surplus to be applied? Regardless of the finer arguments, the popular impression was that there was an attempt to extend the prerogative, that the English were trying to gain complete control of Irish revenues, that huge amounts would be sent to Hanover, and that no more parliaments would be held. All these views were held in fastnesses of ignorance but all of them were in fact based on precedents. The tendency had indeed been for the English government to extend its control in Ireland; Charles II and

61. B.L., Add. Mss. 32,725, fo. 499, Bishop William Barnard to Newcastle, 14 Dec. 1751. See also *Pue's Occurrences*, 17 Nov. 1753; *Universal Advertiser*, 13 Nov. 1753; *H.M.C. Stopford-Sackville*, i, 178, Holdernesse to Dorset, 21 Nov. 1751. The new coach cost £892 10s. 2d., which was more than the cost to Dorset of buying Harrington's entire equipage. Hartington's bill for Dorset's equipage was £1,258 6s. 0d., which represented two-thirds of the purchase cost; see Hartington's receipt in P.R.O.N.I., T.3019.
62. It was customary to have improvements made, new furniture and hangings bought, *etc.* for each visit of a lord lieutenant. The last bill for Devonshire was £646 19s.10¼d., the first for Chesterfield was £1,040 15s.11d., and for Harrington £1,106 6s.4¼d. Dorset's reception in 1751, however, cost £1,879 3s.8d. See *C.J.I.*, v, app., pp ccxviii-ccxxvi. Considerable work was done on the Castle and its surrounds in the 1740s and '50s, as indeed on other public buildings, such as the Parliament House and the Lord Mayor's House in Dublin. The rebuilding and refurbishing under Dorset was not, therefore, a particular exercise of his; but Stone may have been the initiator of many of the improvements. All the work seems to have been entrusted to Nevill up until his replacement by Eyre as surveyor-general (Nevill's account from 1743 to 1751 is given in *C.J.I., loc. cit.*).
63. General increases in army pay were granted in March 1754. Increases had been given to dragoons and battleaxe guards, and to the judges, earlier in Dorset's term.

James II had indeed withdrawn large sums from the Irish treasury to pay English armies; the English presence in the revenue commission had indeed increased; and in 1733, in Dorset's first viceroyalty, there had been an attempt to secure a debt supply for 21 years which if it had succeeded would have weakened parliament's power. The Castle claimed that the popular fears were manufactured and propagated by the Speaker and his colleagues and this, assisted by support from E. S. Pery[64] is a claim which has persisted down the years. But whatever stimulation there may have been was insignificant in comparison with the genuine pressure of public opinion, which accosted members with addresses and representations as they met for the session. Bishop Edward Synge, a fair and reliable witness of the behaviour of the populace, wrote to Lord Limerick: 'I assure your Lordship that upon the utmost enquiry I cannot find they were raised or encouraged.'[65]

7

It has long been thought that the important consequence of the Money Bill dispute was that it taught the Commons to vote specific appropriations in order to prevent surpluses.[66] Together with the lack in the Irish House of Commons of the English standing order prohibiting private Members from introducing financial petitions, the dispute was held responsible for what was later considered mutual spoonfeeding by the Members, leading to the consolidation of 'undertaker' power and even providing fuel for the drive for legislative independence.[67] Clare, in his great speech on the Union, described the consequence thus: 'a system has been gradually built upon [the Members' appropriations] which would beat down the most powerful nation of the earth'.[68] The 'system' was held to have originated in the first session after the Money Bill dispute, in 1755.

This view requires some qualification. First, the specific appropriations of 1755 did not come out of the blue. The voting of

64. *H.M.C. 8th Rep.*, i, 178, Pery to Bedford, c.1757.
65. P.R.O.N.I., Mic 147/9, xvii, 108-9, Bishop Edward Synge to Lord Limerick, 25 Dec. 1753.
66. Kiernan, *Financial Administration*, p. 159; Lecky, ii, 465. L. M. Cullen, *An Economic History of Ireland since 1660* (London, 1972), pp 95-6, is the first writer, to my knowledge, to modify the accepted view.
67. Kiernan, *Financial Administration*, pp 306-7.
68. Francis Plowden, *An Historical View of the State of Ireland* ... (2 vols., London, 1803), i, 306-7, quotes this portion of Clare's speech.

money to private persons for economic purposes was not unusual in Irish parliamentary history, although after the Hanoverian accession it was limited and infrequent for lack of funds. Moreover, in 1753 the supply to the King was declared limited to £347,572-odd and subsidies were agreed for ten manufactures and industries and for two charities. Two of the subsidies involved were very large — £20,000 to the city of Dublin to finish Essex Bridge and the ballast office wall, and the same amount to private enterprisers to make the Lagan navigable.[69] Secondly, the voting of appropriations was not a partisan matter; both government and patriot supporters approved of the appropriations and benefited from them. George Stone and Arthur Hill, for example, were participants in the Lagan navigation, and Stone was also interested in schemes for turnpikes. Thirdly, the possibility of building an 'undertaker system' by the control of specific appropriations did not occur to Stone or Sackville, to Hartington or Conway, or indeed to the 'patriots' themselves.

It is undoubtedly true that there was enormous popular jealousy of any money going out of the country in the years 1753-6. It it also true that the more extreme claims of the Castle propagandists caused a panic which in Thomas Pakenham's view would 'never go down'.[70] Nevertheless, the only concrete evidence of a determination to prevent a recurrence of the argument over previous consent occurs not in the patriot records but in those of the English ministry. This is a paper in Newcastle's hand, marked simply 'Ireland' and probably composed in early 1754:

> That an instruction should be given to the lord lieutenant and Council of Ireland not to transmit any bill or proposition for granting, disposing, *etc.*, of HM revenue or any part thereof, with a proper recital that all grants, gifts, *etc.* of money belonging to HM should be by letter under HM sign manual.[71]

69. Hartington, in fact, did not think the 1755 Money Bill appropriations significantly greater than those of 1753: see B.L., Add. Mss. 32,861, fo. 23, Hartington to Newcastle, 19 Nov. 1755. He also differentiated quite properly between money bill appropriations and royal subsidies requested by addresses of parliament. Not all of the 1755 grants were money bill appropriations: a few were provided from the treasury following parliamentary addresses which **Hartington** thought a welcome gesture by the patriot leaders of confidence in the good intentions of the government.
70. From an essay by Pakenham which he sent to Hartington at the latter's request early in September 1755 (P.R.O.N.I., T.3158/420/1 [Chatsworth Mss.]).
71. B.L., Add. Mss. 32,995, fo. 56. Malone is reported to have threatened to

While many patriot supporters may well have wished for specific appropriations in order to prevent Irish money being put to English uses by the expedient of King's Letters, the principal reason for the 1755 appropriations was less sensational. Chief Secretary Conway explained it thus to Sir Robert Wilmot:

> It would neither have suited the plan or professions of my lord lieutenant, nor the situation of this country or temper of its people, to hoard up and keep undisposed so vast a sum as would probably be found in the treasury accruing for two years to come. You see at once how improper and impractical that would be. It was then a determined thing that a good part of this great overplus was to be laid out; the consideration being to do it in the manner most useful and most agreeable to the country.

It was clear at Lady Day 1755 that the surplus would be sufficient to finance the ordinary expenses of government for two years: this had not been the case in the three previous sessions because the bulk of those surpluses had been used to pay off the national debt. Even before he came to Ireland, Hartington was aware of the likely magnitude of the 1755 surplus and was contemplating whether he should insist on reserving the money for government expenses only or ask parliament to vote additional duties as usual and agree to bounties and grants as a *quid pro quo*. Essentially, the problem of financing the forthcoming war decided the new lord lieutenant in favour of the latter course. Hartington told Wilmot that because of 'the great difficulty' in asking for money 'it was agreed that part of the balance should be laid out in works that were beneficial to the country, leaving about £200,000 for exigencies'. In pursuance of this agreement Hartington recommended to the Commons the encouragement of deserving enterprises in his speech from the throne in 1755. Conway was fully conscious that some bad schemes might be included in the proposals of the Commons but the immediate economic and political requirements were paramount in his mind: 'after all, making seven or eight rivers navigable

grant supplies under precise conditions, which was not a novel idea. If carried out, this plan would have greatly complicated the government's accounts, but it would not necessarily have prevented surpluses, nor would it have forestalled future argument. Opposition to any such attempt was, however, demanded of the Speaker in his negotiations with Dorset in February 1754: see B.L., Add. Mss. 32,733, fo. 259, Dorset to Newcastle, 16 Nov. 1753; Add. Mss. 32,734, fo. 188, same to same, 9 Mar. 1754. In 1710 a strict appropriation of the supply was proposed and rejected: see D. W. Hayton, 'Ireland and the English Ministers, 1707-16' (Oxford Univ. D.Phil. thesis 1975), p. 94.

at once may appear burlesque, and so it does to me as well as others more inclined perhaps to make it so, but I insist this is better than hoarding or appearing to hoard the money.'[72]

Reading the correspondence and pamphlets of the patriots, one concludes that their principal concern was to use surpluses to promote economic development and enlightened enterprises such as public buildings and charities.[73] The main aim of the committee of supply, in modern language, was to reflate a depressed economy. It is certain that the expenditure of public money in this way was inadequately supervised but initially, at least, the basic motives of the undertakers were neither calculating nor corrupt.

The principal importance of the Money Bill dispute lay not in any influence it might have had in encouraging the practice of specific appropriations but in a more general area. The pamphlet debate raised wider issues than the claim of the Commons to have a say, as of right, in the disposal of a surplus on unappropriated revenue. The right of the House to initiate all financial legislation, acquired over the years though not allowed by Poynings' Law or by the third or fourth of Philip and Mary, was challenged; as was the right of the English Privy Council to alter money bills. The debate expanded further into a discussion of the theoretical underpinning of the eighteenth-century constitution, a debate occasioned chiefly by the development of politics in England since the Revolution and the lack of a parallel development in Ireland. The dispute was of significance because it raised the issue of colonial dependency and because the political leadership became allied however reluctantly with religious and economic classes which were prepared to campaign for Irish rights.

To understand the mentality of Henry Boyle and his supporters it is necessary to refer to their origins. Professor McCracken has calculated that over half the members who served in George II's reign were of early Stuart or Cromwellian origin and that over three quarters were of planter stock.[74] Nearly all were landowners

72. P.R.O.N.I., T.3019, Henry Conway to Wilmot, 30 Nov. 1755; *ibid.*, Hartington to Wilmot, 30 Dec. 1755; B.L., Add. Mss. 51,381, fo. 168, Conway to Fox, 25 Feb. 1756; P.R.O.N.I., T.3158/290/39 (Chatsworth Mss.), paper on strategy for Hartington's administration, probably composed Mar./Apr. 1755.
73. See, for example, P.R.O.N.I., D.1606/1/3 (Gosford Mss.), Lady Orrery to Sir Archibald Acheson, 16 Mar. 1752, regarding the completion of the Caledon Bridge; *A Tour Through Ireland by Two English Gentlemen* (London, 1748).
74. J. L. McCracken, 'Central and Local Administration in Ireland under George II' (Queen's Univ. Belfast Ph.D. thesis 1948), p. 110.

and well over half were primarily landowners. Furthermore, in 1753, the House of Commons was as elderly as the reign. Something over 10% of the members had been elected in 1727 and over a third had been born in the previous century. Among the major figures many had direct experience of the Catholic threat. Sir Richard Cox's family had been exiled in Bristol during the reign of James II; Henry Boyle's father had died in Flanders in 1693; Nathaniel Clements's brother had been killed at Fontenoy.[75] To most members, on both sides of the House, England was almost literally the mother country, the protectress of their possessions and their way of life.

This was a factor which heavily influenced political conduct. In Henry Boyle's words, he and his friends had a 'thorough conviction that [their] being as a Protestant and a free people depend[ed] on the establishment of the throne in His Majesty and his royal house'.[76] The importance of opposition on the issue of previous consent was that men like Boyle felt obliged to confront the lord lieutenant, the English ministry and the powers of the King. They held off for as long as they could and even when the conflict was engaged their tactics were to distinguish carefully not only between government and King but between England and her representatives for the time being in Ireland. Their strategy was to demonstrate their strength, not their willingness to oppose. Thus attention was primarily concentrated on the addresses, a time-honoured barometer of the atmosphere in the House of Commons; on elections, then as now, the principle method of showing public support; on creating difficulty for the government by attacking corruption and maladministration; and by showing voting strength, which could be done, in postponing questions, for example, or in inconveniently bringing them on. All of this was accompanied by earnest lobbying of important figures in England, stressing that the attack was not directed at England or the crown. For their part, Stone and Sackville were anxious to convince Whitehall and the court that it was not a question of personalities, but one of the King's honour and England's interest.

Although there was some dislike expressed of the patriot leaders English politicians had no mind to call them rebels. They

75. *Dictionary of National Biography*; T.C.D. Ms. T.6.11 (Clements corresp.), i, Hamilton Lambert to Clements, 23 May 1745, reporting the death of Nathaniel's brother Harry and serious injuries to his nephew Captain Tighe; his relation by marriage, Ralph Gore, was also wounded.
76. P.R.O.N.I., D.2707 (Shannon Mss.), Henry Boyle to Hartington, draft, n.d. [Apr. 1755].

were content to see the struggle as one for power, and so far as the Dorset/Stone allegations of Irish rebelliousness were concerned, thought 'they must be poor or partial politicians who can't see through such a disguise'.[77] Even the ministry itself was largely disinclined to see the struggle in this light and Newcastle in particular bore the same sort of attitude to Boyle and his fellows as he did to English politicians, that all of them could be bought or soothed and that none of them would risk being at odds with the King.

It was the English in Ireland who sensed that the chemistry of the Anglo-Irish relationship was changing. Although there was a strong element of self-interest in the claims of Dorset, Sackville and Stone, there was an element of truth also. They were not alone in their assessment. On hearing of the fate of the Money Bill, the judicious Dr Henry wrote to the archbishop of Canterbury: 'these are terrible things! – I dread fatal consequences. Lord help us!'[78] The exclamations come at the end of a long letter which was painstaking in its account of the problems and allowed merit to each side. William Yorke's letters to Lord Chancellor Hardwicke were insistent on the threat to the English interest in Ireland. Yorke was a judge and through his assize work was well informed as to local opinion. Although he was of course connected to the Castle, it is obvious that his views were formulated and held independently.[79]

In England, Hardwicke and the attorney-general William Murray did take the claims seriously, and Pelham seems to have come round to their point of view just before he died in March 1754.[80] For George Dodington, who knew Ireland, the rejection of the Money Bill was alarming: 'dangerous event! and productive of more mischiefs than I shall live to see remedied.' Prophetically, he warned the Princess of Wales that the shades of the Money Bill would haunt the reign of her son.[81]

By the end of the Seven Years War, the attitude of the English political establishment had changed. After the Money Bill defeat, Fox was inclined to think that 'as soon as we come to humour them

77. *Bedford Corresp.*, ii, 142, Rigby to Bedford, 25 Dec. 1753.
78. B.L., Add. Mss. 35,592, fos. 226-32, Henry to Archbishop Thomas Herring, 21 Dec. 1753.
79. See especially B.L., Add. Mss. 35,591, fos. 371-2; Add. Mss. 35,592, fos. 270-72; Add. Mss. 35,593, fos. 54-7; Add. Mss. 35,595, fos. 214-15.
80. *H.M.C. Stopford-Sackville*, i, 108, Pelham to Dorset, 28 Feb. 1754.
81. *The Political Journal of George Bubb Dodington* eds. J. Carswell and L. A. Dralle (Oxford, 1965), pp 243-44.

The Money Bill Dispute

[the Irish] ... they will be as they always have been, HM's most obedient and affectionate subjects'.[82] In a memoir written about ten years later, Fox believed that at the time of the accession of George III the Irish were 'foolishly and seditiously ... every day aiming at independency'.[83] About the same time, Horace Walpole, who had been admiring of the patriot side, declared in an even-handed obituary of George Stone that 'he was forced to drown his own intellects, that he might govern the no-understandings of the Irish ... I do not think the administration will be disposed to place the metropolitan mitre on an able head again in haste'.[84]

In fact the administration gave the mitre to Richard Robinson, another Dorset appointee, who was by no means incompetent but who had a much more restricted idea of his duties. At the same time it seems to have been decided in principle that the viceroy should have permanent residence in Ireland, a suggestion which William Yorke had tentatively offered to Hardwicke in 1758.[85] The first experiment, under Townshend, of this policy of permanent residence confirmed the English establishment in its wary attitude towards Ireland. In 1755 Chief Secretary Conway had dismissed the Dorset policy in Ireland 'not only as a desperate [game] but one actually played and lost'. In 1773 he wrote to Charles O'Hara: 'there seems to be in your country a kind of natural antipathy to an English governor which nothing but strong acts of government can overcome.'[86]

Many elements were mixing in Ireland during Dorset's lord lieutenancy: an enlightened and improving spirit, economic ideas of *laissez-faire*, better relations between Catholics and Protestants, and resentment of England. For this, the Money Bill dispute provided both an accelerator and a convenient focus. Thomas Pakenham tried to explain its effects on the patriots for the benefit of Dorset's successor, Hartington:

82. Ilchester, *Henry Fox, first Lord Holland* (2 vols., London, 1920), ii, 73, Fox to Lady Hervey, 23 Jan. 1754.
83. *The Life and Letters of Lady Sarah Lennox, 1745-1826* ... eds. countess of Ilchester and Lord Stavordale (2 vols., London, 1901), i, 17-19.
84. *The Letters of Horace Walpole* ed. Mrs Paget Toynbee (19 vols., Oxford, 1903-5, 1926), vi, 159-63.
85. B.L., Add. Mss. 35,595, fo. 214, Yorke to Hardwicke, 15 June 1758. For the development of the residency idea until its implementation under Lord Townshend in 1768 see Thomas Bartlett, 'The Townshend Viceroyalty, 1767-72' (Queen's Univ. Belfast Ph.D. thesis 1976), pp 17-43, 91-7.
86. P.R.O.N.I., T.3158/416/8, Conway to Hartington, 7 Aug. 1755; T.2812/12/30 (O'Hara Mss.), Conway to O'Hara, 21 Feb. 1773.

Independency is a word of offence, and I believe never entered the thoughts of any man in his senses. Yet I must observe that the assertors of the dependency of Ireland upon the crown of England are also the assertors of the unrestrained prerogative of the crown in Ireland.

He warned: 'there are men of spirit, ability and resolution that will go as far as ever their ancestors did in defence of their just rights.' Pakenham and his fellow patriots in the Protestant Ascendancy were moving slowly towards the adoption of a political principle which the Catholic, Charles O'Conor, and his friends were cautiously urging for other reasons: the cause of liberty as the cause of Ireland.[87]

That the period from the 1720s to the 1770s has been called the age of the 'undertakers' is very much due to the historiographical influence of the English in Ireland, and, rather curiously, their asseverations have been accepted in the face of some simple facts. Before the start of the Hanoverian era, it was not unthinkable for an Irishman (that is one whose loyalty was to the interests of Protestant Ascendancy rather than to those of England) to be lord lieutenant, as Ormonde had been, or chief secretary, as Edward Southwell had been; it could not have been possible in 1754 as it was in 1714-15 for all three lords justices to be Irish; nor was it likely that any Irish lawyer would become lord chancellor as Sir Richard Cox or Lord Midleton had been, or primate as Archbishop Boyle had been. In the last years of the reign of Queen Anne, the only constant English attender at the Privy Council – then an even more important body – was Lord Chancellor Phipps; in the 1750s the Council was dominated by active Englishmen. Under Queen Anne, most of the Irish judges were Irishmen; in 1753 scarcely one was Irish. In that early period Irishmen predominated on the bench of bishops; in the 1750s the reverse was the case. The army too, which had been overwhelmingly Irish at top level, was now being reformed by English influence. The business and patronage of the revenue board was controlled by a majority of English commissioners in 1750, and those on the board who were Irish could be relied upon by the Castle; but in William Conolly's day the revenue had been an Irish preserve.[88] This is the pattern of the

87. See P.R.O.N.I., T.3158/420/1, Pakenham's essay on Ireland, composed for Hartington in 1755.
88. For the predominance of Irishmen in the central administration in the early eighteenth century see Hayton, 'Ireland and the English Ministers', pp 81-9, and above, pp 36-7, 49-50.

Hanoverian years and yet Irish politicians could be accused of subjecting the lord lieutenant to *their* power! This aspect of government in Ireland stood out precisely because the only institution which the English had not infiltrated was the Irish House of Commons itself; conversely that was the ground which Irish politicians made their own, devoting attention to the maintenance of parliamentary prerogatives. The Commons was not only the battlefield for rival groups of politicians, but it was the arena in which they as a class could establish political power by their ability to control the financial role of the House, and the degree to which the House could embarress the administration or lower its prestige. One can argue indeed that it was the Castle's attempt under Stone and Sackville to extend *direct* control to the Commons also that forced the majority into opposition. It is difficult not to give the complaints of the patriots more weight. England was coming more and more to see Ireland in a colonial light; indeed, was becoming more and more conscious of her imperial role, and, from the onset of the Seven Years War at least, there was a move towards tougher imperial government.[89] The effect of this colonial ·spirit was to stimulate Irish independent-mindedness, of which there was accumulating evidence.

But, these are movements in the background. While the defeat of the Money Bill in 1753 later came to be seen, quite rightly, as having given a vital impetus, it did not have any immediate effect on Whitehall. It had, however, a most marked effect on George Stone and his Irish allies, who learned that their power-base had to be accommodated to Irish opinion. That had been the experience of all the umbilical settlements that the British had sent to Ireland, and as always Britain was remarkably alive to the danger. It was Stone's shift of alignment after 1756 that really shocked Whitehall; and it is indeed ironical that the primate's opposition to Bedford was probably more urgently effective in persuading the British government to think of closer control of Ireland than all the insistent propaganda for which he himself was responsible in the time of the duke of Dorset.[90]

89. There is a considerable literature on imperial policy prior to the American Revolution: see especially J. M. Sosin, *Whitehall and the Wilderness* (Lincoln, Nebraska, 1961) and L. H. Gipson's monumental *The British Empire before the American Revolution* (12 vols., Caldwell, Idaho and New York, 1936-67).
90. For permission to draw on manuscript material in this article acknowledgement is due to the institutions and depositors of collections mentioned in the footnotes, and to Mr D. W. H. Neilson and the duke of Newcastle, the depositors, respectively, of the Wilmot and Henry Pelham Mss.

THE TOWNSHEND VICEROYALTY, 1767-72

Thomas Bartlett

From 1703 to 1767 it was the usual custom for a lord lieutenant to reside in Ireland only while the Irish parliament was in
session, approximately eight months every two years. This custom
favoured the gradual growth of a system whereby the lord lieutenant contracted with the principal Irish politicians for the necessary
parliamentary majority. The politicians, as we have seen, 'undertook' to see the King's business (principally money bills) safely
through the Commons in return for a large share of royal patronage,
which they distributed among their friends, to their personal
advantage and the increase of their family prestige. By the early
1760s this 'undertaker system' was proving itself to be an extremely
unsatisfactory means of conducting business. For one thing, the
'undertakers' were altogether too exorbitant in their demands; for
another, they were increasingly unable to guarantee their control of
an Irish parliament which was becoming more assertive of its
rights. The 'undertaker system' was replaced during the viceroyalty
of Lord Townshend by a system of direct rule, which remained as
the normal mode of government in Ireland until the Union. It is
with the setting-up of this system of direct control by a resident
viceroy, the work of Lord Townshend, that this paper is concerned.[1]

2

The standard interpretation of the Townshend viceroyalty is
as follows.[2]   From the early 1760s, it is said, successive British
governments had become both dissatisfied and alarmed at the way

1.   I am grateful to Dr P. J. Jupp and Professor J. C. Beckett for their
helpful comments on various drafts of this paper.
2.   This standard account is based on the following authorities: F. Plowden,
*The History of Ireland from its Invasion under Henry II to its Union with
Great Britain* (2 vols., London, 1809); J. A. Froude, *The English in Ireland in
the Eighteenth Century* (3 vols., London, 1881); Lecky; J. C. Beckett, *The
Making of Modern Ireland, 1603-1923* (London, 1966); E. M. Johnston,
Great Britain and Ireland, 1760-1800 (Edinburgh, 1963), and *Ireland in the
Eighteenth Century* (Dublin, 1974); J. L. McCracken, 'The Undertakers in
Ireland and their Relations with the Lords Lieutenant' (Queen's Univ. Belfast
M.A. thesis 1941), 'Central and Local Administration in Ireland under
George II' (Queen's Univ. Belfast Ph.D. thesis 1948), 'The Irish Viceroyalty,
1760-73', *Essays in British and Irish History in Honour of J. E. Todd* eds.
H. A. Cronne, T. W. Moody and D. B. Quinn (London, 1949) and 'From

affairs were being conducted in Ireland. In February 1765 the British government seized the opportunity offered by the deaths, within days of each other, of the two leading undertakers, Archbishop Stone and the earl of Shannon, and decided to re-form the way Ireland was governed. At a Cabinet meeting it was decided that, for the future, lords lieutenant should reside con-stantly in Ireland. A resident lord lieutenant would abrogate the need for lords justices, who were appointed to carry on the govern-ment in the absence of the lord lieutenant, and it was hoped that he would be able to curb the power of the undertakers and, in general, bring administration back to the Castle. The implementa-tion of this decision, however, proved to be a difficult matter. Lord Weymouth was appointed lord lieutenant but resigned with-out ever coming to Ireland; his successor, Lord Hertford, did make the journey to Ireland but only stayed for one session of parlia-ment and then resigned. With the appointment of Lord Bristol, however, late in 1766, it seemed that the decision taken eighteen months previously would at last be implemented. Constant residency in Ireland was made a condition of Bristol's appointment and he seemed agreeable to this.[3] He made it known to various people in Ireland that the 'old system' of conducting business in the Irish parliament was at an end.[4] The power of the undertakers was to be curbed and the position and authority of the English government in Ireland re-established. In view of this, it came as something of an anti-climax when Bristol resigned the lord lieuten-ancy in July 1767: he had not set foot in Ireland during his term of

Swift to Grattan', *The Irish Parliamentary Tradition* ed. B. Farrell (Dublin, 1973), pp 146-7; L. H. Gipson, *The British Empire before the American Revolution* (14 vols., New York, 1936-69), xiii; F. G. James, *Ireland in the Empire, 1688-1770* (Cambridge, Mass., 1973).
3.   *The Correspondence of George III, 1760-83* ed. Sir John Fortescue (6 vols., London, 1928), i, 388, George III to Chatham, 22 Aug. 1766. See also *The Correspondence of William Pitt, Earl of Chatham* eds. W. S. Taylor and J. H. Pringle (4 vols., London, 1838-40), iii, 51, Chatham to the earl of Bristol, 26 Aug. 1766.
4.   · *Corr. of George III*, i, 484-6, Bessborough to John Ponsonby, 3 June 1767. Sir Lewis Namier, in his *Additions and Corrections to Sir John Fortescue's Correspondence of George III* (London, 1937), pp 77-8, incorrectly attributes this letter, stating that the copy in the Royal Archives was sent by Theophilus Jones, Bristol's chief secretary, to John Ponsonby. What in fact happened was that Jones managed to obtain a copy of Bessborough's letter to Ponsonby (Ponsonby had several copies made, for propaganda purposes) and sent this to Bristol who in turn passed it to the King (see Derby Borough Library, Catton collection (Ireland), 1767 box, Sir Robert Wilmot to Thomas Waite, the Irish under-secretary, 21 July 1767).

office. In August 1767 Lord Townshend was appointed to succeed Bristol and, according to the standard account, was instructed to reside in Ireland, to re-establish the power and influence of the lord lieutenancy and to curb the power of the undertakers.[5] In short, Townshend set out for Ireland to do all the things that Bristol had threatened to do but which, in the end, he had not done. A new system was to be established in Ireland. And from October 1767 to December 1772 — a period which took in four sessions of the Irish parliament — Townshend struggled to implement this new system. On his arrival in Ireland his immediate aim was to obtain the consent of the Irish parliament to an augmentation of the number of soldiers paid for by Ireland. The leading undertakers of the time — John Ponsonby, the Speaker of the Commons and 'first' commissioner of the revenue; the earl of Shannon, master-general of the ordnance and, like Ponsonby, the leader of a large parliamentary connection; and government managers such as Philip Tisdall, the attorney-general, and John Hely-Hutchinson, the prime serjeant — agreed to undertake the measure only if their demands for favours were met. These demands were refused by the British ministry and the undertakers then turned their parliamentary forces against Townshend's administration.

In May 1768 the augmentation proposal was rejected by the Irish House of Commons. Townshend then set about trying to establish a new system of conducting affairs in Ireland, but was hampered by lack of support in England, with the result that when the Irish parliament met again in October 1769 the relative strengths of lord lieutenant and former undertakers had not changed. In order to demonstrate that government was impracticable without their support, the former undertakers contrived to have a money bill rejected, a very serious step and one which directly challenged the British government. Townshend entered a protest against the Commons' action and prorogued the House at Christmas 1769. It was not to meet again until February 1771, by which time Townshend had made himself master of the political situation in Ireland.

According to the standard account, during the thirteen months interval between these two sessions of parliament Townshend embarked on a campaign of wholesale dismissal against those who were in opposition and who held government positions. More important, pensions, peerages and promotions of one sort or an-

5.   McCracken, *'Irish Viceroyalty'*, p. 158; Lecky, ii, 79; Gipson, *British Empire*, xiii, 17.

The Townshend Viceroyalty

other were distributed on a lavish scale. Additional offices were
created by Townshend so that he could win over more supporters.
By February 1771 the viceroy had, in effect, bought himself a
majority. In the session of parliament which opened in February
1771 his majority proved its worth. The opposition of Ponsonby
and Shannon was crushed; Ponsonby in disgust threw up the
Speakership; the government, claimed Townshend, 'hath fairly
driven him out of the field'.[6]

Henceforth matters proceeded in a reasonably quiet fashion.
Admittedly, the opposition continued to 'distress and teaze' the
viceroy,[7] but even that grew less as time passed. Townshend's
fourth session of parliament, from October 1771 to May 1772, saw
him fully in control, negotiating directly with groups in the Irish
parliament and distributing patronage as he saw fit. No longer, it
appeared, would the lord lieutenant contract out the King's
business to independent magnates. In future he would carry it
through with the help of dependent servants who looked to him for
all rewards.

This is the received version of the Townshend viceroyalty. It
is not one which the present writer finds very convincing, and in
this paper its weaknesses will be exposed and a new interpretation
of the viceroyalty propounded; finally, some conclusions will be
attempted about the 'place' of the Townshend viceroyalty in the
history of eighteenth-century Ireland. The standard account can
conveniently be divided into two parts: the making of policy and
its execution. Each is dealt with in turn.

3

There is no direct contemporary evidence for the assertion
that Townshend was sent to Ireland with instructions to reside
there constantly.[8] There are, however, two important pieces of

6.   Quoted in McCracken, 'Irish Viceroyalty', p. 166.
7.   Quoted in *ibid.*, p. 166.
8.   Grafton in his autobiography wrote that Townshend was appointed lord
lieutenant 'under the same stipulations for permanent residence as Lord
Chatham had intended' (*The Autobiography and Political Correspondence of
Augustus Henry, Third Duke of Grafton* ed. W. R. Anson [London, 1898],
p. 137). However, Grafton's autobiography was written some 40 years after
the event, and its testimony cannot be regarded as contemporary. Moreover,
its reliability has been questioned: P. D. G. Thomas writes that 'Grafton's
account [of the genesis of the Townshend duties] does not inspire much
confidence in his 40-year-old memory' (P. D. G. Thomas, 'Charles Townshend

91

indirect evidence which have been adduced by historians in support of it. The first is the decision arrived at by the Grenville Cabinet in February 1765:

> It was the opinion of all the Lords that there was a necessity as well as propriety at this conjuncture to advise the King that whenever a new lord lieutenant should be appointed by His Majesty he should be directed to reside ['almost' deleted] constantly ...[9]

Two points should be made about this decision. In the first place, it was taken more than two and a half years *and* two changes of administration – the Rockingham and Chatham ministries intervened – before Townshend was sent to Ireland. Again, the fact that the decision was taken is not in itself evidence that anyone tried to implement it, nor indeed is there any such evidence. The decision merely indicated that at a certain point the question of requiring residence of a lord lieutenant was actively considered. Beyond that point it would be unwise to go.

A second piece of evidence which is usually brought up to support the assertion that Townshend was commanded to reside constantly in Ireland, is the fact that his predecessor, Bristol, had been commanded to do so. It has been assumed that because Bristol was ordered to be a resident so too was Townshend, but there is no evidence for this assumption: indeed, there is a good deal of evidence to the contrary. In December 1767, for example, Townshend sent over to the British ministry a list of requests put forward by Ponsonby and Shannon. Shannon asked to be appointed a lord justice when Townshend returned to England at the end of the parliamentary session. In his reply Shelburne, the secretary of state for the southern department, explained that the end of the parliamentary session would be the proper time to consider the appointment of lords justices.[10] If Townshend had been commanded to reside constantly in Ireland during his term as lord lieutenant,

and American Taxation in 1767', *E.H.R.*, lxxxiii (1969), 39). More generally, the account has been described as an 'untrustworthy apologia' (R. J. Chaffin, 'The Townshend Acts of 1767', *William and Mary Quarterly* (ser. 3), xxvii (1970), 91).
9.   Printed in *Additional Grenville Papers* ed. J. Tomlinson (Manchester, 1962), pp 335-6.
10. W. L. Clements Library, Ann Arbor, Michigan, Townshend Mss., Townshend Letter-book iv, Townshend to Shelburne, 13 Dec. 1767, and the latter's reply, 14 Mar. 1768. All further references to Townshend letter-books are to those in the W. L. Clements Library.

it is remarkable that he should have written to recommend someone to be a lord justice. Moreover, Shelburne's reply clearly implied that the 'old system' of lords justices would be continued after this session of the Irish parliament. Finally, and conclusively, in February 1768 Townshend sent his chief secretary, Lord Frederick Campbell, to London with a list of proposals for making government easier in Ireland. The fourth proposal ran as follows:

> Whether the lord lieutenant should not be ordered to continue his residence here or a deputy be appointed under whom HM may form such an administration as will hereafter carry on the business to HM's honour and quiet as well as to the advantage both of Great Britain and Ireland.

In answer to this proposal Shelburne wrote to Townshend in the following month telling him that he was to consider himself a resident lord lieutenant.[11] It was from March 1768, some six months after he arrived in Ireland, that Townshend knew he was to be kept on in the kingdom, and it was at his own suggestion that this was done. Just as Townshend was not instructed on his appointment to reside in Ireland, neither was he specially chosen for the position. Professor McCracken states that Townshend was appointed lord lieutenant because he was 'prepared to accept the viceroyalty on the new terms'.[12] This is misleading. Townshend was appointed because the ministry felt that such a mark of favour would have an influence on his brother Charles, the chancellor of the exchequer.[13] Charles was a very unstable member of the Chatham ministry and by obliging his brother it was hoped to fix Charles's loyalty to it. Nor was Townshend instructed on his appointment to 'bring back administration to the Castle' or to effect any changes in the system of government in Ireland. The fact remains, however, that he did introduce a new system. How can this be explained?

Townshend was sent to Ireland with one clear instruction: to obtain the consent of the Irish parliament to an augmentation of the number of troops paid for by Ireland. George III himself was the author of this scheme and he and his ministers were most anxious

11. Townshend letter-book iv, Townshend *for* Lord Frederick Campbell, 20 Feb. 1768. For Shelburne's reply, see Townshend letter-book viii, Shelburne to Townshend, 14 Mar. 1768. This point is more fully discussed in Thomas Bartlett, 'The Townshend Viceroyalty, 1767-72' (Queen's Univ. Belfast Ph.D. thesis 1976), pp 24-43.
12. McCracken, *'Irish Viceroyalty'*, p. 158.
13. Or perhaps as a reward for devising the Townshend duties (Chaffin, *'Townshend Acts'*, p. 120).

that the Irish parliament agree to it.[14] It was as a result of the difficulties encountered in implementing this scheme that Townshend decided that the system of government in Ireland needed to be radically reformed. But, having convinced himself that radical reform was needed in Ireland, he still had to convince the British ministers, for he required their approval of and support for his proposals. This was to take over three years. So far from ordering him to Ireland to bring administration back to the Castle, British ministers continually counselled against 'extreme measures' to deal with those in opposition. Time and again they advised Townshend to come to an understanding with the opposition. As late as April 1769 he was ordered to meet with the leading opponents of his administration in order to discuss their future conduct.[15] It was as a result of the rejection of the Money Bill in November 1769, and the reason adduced for this, that the British ministry accepted Townshend's proposals for the reform of the system of government in Ireland and gave him the go-ahead to implement them.[16] His perseverance had at last been rewarded.

Why did Townshend feel so strongly about Ireland? In opposition tracts he was portrayed as little more than a fool – and a corrupt fool at that. His nickname was Sancho, after Don Quixote's servant who later became governor of Barataria.[17] It is true that Townshend could on occasion play the fool. He was a bluff, blunt-spoken, hard-drinking army officer, mercurial in temperament and prone to instant approval and disapproval of people and things, but there was much more to his character and personality than this. He had a strength of character and an inflexibility of will that the opposition in Ireland totally underestimated. Their attempts to intimidate him only aroused his anger and strengthened his determination to resist. Moreover, he had a strong sense of duty – even a sense of mission – which sustained him against the difficulties he encountered in Ireland. He saw it as his duty to place English government in Ireland on a sound footing, and from early 1768 never wavered from this aim.[18] America, he believed,

14. *Corr. of George III*, i, 503-4, George III to Grafton, 1 Sept. 1767.
15. Townshend received his orders verbally from Macartney (Townshend letter-book iv, Townshend to Grafton, 21 Apr. 1769).
16. It was rejected because it did not take its rise in the Irish House of Commons (*C.J.I.*, xiv, 641).
17. A collection of anti-Townshend pamphlets was published in Dublin in 1773 under the title *Baratariana*.
18. Information on Townshend's early life and military career can be found in C. V. Townshend, *The Military Life of Lord Townshend* (London, 1901). Thomas Waite has left us this description (Derby Borough Library,

had all but shaken off her dependency on the mother country; English politics were bedevilled by factious groups of politicians: a stand had to be made to prevent Ireland going the same way. 'Ireland', he wrote, 'hath not yet caught the English or American distemper'; but there could be no cause for complacency, preventative measures had to be taken.[19] It is instructive that the two men who had most influence on Townshend were his brother Charles and Lord Bute. Charles Townshend was the originator of the Townshend duties and, as might be expected, had very fixed and firm ideas concerning the dependence of the British colonies on the mother country. His brother shared these views fully. Indeed, Lord Townshend's revenue proposals for Ireland bore a marked resemblance to those of Charles for the American colonies. In both cases the aim of the proposals was as much political as financial, a means of curbing the power of the colonial assembly.[20] Lord Townshend was also very close to Bute, whom he described as 'the first friend I met with in public life', and during his viceroyalty he did Bute several favours.[21] The 'Butean system of government', as it was referred to, was not based on an extension of the King's prerogative but on the clearing out of government of the old party hacks who for many years had enjoyed a near monopoly of patronage and who were motivated by no concept of public service: these were to be replaced by men whose disinterestedness and virtue were obvious to all. Townshend told Bute that he would do his best to 'suppress the rage of factionalism' in Ireland.[22] From his leters to Bute it is clear that in some ways Townshend saw himself as engaged in the same kind of struggle in Ireland as Bute had been engaged in at Westminster. Bute had failed: in

Catton coll. [Ireland], xlviii, Waite to Wilmot, 7 June 1769, 'Most private and to be burnt'):
> I have been young and am now old, yet never saw I such a composition of agreeable and disagreeable, of bitter and sweet, of starts, whims, irregularity, and indecisions without any ideas of time or place, now surly, now placid and gentle. Everything by fits and nothing long. There are days in which he wearies every person to death. There are others in which he blazes to such a degree and is so bright and able that you are astonished and think him the most entertaining man in the world.
19. Townshend letter-book ii, Townshend to Weymouth, 4 Aug. 1770.
20. Sir Lewis Namier and John Brooke, *Charles Townshend* (London, 1964), pp 103, 40; P. D. G. Thomas, *British Politics and the Stamp Act Crisis* (Oxford, 1975), p. 357. Lord Townshend's plans for the Irish revenue service had both a financial and a political purpose. He sought to increase the King's 'hereditary revenue' by altering the duty on rum, and in so doing to lessen the crown's dependence on parliamentary supply.
21. Townshend letter-book v, Townshend to Bute, 2 Jan. 1770.
22. Townshend letter-book i, Townshend to Bute, 9 July 1768.

England 'faction' flourished as never before. Townshend was resolved to succeed.

The viceroy's character and political ideas — instincts might be a better word — help to explain why he stayed in Ireland, almost bankrupting himself in the process. His sense of duty drove him on, and his political instincts determined the nature of the proposals he put forward to reform the system of government in Ireland. It was Townshend who convinced the British government that change was necessary, and it was he who put forward proposals on which the new system was to be based. At almost every point in his viceroyalty, Townshend's character and political beliefs were the vital factors. The British government had no discernible policy for Ireland: Townshend presented it with one, and put that policy into effect.

4

In November 1769 the Irish House of Commons rejected a money bill on the grounds that it had not taken its rise in that House. Ponsonby and Shannon were widely suspected of having engineered this government defeat in order both to demonstrate their power and to enlist public opinion on their side. The British government, alarmed by this attack on Poynings' Law, gave Townshend the go-ahead to take the offensive against those in opposition. In December 1769 the lord lieutenant entered a protest against the Commons' action and prorogued parliament. By the time it met again, some thirteen months later, he had secured a majority.

During the interval Townshend built up a strong 'Castle' party — or party of 'lord lieutenant's friends'. Throughout the period of the augmentation dispute, and during the short session of 1769, he had been impressed by the way that a large number of independent country gentlemen and several of the lesser interests in the Irish parliament had supported the government and he became convinced that, properly encouraged and rewarded, these two loose groupings could be brought together to form a 'Castle' party. Such a party would enable the government to dispense with the service of the undertakers. The independent members had for some time been weary of the rule of the great families and were disgruntled at the mismanagement and jobbery which seemed inseparable from it. Moreover, they longed for direct access to the Castle. The lesser or secondary interests, such as the Tyrone, Gore or Drogheda connections, also longed to break the monopoly which Shannon and

Ponsonby seemed to enjoy of government patronage and influence. However, they were motivated less by a desire to serve Townshend than to further their own ends.

Supported by this new 'Castle' party, Townshend aimed at destroying the undertaker system and instituting a new system in which the lord lieutenant and Dublin Castle would directly control a parliamentary majority. Henceforth, the lord lieutenant would be the chief undertaker, and power and patronage would flow from the Castle.

5

Townshend's critics — both contemporary commentators and later historians — are in agreement as to the means he used to build up his party: bribery and corruption. The *Freeman's Journal* declared that:

> Never were the modes of seduction and corruption practised with more art and assiduity than at present. Promises and threats know neither measure nor bounds. Peerages, seats at the board of Privy Council, commissionerships of all kinds, with all manner of places and pensions are held out indiscriminately to all who can give or secure a vote in the senate.[23]

Historians have echoed these remarks. Lecky wrote that 'no previous administration had done so much to corrupt and lower the tone of political life in Ireland'; Froude described Townshend's methods as scandalous; while J. G. Swift MacNeill, his pen shaking with indignation, declared that 'coarse metallic corruption' was the secret of the viceroy's success, and quoted without comment a report that up to £500,000 had been spent in 'bringing this parliament into harmony with the government. At length, wrote MacNeill, 'on the 26 February 1771, the Irish parliament, whose members had been in training for upwards of a twelvemonth in a course of corruption, met', and the result was a victory for Townshend.[24]

23. *Freeman's Journal,* 19 Feb. 1771.
24. Lecky, ii, 115; Froude, *English in Ireland*, ii, 104-5; J. G. Swift MacNeill, *A Constitutional History of Ireland till the Union* (Dublin, 1917), pp 121-2, 124. F. J. Fisher, *The End of the Irish Parliament* (London, 1911), pp 76-7, provides the only important dissenting view. Townshend, he writes, did not corrupt Irish politicians, rather 'he threw a flood of light on the dishonesty, greed and lack of true patriotism which characterised them and all their works'; that is, Townshend should not be blamed for 'buying' Irish politicians, on the contrary they should be blamed for allowing themselves to be bought.

This explanation is hopelessly inadequate. It is true that Townshend distributed pensions to the value of some £2,000, and that he handed out peerages and created and bestowed offices on his supporters, but such actions can hardly be classed under the emotive and pejorative term 'bribery and corruption'. They were the very stuff of eighteenth-century politics.[25] In the period before the rise of a strong party system they were the means by which both the government and opposition groups commonly sought to increase and confirm their supporters. Ponsonby and Shannon could have no justifiable complaint against Townshend's methods, for theirs had been no different. The moral indignation of Lecky, Froude and MacNeill is thus largely misplaced, and by concentrating on one aspect of the situation, they have ignored other, more important, considerations.

The changed political situation in England worked greatly to Townshend's advantage. The 1760s had been years of acute political instability in England. Short-lived ministry had succeeded short-lived ministry, and this had had its effect in Ireland, every change in administration in England resulting almost invariably in a new lord lieutenant. It was this continuing uncertainty in England which made the opposition to Townshend at first so formidable; for a new lord lieutenant might perhaps reverse his policy and seek an accommodation with the undertakers. In these circumstances many of the independent country gentlemen whom he sought to bring into a 'Castle' party were understandably reluctant to commit themselves. However, in January 1770 Lord North became first lord of the treasury in succession to Grafton and his appointment heralded a long period of political stability in England. Townshend derived considerable advantage from this for it reflected on his own administration in Ireland. Independent members, once they saw that Townshend was to stay as viceroy, that his policy was to be supported in England and that, in large measure, he was to be given those powers over patronage he had requested, were no longer hesitant before promising him their support. By the same token, the Irish opposition groups were correspondingly disadvantaged. As Townshend himself explained, 'it has been long the language of opposition here that the English ministry were in too weak difficulties at home to give much attention to the affairs of this country and that men and measures would remain upon the old footing'.[26] This was only one of many reversals which the Irish

25. On this point, see Betty Kemp, *King and Commons 1660-1832* (London, 1968), pp 88-90.
26. Townshend letter-book ii, Townshend to Weymouth, 7 Mar. 1770.

opposition groups experienced in 1770.

When Townshend had prorogued the Irish parliament in December 1769 the Irish opposition appeared to be in a strong position. The prorogation seemed certain to arouse a great deal of resentment in the country. Again, the political instability in England led the opposition leaders to believe that it was only a matter of time before Townshend was recalled and another lord lieutenant sent out who would bring about a settlement with them. This in itself helped weaken their position. Shannon and Ponsonby and their allies were over-confident, and they sank into inactivity and allowed Townshend to seize the initiative and call upon them to justify their opposition.[27] Nor were they able or willing to form a united front. There was at best a tenuous alliance between the groups of Ponsonby, Shannon, Loftus, Flood and Leinster. At all times the issues dividing them were as important as those which bound them together. Shannon, for example, regarded his connection as constituting the natural support of government. He believed that his proper place was on the lord lieutenant's right hand: opposition was distasteful, temporary and designed to achieve a limited end. Shannon was in opposition because his natural position in government was threatened; once that position was again accepted he would be, as his father had been before him, one of the mainstays of the government in Ireland. On the other hand, the 'patriot' group led by Flood and Sir Lucius O'Brien wished for a vigorous opposition. They were not worried by the prospect of a dissolution of parliament and felt that the situation in Ireland gave them a good opportunity to bring forward constitutional points. It seems fairly certain that it was this group that engineered the rejection of the Money Bill in November 1769. There was no love lost between the groups of Flood and Shannon; they jogged along together for mutual convenience, not out of conviction.[28] The other opposition factions had likewise their own interests to safeguard. The Loftus connection, for example, could

27. Government-sponsored pamphlets were produced and distributed with some success. Townshend to Weymouth (Townshend letter-book ii, 2 Mar. 1770):
> it has been my utmost endeavour to convince the general sense of the public that the late interruption of the course of parliament was entirely owing to the spirit and extravagance of party here and not to any unkind disposition of our gracious sovereign or his ministers and I have the satisfaction to inform your lordship that this opinion generally prevails.

28. A futile attempt was made to unite the Irish opposition groups on a more regular basis (P.R.O.N.I., D.1707/5/41A [Shannon Mss.], Shannon to James Dennis, 10 May 1770).

hardly afford the luxury of opposition for they were too vulnerable to government pressure; in May 1770 they deserted, and joined the Castle forces.[29] This disunity among the various opposition groups made it impossible for them to agree on either tactics or aims. They allowed, or were forced to allow, matters to drift along, continually hoping for that political convulsion in England which would restore their credibility.[30]

Given this approach, it is not surprising that the Irish opposition completely failed to whip up public opinion on its behalf. The anticipated outcry against the prorogation did not materialize. If anything, the evidence suggests that there was a certain amount of feeling against the opposition leaders for provoking it. In January 1770 the young Henry Grattan complained that 'the measures of parliament have not enough engaged the attentions or affected the passions of the people'. By February the situation appeared worse to him: 'Ireland seems to have forgotten her injuries.'[31] The spring assizes passed off without incident, and an attempt by one of Leinster's friends to get up an address in County Kildare against the 'Protest and Prorogation' was easily defeated.[32] In February 1771, on the very eve of the parliamentary session, the *Freeman's Journal* was moved to criticize its readers for their apathy: 'what have we done to counteract their [*i.e.* the administration's] plots? What public meetings held, to convince, to confirm, to inspire our minds?'[33]

This lack of public concern in the fate of the former parliamentary managers was a consequence of the small reputation Shannon and Ponsonby enjoyed. Many were pleased to see them humbled and news of their dismissal was greeted with a certain satisfaction. The *Freeman's Journal*, despite its opposition leanings, could hardly forbear sneering at Shannon's humbled position. It pictured him arriving at the great St Patrick's Night ball at the Castle dressed in 'an old hospitalman's coat with a wooden leg, bearing several scars on his face and a label on his breast with the words: "Thus am I rewarded for my services" '.[34] The opposition of Shannon and Ponsonby seemed to many to be self-interested and

29. Townshend letter-book ii, Townshend to Weymouth, 2 Mar. 1770.
30. For further information on the opposition groups in 1770 see Bartlett, 'The Townshend Viceroyalty', chapter 8, pp 221-44.
31. H. Grattan, *Memoirs of the Life and Times of ... Henry Grattan* (5 vols., London, 1839-46), i, 152, 154, Grattan to Day, Jan., 11 Feb. 1770.
32. For the 'squib at Athy', see Townshend letter-book ii, Townshend to Weymouth, 17 Aug. 1770.
33. *Freeman's Jnl.*, 21 Feb. 1771.
34. *Ibid.*, 15 Mar. 1770.

not rooted at all in genuine grievances. There was no reason why the impending departure of these men from the corridors of power should be lamented by the people at large. In fact, as Henry Grattan pointed out, a good many had reason to cheer the dismissal of Ponsonby and the rest. 'The changes in this country', wrote Grattan, 'have given satisfaction to many – to those who were not themselves in place and who considered the oligarchy here as a degrading oppression – and to those who wished a more effectual opposition and expect it from the sanguine resentment of the dismissed.'[35] When Townshend summoned parliament to meet in February 1771 the opposition were in disarray and posed little threat.

Finally, the creation of a 'Castle' party by Townshend was a tribute to his and Sir George Macartney's efforts at management. The traditional account of the viceroyalty distorts the whole business of management by focusing on only one, albeit an important, element in it. There was more to the business of management than simply distributing patronage. Townshend's success in winning a majority during 1770 can largely be attributed to management, but it was management of a kind that was rare in eighteenth-century Ireland. He saw that expert political management was needed not only in Ireland but, more significantly, in England as well, and this he provided. In his first parliamentary session (October 1767-May 1768) Townshend had relied on the support of Irish politicians, but they had let him down. In his second session (October-December 1769) he had placed his trust in the promises of British ministers but they too had failed him, and he had been unable to prevent the rejection of the Money Bill. He had learned from these failures; now the offensive would be carried on simultaneously in both countries.

At the most basic level, management in Ireland required Townshend's residence there throughout the year. By staying in Ireland he gave heart to his supporters and dismayed his enemies: seeing was believing. Moreover, it was important that the government's case was not allowed to go by default. Hence, government-sponsored pamphlets were produced which challenged the opposition's motives and attacked their actions. Attempts were also made to have government supporters selected on to grand juries so as to prevent, if necessary, resolutions critical of government policy being

35. *Life ... of ... Grattan*, i, 162, Grattan to Day, 30 Mar. 1770. See also *Broghill's* reply to *Sindercombe* in the *Freeman's Jnl.*, 6 Mar. 1770: 'to see the business of the nation conducted without the venal concurrence of a rapacious confederacy, had long been the wish and despair of the people.'

passed.[36] Apart from this, there was the important matter of distributing government patronage, what little of it there was, in order to gain the maximum advantage. Every scrap of patronage in Townshend's hands was disposed of with the utmost discrimination. There was little trace of sentiment, or indeed of merit, in his promotions and recommendations. The sole criterion was the advantage of the King's service. In following this rule, Townshend turned down several close friends. Indeed, so resolute was he that he even refused his own son four successive cornetcies in order to oblige people who could be of use. In general, Townshend and Macartney took every opportunity of confirming their supporters, by flattering, obliging or threatening them.[37] They were prepared to exert every effort and strain every connection in order to influence the doubtful members and improve the Castle's numbers,[38] and they were ready to suborn members of the opposition should any opportunity offer.[39]

Management was equally important in England. Townshend's plans for the remodelling of the Irish revenue board, the creation of an accounts board and promotions in the peerage, all required Cabinet approval, and hence ministers had to be convinced of their merits. Moreover, in view of the notorious reluctance of British ministers to pay more than a minimum amount of attention to Irish affairs, it was necessary to coax and cajole them into considering Irish affairs fully. An agent was needed in London, and this position was admirably filled by Townshend's choice, Thomas Allan.[40] Allan's duties were manifold. He sought to persuade ministers of the necessity of adopting Townshend's proposals;

36.   W. L. Clements Library, Townshend Mss., Gorges Howard to Townshend, 22 Mar. 1770.
37.   Bartlett, 'The Townshend Viceroyalty', chapter 7, pp 194-220, *passim*.
38.   For example, Townshend wrote to his mother (Townshend letter-book v, 14 Feb. 1771):
>   There is a Mr Charles Lambert, a son of a very worthy gentleman, Mr Gustavus Lambert of Beauparc, who is upon the point of marrying a relation of yours, Miss Dutton. It may be difficult at such a time to persuade a young lady to part with her lover but if your ladyship pleases to hint how much it may *coincide* with my wishes to *Mr Lambert's family* as well as for the King's service here at so critical a time as the first day of the session, it may be of use.
39.   They attempted in vain to win over the Jephsons of Mallow, who were supporters of Shannon (W. R. Perkins Library, Duke University, N. Carolina, Townshend Mss., Robert Waller to Townshend, 24 Dec. 1770; P.R.O.N.I., D.1707/5/41A, Shannon to James Dennis, 29 Jan. 1771).
40.   For Thomas Allan, see E. M. Johnston, 'The Career and Correspondence of Thomas Allan, c.1725-1798', *I.H.S.*, x (1957).

patiently explained these proposals to all who could be of use; sent back information on the political scene in England; supplied North and other British ministers with arguments in favour of Townshend's policy; investigated and scotched rumours; and kept an eye on Irish M.P.s who were in London. In short, Allan fully complemented Townshend's efforts at management in Ireland.[41]

There was one further element of parliamentary management which was of considerable importance to Townshend in his endeavour to build up a government party in the Irish House of Commons. It was widely recognized that the Irish opposition drew great advantage from the fact that they were able, in large measure, to choose the issues on which to launch their attacks. In the 1769 session of parliament, for example, Townshend had expected and prepared for an attack on his augmentation proposal; instead, the opposition had directed their energies towards rejecting the Money Bill. It is often overlooked, however, that Townshend possessed a comparable advantage, and one which he made full use of in 1770. The opposition might have been able to choose the ground on which to fight, but Townshend was able to choose the time. He now recalled the Irish parliament at a time when opposition in England was at a low ebb, and at a time when there were no contentious measures to be introduced, not even a money bill. He correctly forecast that the opposition would have 'nothing to unite on or against' and would therefore be all the more vulnerable to his attack.[42]

6

The outcome of the session of parliament which opened in February 1771 and lasted until May seemed to bear out Townshend's most optimistic forecasts and to provide a complete vindication of his methods of management. Early in the session a motion complimentary to him was carried and Ponsonby, rather than deliver it, chose to resign his office of Speaker.[43] This had been the last office of importance held by one of the former undertakers and Ponsonby's resignation seemed to set the seal on Townshend's triumph. Edmond Sexten Pery was elected as successor to Ponsonby and this too was considered as a government victory.[44] The session

41. Allan's correspondence (P.R.O.N.I., D.572/3/1-117 (Macartney Mss.) and Public Record Office of Ireland, M 730/1-104) gives details of these.
42. Townshend letter-book ii, Townshend to Rochford, 31 Jan. 1771; *ibid.,* Townshend to North, 4 Feb. 1771.
43. Ponsonby resigned on 4 Mar. 1771.
44. Townshend letter-book ii, Townshend to North, 7 Mar. 1771.

as a whole passed quietly and large government majorities were routine.[45]   Townshend's victory in this session was, however, diminished by three important considerations.

This session of parliament was an extraordinary one. It was called simply because Townshend wanted a showdown with the former undertakers. Government forces were at their strongest and those of the opposition at their weakest. Moreover, there were no contentious proposals to put before parliament.[46] These circumstances would hardly operate in the next session. There would then be many contentious matters to be discussed: the division of the Irish revenue board, for example, or the creation of a new board of accounts. Was it not possible that opposition might revive? Again, it seems strange to look on the election of Pery to the Chair as a victory for the viceroy. Pery had long been a thorn in the side of English government in Ireland and in many ways he was a more formidable politician than Ponsonby.[47] Was it not possible that, using his office as a power-base, he could turn out to be even more dangerous than Ponsonby? Finally, and most important, there were signs in this session that Townshend's supporters were, on occasion, prepared to play fast and loose with government business. His managers had permitted an amendment to the address to be carried unopposed, which referred to the 'protest and prorogation', a subject which Townshend had given explicit instructions was not to be raised.[48]   Moreover, the amendment (penned by Pery) turned out to be 'an artful justification' of the Commons' action at that time.[49]   It was overcome with some difficulty.   And three bills which required financing out of the 'hereditary revenue' were allowed to pass with only token resistance; again, this was contrary to Townshend's instructions.[50]

It seems clear that the groups who had been regarded for a

45.   In the 25 divisions noticed in *C.J.I.* from 26 Feb. to 18 May 1771 government numbers averaged 100 to the opposition's 63 (*C.J.I.*, xiv, 751-808).
46.   Wilmot, for example, pointed out that the Irish opposition groups in this session 'lacked a proper and true Irish point on which they could agree' (Derby Borough Library, Catton coll. [Ireland], Misc. Mss., note by Wilmot on a letter from Waite, 27 Feb. 1771).
47.   Waite described him as 'the most inveterate enemy' to English government in Ireland (Derby Borough Library, Catton coll. [Ireland], Misc. Mss., Waite to Wilmot, 11 Mar. 1771).
48.   *C.J.I.*, xiv, 759.
49.   Townshend letter-book ii, Townshend to Rochford, 6 Mar. 1771.
50.   *Ibid.*, same to same, 28 Mar. 1771; Townshend letter-book iii, same to same, 13 Sept. 1771.

time as the secondary connections, forced to play second fiddle to
Ponsonby and Shannon, now aspired to become undertakers
themselves, negotiating with the Castle as equals if not superiors.
In justifying his reliance on these groups, Townshend had written:
'if we do not support and combine with us the secondary interests
here, we must submit to be ruled by the first.' What the session of
February-May 1771 showed was that there was a danger of being
ruled by the second interests *in place of* the first.

The 1771 session was much less than a total triumph for
Townshend; in particular, the indiscipline of the government
supporters was an ill omen. Townshend recognized the problem
and believed that he would have a solution for it by the time the
Irish parliament re-assembled in October 1771, for it was his hope
that by that date Shannon would have brought his connection back
to the government side. Townshend believed that Shannon now
realized that the game was up and that he would be only too glad
to settle if suitable terms were offered him. Shannon's accession to
the government ranks would finally shatter opposition, and, perhaps
more important, would serve to overawe the government's other
supporters and check their pretensions. Townshend also expected
that by October all his leading supporters would be rewarded with
offices, peerages and pensions and would be thereby confirmed in
their allegiance to the government. He wrote:

> A well-timed and ample advancement of those who have
> distinguished themselves at this important crisis, will establish
> the authority and influence of English government upon a
> permanent basis. Otherwise, the stone will immediately roll
> back on English government here and all future faith in it will
> forever explode.[51]

When the Irish parliament re-assembled Townshend's expectations were fulfilled only in part. Many of his supporters had been
rewarded, but Shannon remained aloof[52] and the result was, from
the government point of view, a very troubled and confused session,
in which the indiscipline of the so-called government supporters was
almost unlimited. On the first day of the session some of the more
prominent government supporters did not attend. John Beresford,

51. Townshend letter-book v, Townshend to Lord Frederick Campbell, 24
Apr. 1771.
52. Shannon rejected Townshend's overtures because he believed that
Townshend was 'endeavouring to do his business as cheaply as possible' and he
resolved to hold out for more lucrative terms (P.R.O.N.I., D.2707/5/41A,
Shannon to Dennis, 26 May 1771).

a revenue commissioner and a leading member of the Tyrone connection, was not there; nor was Theophilus Jones, a former chief secretary and member of the Tyrone connection; Lord Drogheda was also absent.[53] These absences served as a warning to the viceroy that the support of the new 'King's servants' could not be taken for granted. Dramatic confirmation of this appeared in a series of major defeats sustained by Townshend in the period up to Christmas. A majority of over 40 was recorded against the Castle on the proposal to divide the Irish revenue board; a pension for the English politician Jeremiah Dyson was thrown out; and there were other defeats.[54] In each case a major feature was the wholesale defection of government supporters, either into the ranks of the opposition or as absentees. The secondary interests, it was now clear, aspired to be the new undertakers and sought to build up their strength in order to be in a position to dictate to the crown. As Townshend put it, explaining their conduct,

> The fact is that these noblemen, having now aided English government to reduce the former cabals and conceiving them alienated from any future communications, begin now to entertain the same views and would fain form their own parties with the materials of government that they may be the managers in their turn.

Lord Tyrone's conduct offers evidence of this. His connection had received numerous favours from Townshend; his brothers, for example, had been advanced in the revenue service and the Church. Yet despite these favours, neither John Beresford nor Richard Underwood attended during the session; two members of the Tyrone connection voted against the government on a motion relating to the division of the revenue board; and Tyrone himself, for his part, presented Townshend with a list of six great employments which he desired on their falling vacant, and, on being refused these, left Dublin at a critical moment for the government.[55] His motives seem clear. Neither he nor Beresford wished the revenue board to be split up into separate boards for customs and excise, for that would halve their power. For similar reasons, they opposed Townshend's plan to bring the patronage of the revenue

53. Townshend letter-book iii, Townshend to North, 10 Oct. 1771.
54. *C.J.I.*, xv, 112; Townshend letter-book iii, Townshend to Rochford, 28 Nov. 1771.
55. *Ibid.*, Townshend to North, 10 Oct. 1771; *ibid.*, Townshend to Rochford, 12 Dec. 1771. The two members of the Tyrone connection who voted against the proposal to divide the revenue board were Edward Cary, M.P. Co. Londonderry, and Richard Gorges, M.P. Enniskillen.

service under viceregal control. Townshend wrote bitterly: 'it should seem as if those who loudly exclaimed against [John Ponsonby as 'first' commissioner] ... cannot bear the disappointment of sharing only a proportion of that gentleman's power.'[56]

If the secondary interests had shown that they could not be be relied on, so too had the independent members whom Townshend had once considered his first friends. Where an 'Irish point' was at stake they courted popularity. Many of them had sided with the opposition over Dyson's pension and the division of the revenue board.

To these problems Townshend produced two answers. He decided to ignore the Commons' resolutions against his measures and went ahead and implemented them by King's Letter. The revenue board was divided and the viceroy given control of its patronage. To a large extent it had been the independence of the Irish revenue board, especially in patronage matters, which had made Ponsonby so formidable, and while the revenue board remained independent it was possible, even probable, that another would seek to create or strengthen a personal following from its patronage. Henceforth the lord lieutenant would be the *de facto* first commissioner of the revenue. Townshend also decided to re-open negotiations with Shannon, and this time he met with success. Shannon's terms for coming over to the government were steep, but the viceroy believed it necessary to comply. As he explained to Lord Rochford, if Shannon came over it would mean a loss of some 15 members from the ranks of the opposition and, moreover, 'would curb the endless importunity and ingratitude of many lesser interests'.[57]

The conclusion of the treaty with Shannon was to be the work of Lord Harcourt, the next lord lieutenant, but the credit

---

56. *Ibid.*, Townshend to Rochford, 12 Dec. 1771.
57. *Ibid.*, Townshend to North, 10 Apr. 1772; *Calendar of Home Office Papers, 1770-72*, pp 478-9, Townshend to Rochford, 10 Apr. 1772. The terms asked for were as follows: (1) Sentleger Sentleger, nephew and heir to Lord Doneraile, to be made a baron (2) Denham Jephson to be granted a pension of £600 p.a. (3) Nicholas Lysaght, M.P. Tallow, to be made a lieutenant-governor of Cork (4) James Dennis, Shannon's counsellor, and second serjeant-at-law, to be made prime serjeant, solicitor-general or attorney-general, whichever became vacant first (5) Richard Townshend to have the first vacant commissionership of the revenue (6) the dean of Cork to be made bishop of Cork at the first opportunity.

properly belongs to Townshend.[58] From early in 1772 it was clear that Shannon's thoughts were turning more and more towards an accommodation with the government. When parliament had re-assembled after the Christmas recess Townshend had faced a formidable opposition and, for a time, it had seemed as if this opposition, enraged by his high-handed action over the revenue board, would carry all before it. Then opposition had faded away. Froude, in *The English in Ireland in the Eighteenth Century,* writes that 'suddenly, the ranks of opposition wavered, a combination which had threatened to be irresistible dissolved like a mist. Neither the Commons' Journals nor the Irish histories explain this change'.[59] The explanation was, in fact, the well-founded belief that Shannon was contemplating a return to government. The opposition ranks were split, while government supporters looked to their places. In the last act of this session Shannon indicated where his loyalty lay when he carried the sword of state. Townshend made much of this.[60] Finally, during his last months in Ireland, Townshend appointed one of Shannon's men, Richard Townsend, to be a commissioner of the Irish excise board.[61]

Possibly of greater significance than the appointment of Richard Townsend, however, was the identity of the person whom the lord lieutenant dismissed, Sir William Osborne. Osborne, in common with other 'King's servants', had caused trouble both during and after the session of parliament, and Townshend decided that he had to go.[62] Yet this was more than the mere replacement of an ingrate by someone who could be relied on. Osborne was a former member of the 'patriot party' and was one of those independent country gentlemen whom Townshend had at one time looked to as potential pillars of a 'Castle' party. The experience of the two previous sessions had shown him how unfounded was this belief, and the dismissal of Osborne and his replacement by one of Shannon's men marked the rejection of this earlier policy. Townshend still looked for support to the secondary interests and the independent members, but he now realized that only the

58. *The Harcourt Papers* ed. W. E. Harcourt (9 vols., privately printed, 1888-1905), ix, 51, 60-63, Harcourt to North, 20 Dec. 1772, North to Harcourt, 31 Dec. 1772.
59. *C.J.I.*, xv, 214-215; Froude, *English in Ireland*, ii, 112-113.
60. Townshend letter-book iii, Townshend to Harcourt, 29 June 1772.
61. *Ibid.*
62. P.R.O.N.I., D.572/4/19 (Macartney Mss.), Godfrey Lill to Macartney, Dec. 1772; D.572/5/20, 29, 30, Robert Waller to Macartney, 3 Oct., 21, 23 Nov. 1772; Townshend letter-book iii, Townshend to North, 29 Nov. 1772. Significantly, Townshend remarked that Osborne's dismissal would cause little trouble as he had no following in parliament.

additional support of a large and disciplined group, such as Shannon's, could provide the government with a stable working majority. Townshend had hoped that the accession of Shannon to government would help stabilize Irish politics and finally establish 'the Castle' as the leading undertaker, in practice as well as in theory. And so it proved. During the next 30 years Irish politics operated in general within the framework set down by Townshend during his viceroyalty.

7

In this paper attention has been concentrated on the two aspects of Townshend's viceroyalty which have figured most prominently in the historiography of the period: the decision to 'bring administration back to the Castle'; and the methods by which Townshend achieved this end.

The argument has been against the received view that Townshend was sent to Ireland with instructions to reside there constantly and break the power of the undertakers. Rather, his lengthy stay in Ireland was brought about by the opposition he encountered over the augmentation proposal; and the policies he pursued were essentially his own, shaped by his character, connections, political principles and his experiences in Ireland. He took the major decisions himself – to reside in Ireland constantly, to curb the power of the great undertakers and to create a 'Castle' party. The role of the British Cabinet (and ministers) was merely one of granting formal approval to the policies which Townshend put forward.

It has also been argued here that the notion of the Townshend viceroyalty as being a byword for corruption is a mistaken one. Townshend's majority in the session of February 1771 was a product of many factors: painstaking management in Ireland and England during the previous year; the dismissal of the leading undertakers in May 1770 and Townshend's evident determination not to be intimidated by them; promises of offices and pensions to some supporters; the timing of the parliamentary session; and the weakness and disunity displayed by the opposition groups. But more than anything it was the changed political situation in England which ensured Townshend's victory. The formation and consolidation of North's ministry in the spring of 1770 marks the true turning-point in Townshend's fortunes, and in the viceroyalty as a whole. 'Corruption' had little to do with it.

Finally, it has been shown that Townshend's difficulties were by no means over at the end of this session. Having crushed the former undertakers, he was now faced with the problem of disciplining and restraining his own supporters, 'who would be the managers in their turn'.[63]   As a result of the indiscipline of his supporters, opposition revived during the session which opened in October 1771, and several important defeats were inflicted on the administration. It was only towards the end of his viceroyalty, by his *rapprochement* with Shannon, that Townshend was able to solve this problem. Shannon came over to government not as an equal of the lord lieutenant but as his private servant, and his defection from the opposition ranks, besides completing the destruction of the opposition grouping, freed Townshend from his dependence on the unreliable country gentlemen and also had a chastening effect on the secondary interests. Harcourt was to reap the benefit of Townshend's actions.

This new interpretation not only revises considerably the earlier accepted views of the viceroyalty but it also has a wider significance, in that it sheds light on the knotty problems of the making and implementation of policy within the first British empire. In recent years the policies − or lack of them − of the various ministers of the 1760s towards the colonies, along with the individual decisions which were reached during this period, have been subjected to close scrutiny in a number of monographs and articles; and the result has been, cumulatively, an important addition to the historiography of the old empire.[64]   So far as policy-making is concerned, two broad conclusions may be drawn from these studies. Firstly, it is now clear that the process of policy-making was extremely complex; glib assumptions have had to be discarded. P. D. G. Thomas writes that

> In the period of the Stamp Act crisis, Britain's American policy was influenced in varying degrees by the King; his ministers; lesser politicians in office; permanent officials in government departments; unofficial advisers of ministers;

63.   Townshend letter-book iii, Townshend to North, 10 Oct. 1771.
64.   Thus the decision to keep up an army in America after 1763; the Proclamation of 1763 and British policy on western lands; the Stamp Act; and the Townshend duties of 1767 have all been considered in detail: see J. W. Shy, *Towards Lexington* (Princeton, 1965); J. Sosin, *Whitehall and the Wilderness* (Lincoln, Nebraska, 1961); E. S. and H. M. Morgan, *The Stamp Act Crisis* (Chapel Hill, 1953); P. Langford, *The First Rockingham Administration, 1765-1766* (Oxford, 1973); Chaffin, *'Townshend Acts'*. See also Thomas, *British Politics and the Stamp Act Crisis*.

outside pressure groups; the need to secure the approval of parliament.[65]

A second broad conclusion that has emerged is that at almost every stage in the decision-making process, the role of personality – whether it be that of Rockingham or of Charles Townshend – was of critical importance.[66] By their ideas, beliefs, ambitions and connections, ministers such as these were able to influence greatly the nature and timing of the decisions affecting the colonies which were taken during the 1760s. As a corollary of this, the importance of the Cabinet as a policy-making body has now been denied. It is seen as a body which granted 'merely formal approval to policies formulated by politicians of lesser rank, permanent officials and even unofficial advisers'.[67]

Both these conclusions are at variance with what was the accepted account of British policy towards Ireland in the 1760s. British policy, so vacillating elsewhere, has hitherto appeared orderly, coherent and rational so far as Ireland was concerned, and this contrast, always a central weakness of the old interpretation, has so far remained unexplained. The interpretation put forward in this paper shows that there is in fact no contrast to be explained. Policy towards Ireland and the American colonies was equally indecisive – and the policy that did emerge was essentially the work of one man, in the case of Ireland, Lord Townshend.

What is the importance of the Townshend viceroyalty in the history of eighteenth-century Ireland? Paradoxically, the vice-royalty marks the end of 'the age of the undertakers' but not of the undertakers themselves. Given that the main feature of the Irish governmental structure was the separation of executive from legislature, undertakers (or 'managers', as Townshend called them) were essential and, as we have seen in a previous essay, had in fact been a feature of Irish parliamentary life ever since the Glorious Revolution. What had changed between 1767 and 1772 was that by the latter date the great undertakers such as Ponsonby and Shannon were no longer in a position to dictate terms to, or negoti-ate as equals with, the lord lieutenant for the purpose of under-taking the King's business through parliament. The oligarchy had been broken. From 1772 the lord lieutenant headed, and his chief secretary controlled, a 'Castle' party in parliament, which could

---

65. Thomas, *British Politics and the Stamp Act Crisis*, p. 21.
66. Langford writes, 'the critical factor at every turn is the role of person-ality' (Langford, *First Rockingham Administration*, p. 3).
67. Thomas, *British Politics and the Stamp Act Crisis*, p. 113.

undertake the King's business. Other groups could assist in this task and would be rewarded for their efforts, but there was no doubt as to who was in control. From 1772 onwards, the lord lieutenant was the leading undertaker in Ireland and also the chief dispenser of patronage, whether in the Church, in the army or in the revenue service.

Townshend established control over the revenue board and its patronage, and this was his great achievement. The Irish revenue board — more comparable to the British treasury than to the English boards of customs and excise — had been Ponsonby's power-base, and its patronage had given him immense influence in parliament and in the country at large. Townshend brought back the revenue board to the Castle. Henceforth, letters requesting offices in the revenue — many of them written by revenue commissioners — regularly formed part of the viceroy's postbag. Without this patronage, the task of maintaining a 'Castle' party would have been almost impossible. As it was, the 'Castle' party survived the Constitution of 1782, the Regency Crisis and the Fitzwilliam episode, and in fact was instrumental in undertaking the greatest project of all — the Union.[68]

It was appropriate that the party built up by Townshend should have had a role to play in carrying the Union, for in a real sense the seeds of the Union were sown during his viceroyalty. For the central weakness of the Anglo-Irish governmental structure — the separation of executive from legislature — was not only unremedied at Townshend's departure, but had in fact been exacerbated by his new system. Henceforth the 'English' executive would attempt to control directly the Irish legislature. Ireland's constitutional subordination could scarcely have been made more explicit, and for that reason was more capable of being resented. The American war gave both stimulus and opportunity to those who wished to attack the constitutional relationship laid bare by Townshend's reforms. That relationship was altered by the Constitution of 1782, but the system of direct control remained and hence Ireland's informal constitutional subordination continued. When the system established by Townshend proved too costly, too troublesome or too dangerous, there would be no alternative but Union. This is where the real importance of the Townshend viceroyalty lies.

68. G. C. Bolton, *The Passing of the Irish Act of Union* (Oxford, 1966), *passim*.

THE VOLUNTEERS AND PARLIAMENT, 1779-84

P. D. H. Smyth

The relationship which existed between the Volunteers and the Irish parliament from 1779 to 1784 was an example rare in the politics of any country, and certainly unique in Ireland, of co-operation between an armed force and a representative assembly. There were no obvious parallels upon which the Volunteers could draw. The Cromwellian period in English history was both distant in time and distasteful in example, while the implications of the American revolutionary experience were too recent – and probably too drastic in any case – to have been assimilated. Ultimately the partnership of 1779-84 was the result more of short-term improvisation than of long-term planning. Because of, or perhaps despite that fact, it was an extremely complex relationship. On the surface, armed men working towards the same objectives as parliament was an impressive example of national unity, and it certainly produced results: it is impossible to visualize the Constitution of 1782 having been achieved without this apparent harmony. Below the surface, however, there existed a complex substratum of conflicting ideas on the role which it was acceptable for an armed force to assume in politics, and long and bitter arguments raged over the constitutional propriety of the Volunteers holding political opinions and acting upon them. Numerous members of the Irish parliament were also Volunteers – around 1782 there were at least 23 Volunteer officers, from Ulster alone, sitting in the Commons, and almost a dozen in the Lords[1] – but this only served

1. In the Commons – Hon. C. Skeffington, C. R. Dobbs, J. O'Neill, Hon. R. Rawdon, W. Brownlow, T. Dawson, H. Grattan, G. Montgomery, Hon. J.J.B. Maxwell, Sir H. Hamilton, A. Montgomery, R. Stewart, Hon. E. Ward, R. Blackwood, R. Ross, I. Corry, Sir A. Brooke, M. Archdall, H. Flood, T. Conolly, E. Cary, R. Jackson, J. Stewart, N. Montgomery, Sir C. Molyneux, T. Knox, H. T. Clements, Hon. R. Ward and H. L. Rowley; in the Lords – the earls of Antrim, Bristol, Charlemont, Donegall and Moira; Lords Belmore, Enniskillen, Erne, Farnham and Glerawly. There was a rumour (unconfirmed) that the duke of Buccleuch had enrolled as a private in a Dublin Volunteer company in 1782.
   Included in the Commons list are men who sat for Ulster constituencies but commanded Volunteer units elsewhere – Flood and Grattan, for instance; also men who commanded units in Ulster but sat for constituencies elsewhere – H. T. Clements, Hon. R. Ward and H. L. Rowley. Both lists should be treated with caution: (a) because the paucity of information which relates to companies in Counties Donegal, Monaghan, Cavan and Fermanagh leaves plenty of scope for mistakes; and (b) because the mere fact of a man being a Volunteer officer is not proof of his commitment to the movement's principles and objectives.

to cloud the issue with dual loyalties. Historians have tended to view the period as something of a new departure in Irish politics – and in a sense it was – but the point to be firmly established is that the politics of these years were governed by old, traditional ideas as much as they were animated by new ones. The Volunteers and parliament formed a new and significant relationship, but their partnership was none the less dominated by well established terms of reference. This paper takes as its theme the constant interplay between what were essentially old and new political philosophies.

A feeling of uncertain values had enveloped the Volunteer movement almost from the beginning. The Belfast Volunteer Company, formed on 17 March 1778, drew up a statement asserting its independence from government control, and enough companies followed this lead for Volunteering to acquire a philosophy of independent armed service, with Belfast as the initiator of the new movement.[2] Generations of historians in later years would look back, misty-eyed, on a nation of broad-shouldered freemen whose pockets were as empty of government gold as their hearts were full of the national good.

This independence was undoubtedly a bonus in nineteenth-century terms, but whether it was quite so desirable in 1778 is open to question. The central fact about the Volunteer companies of 1778 – and it is a fact of which it is all too easy to lose sight – is that they were bodies of armed men who had specifically placed themselves outside the sphere of government influence. In the event, this proved to be no bad thing, but no-one in 1778 could have anticipated such a happy outcome. Even in Belfast, for the first few weeks, there seemed to be doubts about the morality of Volunteering, and in the first year of their existence there was certainly no massive tide of public reaction in favour of the companies.[3] The early Volunteers undoubtedly felt this lack of

2. Henry Joy, 'History of the Volunteers of Ulster originating in Belfast 17 March 1778': Joy Mss., v, 56, on temporary deposit in P.R.O.N.I. (T.D. 2777). See also the Articles of Association of the Armagh Volunteers, asserting the same kind of independence. These were published by request in the *Belfast Newsletter* in December 1778, so that other companies then forming could have a model to follow (T. G. F. Paterson, 'The County Armagh Volunteers of 1778-1793', *Ulster Journal of Archaeology* (ser. 3), v (1942), 40-1).
3. P.R.O.N.I., T.D. 2777 (Joy Mss.), v, 56. So far as can be estimated,. there were only about 12,000 Volunteers by the spring of 1779 (*Belfast Newsletter*, 23 Apr. 1779). In this connection see also a letter on the state of Volunteering in Belfast in the *Londonderry Journal*, 25 June 1779: 'the Volunteers of this place are as tired of military exercise as children are of a

warmth. The very earnestness with which they celebrated royal birthdays, and every other public festivity, with almost feverish protestations of loyalty, bespoke an uneasy conscience.[4] Politics, it must be emphasized, formed no part of the Volunteers' outlook in 1778; that would have put far too great a strain on public tolerance. So far as can be judged, public opinion in 1778 generally regarded the Volunteer companies as a transitory phenomenon, to be countenanced only until such time as the government decided to begin organizing the militia. Throughout the summer and autumn of 1778 there was a steady stream of reports that the militia would be called out, and it was assumed that, when that happened, the local Volunteer companies would be absorbed into the national organization.[5] In Dublin, for instance, it was only when it became fairly clear that the government was not going to organize the militia that the first Volunteer company was formed in October 1778, and as late as June 1779 the gentlemen of Clare and other counties were offering to pay for their own companies of militia until parliament could meet to reimburse them.[6]

As it became increasingly apparent that the government intended neither to suppress the Volunteers nor organize the militia, men came forward who had previously held back, and it was this influx of the less impulsive that altered the whole character of the movement and steered it away from its earlier subversive image. From the beginning of 1779 Volunteering began to become 'respectable'. In January, for instance, the earl of Antrim reviewed and presented colours to Volunteer bodies in County Antrim.[7] A man of his standing — he was governor of the county — did not have to go to such lengths merely to gain cheap popularity; nor, by

rattle ... Our cloud-cap't grenadiers and our gorgeous infantry are dissolving apace as the summer approaches ... After the amusement of a year our Volunteers rest satisfied with a fine coat and a firelock ...' A scrap book of notes, newspaper cuttings, *etc.*, on the Volunteers (P.R.O.N.I., T.962/6) suggests that the author may have been William Drennan.
4.   *Belfast Newsletter,* 5 June, 3, 7 July, 3, 6 Nov., 11 Dec. 1778; 19 Jan., 23, 26 Feb., 19, 26 Mar., 30 Apr., 8 June 1779; *Londonderry Jnl.,* 5, 19, 23 June, 3, 10 July, 4 Aug., 6 Nov. 1778; 23, 26 Feb., 2, 26 Mar., 20, 27 Apr., 4, 8 June 1779.
5.   *Belfast Newsletter,* 2 June, 17 July, 15 Sept. 1778; *Londonderry Jnl.,* 6 Oct., 24 Nov. 1778; *H.M.C. Lothian,* p. 337, Hillsborough to Buckingham- shire, 22 Aug. 1778; P.R.O.N.I., D.607/161 (Downshire Mss.), John Slade to [Hillsborough] , 8 Sept. 1778.
6.   *Belfast Newsletter,* 24 July, 13, 16 Oct. 1778; Buckinghamshire to Weymouth, 30 June 1779, enclosing a memorial to this effect which had been received from Sir Lucius O'Brien, quoted in H. Grattan, *Memoirs of the Life and Times of ... Henry Grattan* (5 vols., London, 1839-46), ii, 394-5.
7.   *Belfast Newsletter,* 22, 26 Jan. 1779.

the same token, is it likely that a county governor would have bestowed official recognition on bodies of disreputable men with anti-government leanings. In June 1779 the Volunteer companies of Dublin were called upon by the authorities to dispel a mob and to mount guard on the Royal Exchange.[8] At about the same time even the lord lieutenant, Lord Buckinghamshire, was having to admit that, while the whole idea of the Volunteers was 'unpleasing' to him, the companies could be of 'the most material utility'.[9] In Larne an army captain acted as reviewing officer while the local company went through its paces. In Cork the local companies were appointed to garrison the town while the army marched out to investigate an invasion scare.[10] By the middle of the summer the Irish Privy Council yielded to the pressure, and authorized county governors to issue militia arms to Volunteer companies: these were gratefully accepted, and no murmur was heard about dependence on government.[11] By the end of the summer of 1779, when the threat of invasion had sent Volunteer numbers surging towards the 40,000-mark,[12] and talk began to be heard of the scattered companies forming themselves into regiments and battalions,[13] the Volunteers more resembled the militia than they did the rather self-consciously 'independent' force of a year before.

The government was thus placed in a dilemma concerning its official attitude towards the Volunteers. The problem crystallized in October 1779 when a grateful parliament, realizing that the Volunteer companies had performed a real service during the

8. *Ibid.*, 8 June 1779.
9. P.R.O.N.I., D.607/198 (Downshire Mss.), Buckinghamshire to Hillsborough, 10 May 1779.
10. *Belfast Newsletter*, 18, 29 June 1779.
11. *Life ... of ... Grattan*, i, 368; P.R.O.N.I., T.D. 2777 (Joy Mss.), iv, 178, Henry Joy, 'Scattered materials for Annals of the Province of Ulster. Volume iv: from the year 1689 to 1800'; *Londonderry Jnl.*, 2 Nov. 1779; *H.M.C. Charlemont*, i, 355, Sir Richard Heron to Charlemont, 21 Sept. 1779; *ibid.*, 361-2, William Brownlow to same, 23 Oct. 1779; *ibid.*, 365, David Bell to same, 5 Nov. 1779; N.L.I., Ms. 838, records and accounts of the Ennis Volunteers, 1778-92.
12. *Parliamentary History*, xx, 1159, 1198; *Belfast Newsletter*, 17 Aug. 1779; *Londonderry Jnl.*, 28 Sept. 1779. Accurate estimates of Volunteer strength were almost impossible to make, especially before the Volunteers acquired some kind of large-scale organization.
13. *E.g.*, *Belfast Newsletter*, 17 Sept., 5 Oct. 1779; *H.M.C. Charlemont*, i, 177. See T. G. F. Paterson, 'The Volunteer Companies of Ulster, 1778-1793', *The Irish Sword*, vii (1965-66), 90-116, 204-230, 308-12; viii (1967-8), 23-32, 92-7, 210-7; and 'The County Armagh Volunteers of 1778-1793', *Ulster Jnl. of Arch.* (ser. 3), v (1942), 31-61; vi (1943), 69-105, for details of this regimentation in Ulster.

summer by the assumption of the role of the militia, felt obliged to pass votes of thanks to them. In both Houses a form of words was chosen which managed to convey the maximum gratitude to the Volunteers with a minimum of embarrassment to the government: a simple message of thanks to the armed companies for their spirited exertions in defence of the country.[14]   The Commons were, it would appear, happily unanimous, but in the Lords a significant debate occurred. The vote of thanks was moved by the duke of Leinster, by this time the idol of the Dublin Volunteers. However, the lord chancellor, Lord Lifford, insisted that as control of the Volunteer companies did not reside in the crown the companies themselves must be outside the law, and Viscount Valentia flirted with the same issue, wondering if a vote of thanks such as had been proposed might not confer some sort of legal recognition on the companies. Lord Mountmorres cut through all the arguments by saying that the point at issue was whether the conduct of the Volunteers had been meritorious or not, and, since it obviously was, a vote of thanks was perfectly proper.[15]   The House eventually agreed with him, but the important thing was that the central issue − the legal standing of the Volunteer companies − had been swept under the carpet at a time when it would have been feasible to have thrashed out an official attitude.

This point is of fundamental importance. Because of the peculiar circumstances of 1779, neither side defined its position. The Volunteer companies were frankly and unashamedly delighted with the votes of thanks from parliament: in County Armagh, for instance, the Volunteering spirit and numbers 'increased greatly' as a direct result, and in County Londonderry loud public complaints were issued when the county governor was slow in bringing the official message down from Dublin.[16] Nevertheless, the Volunteers as a whole still remained independent of government control, and made no move to alter the situation. If by the autumn of 1779 there appeared to have been a *rapprochement*, it had not been due to the Volunteer companies deliberately abandoning a position of hostility towards the establishment and adopting a more conciliatory attitude; nor, on the other hand, had the government made a clear decision to alter its stance in the face of the realities of the situation.   Neither side appears to have taken a decision; they simply drifted into an undefined relationship.

14.   *C.J.I.*, xix, 15; *L.J.I.*, v, 133.
15.   *Belfast Newsletter,* 26 Oct. 1779.
16.   *H.M.C. Charlemont*, i, 361-2, Brownlow to Charlemont, 23 Oct. 1779; *Londonderry Jnl.*, 2 Nov. 1779.

The official 'working relationship' between the Volunteers and parliament began at this time and with no clear guidelines. As we have already seen, it was not until near the end of 1779 that the Volunteers gained some form of national identity, and became capable of concerted action; and, that apart, the companies may have had genuine scruples about becoming involved in the Free Trade agitation. With unification and large-scale organization, however, came political potential, and some men realized that this was worth encouraging.[17] Grattan was warm in the praise he bestowed on the Volunteer companies in his famous Free Trade speech in the Commons on 12 October 1779, and he practically defied the British parliament to withhold commercial concessions in the face of armed men.[18] A few weeks later, Hussey Burgh uttered the best known metaphor of the period, when he called upon all to behold how the dragon's teeth of England's oppressive laws had sprung up in a crop of armed men.[19] The duke of Leinster organized the Dublin Volunteers into a triumphal guard to escort the amended King's Speech of 14 October from parliament to the Castle, and it was the men under his command who organized the celebrated 'Free Trade or This' demonstration around King William's statue on 4 November.[20] The Volunteers quite naturally relished these marks of attention from the leading figures of the day, and as a result began to think themselves of some political consequence.

It was the 4 November demonstration which passed into Volunteer folklore as the decisive event in the winning of Free Trade. However, it was only when this show of force (with of course the implied threat of further Volunteer action) was combined with a continuing show of recalcitrance by the Irish Commons, that Lord North was persuaded of the wisdom of making concessions.

17. See Lord Charlemont's remark, made with the hindsight of some years, that the potential of the Volunteers as a political force 'was quickly perceived ... by those who panted after the prosperity and emancipation of their country' (*H.M.C. Charlemont*, i, 51). In this connection it is also worth noticing that the Dublin society 'The Monks of the Screw', founded in mid-1779 with a membership which included Flood, Grattan, Charlemont, Yelverton, Burgh and other enlightened politicians, was said to have been responsible for introducing the Volunteers to politics (W. H. Curran, *The Life of the Right Honourable John Philpot Curran* (2 vols., London, 1819), i, 121-5, n.; 150-1, n.).
18. W. W. Seward, *Collectanea Politica* (3 vols., Dublin, 1801-4), i, 169.
19. *Belfast Newsletter*, 7 Dec. 1779.
20. Buckinghamshire to Weymouth, 14 Oct. 1779, quoted in *Life ... of ... Grattan*, i, 395-6; Brian Fitzgerald, *Emily, Duchess of Leinster, 1731-1814* (London, 1949), pp 162-3.

The 'patriot' members of the Irish Commons were carrying all before them in the opening weeks of the 1779 session, forcing through a six-month money bill inside parliament and organizing meetings of constituents outside, in order to maintain the pressure for Free Trade.[21] It was the combination of public and parliamentary demand which North and the British parliament decided not to resist — and not simply the Volunteers on their own: that was the essential lesson to be learned from the events of 1779. Grattan, and possibly a few of the other 'patriot' leaders, realized this, and worked hard subsequently to promote the same unity of purpose between the Volunteers and parliament; but the events of the next few months were to give an indication of the difficulties they would encounter.

In the weeks following 4 November, different Volunteer companies responded to the lead which they believed they had been given, and began to assume their own political initiative. Numerous companies demonstrated in favour of the short money bill in November, and went on to express their approbation at the eventual granting of Free Trade in the following month.[22] Some Volunteer companies were explicit about their aim. The Newry Volunteers met late in December to proclaim that Ireland needed legislative independence in order to protect the commercial concessions so recently wrung from Britain.[23] In January 1780 there was published an outspoken pamphlet by Francis Dobbs, captain of a County Armagh company, entitled *A Letter to Lord North*, in which Britain was urged to concede legislative independence to Ireland before she took it for herself by force of arms. Numbers of companies found it incumbent on them to declare publicly their support for Dobbs's sentiments and selflessly offered to support parliament in the great work of attaining the goal of legislative independence.[24]

Parliament's response to this was to execute a speedy volte-face, an understandable reaction: Volunteers supporting parliament's demands for Free Trade was one thing; Volunteers making their own political demands quite another. The lyrics of a ballad entitled 'Patriot Paddy' were widely circulated:

Arragh, where is the reason good neighbour I pray,

21.   *C.J.I.*, xix, 152-4; *Belfast Newsletter*, 26, 29 Oct., 2 Nov. 1770.
22.   *Belfast Newsletter*, 3, 7, Dec. 1779, 4, 7, 11, 14 Jan., 4 Feb. 1780.
23.   *Ibid.*, 31 Dec. 1779.
24.   Francis Dobbs, *A Letter to the Right Honourable Lord North, on his Propositions in Favour of Ireland* (Dublin, 1780); *Belfast Newsletter*, 8, 15, 18, 22, 29 Feb. 1780.

E

That Paddy should work while the Englishmen play?
Who gave them the right to make Irishmen slaves,
To ride us to death and then dance on our graves ...?
I'll shoulder my hangar, and blow out some brains,
My musket I'll draw, and then — off with my chains ...25

Burgh, Daly, Yelverton, Conolly and Leinster vied with one another in the closing weeks of 1779 and early in 1780 in expressing righteous indignation at the thought of constitutional issues being raised by armed men. Grattan alone urged the wisdom of 'an application to the people, and reliance upon their spirit'.26 The consequences of his adopting this stance are difficult to judge, but certainly for the duration of the session he and the rest of the 'patriots' were heavily defeated on almost every question.27 The news that came in from Britain in June of the results of Lord George Gordon's appeal to extra-parliamentary opinion certainly did not heighten the attractiveness of Grattan's viewpoint.28

The parliamentary session in fact ended with a fairly forthright repudiation of 'patriotism', when, in August, in spite of the ragings of Grattan, the despair of Burgh and the threats of Yelverton to resign from the House, the Commons accepted by 114 votes to 62 a mutiny bill returned from England with a clause inserted to make its operation perpetual.29 This vote provoked an incident which brought to a head the bad feeling developing between the politically active Volunteers and parliament. A meeting of the Dublin Merchants Volunteer Company issued a public declaration that the Commons' acceptance of the perpetual Mutiny Bill was a subversion of the constitution, and for a time it looked as if the Merchants' example would be widely followed.30 Both Houses of parliament were stung by the Merchants' resolution and contemplated taking vigorous legal action against them, but eventually so little support for the outspoken company was generated outside Dublin that it was thought better to drop the affair without enlarging it to the status of a confrontation.31 A letter published

25. *Londonderry Jnl.*, 17 Dec. 1779. Normally the hangar (sword) would be drawn and the musket shouldered: the confusion here is a sarcastic comment on the Volunteers' pretensions.
26. *Some Authentic Minutes of the Proceedings of a Very Respectable Assembly, on the 20th December, 1779* (Dublin, 1780), pp 10, 33, 39-46; *Belfast Newsletter*, 7 Mar. 1780; *L.J.I.*, v, 162; Buckinghamshire to Hillsborough, 2 Mar. 1780, quoted in *Life ... of ... Grattan*, ii, 25-6.
27. *C.J.I.*, xix, 325, 335; *Life ... of ... Grattan*, ii, 38-9, 50; Buckinghamshire to Hillsborough, 21 Apr. 1780, quoted in *ibid*., ii, 52-3.
28. *Belfast Newsletter*, 13, 16, 20 June 1780.
29. *C.J.I.*, xix, 452, 457; *Belfast Newsletter*, 15, 22 Aug. 1780.
30. *Belfast Newsletter*, 22 Aug. 1780.
31. *C.J.I.*, xix, 461-3; *L.J.I.*, v, 218.

in the *Belfast Newsletter*, and addressed to the Volunteers of Ireland, pointed up the moral of the incident. The Volunteers, the writer said, could be regarded in two distinct ways: as armed citizens, and as freemen of Ireland. In the case of the Merchants Company the roles had become confused: they had censured parliament in their capacity as armed men, when constitutionally they were only entitled to object as freemen and electors to the behaviour of their representatives.[32] The letter in fact stated the dilemma which lay at the heart of all relations between the Volunteers and parliament, but it suggested no easy way in which the dilemma could be resolved.

Parliament was prorogued from September 1780 to October 1781, and the silence of the Volunteers on political matters during that time was an indication of how much they still thought in terms of working through parliament to achieve their objectives. Indeed, there may have been a desire among them at this point to erase whatever bad impression may have been created earlier, for in 1781 the Volunteers, if they did not actually strive for respectability, at least succeeded in having respectability thrust upon them. By early in the year the British Cabinet was reported to be considering the employment of the Volunteers as a reserve force when six regular army regiments were withdrawn for American service; it was confidently asserted in Dublin that the Prince of Wales was 'in raptures' with the Volunteer spirit; and the King himself was used to add lustre to the already impressive reputation, when he was rumoured to have celebrated St Patrick's Day at St James's Palace resplendent in full Volunteer uniform, complete with a bunch of shamrocks in his hat.[33] The truth of these stories is difficult to assess, but that they circulated at all, without ridicule, is in itself a comment on the changed public attitude to Volunteering.

Evidence of the Volunteers' own response to their enhanced reputation came during the summer of 1781, when the annual invasion-scare led to the new lord lieutenant, Carlisle (who had succeeded Buckinghamshire in October 1780) being overwhelmed with offers of service from Volunteer companies all over Ireland, with the notoriously undeferential Belfast companies well in the van.[34] There were other indications too. The duke of Leinster and

32. *Belfast Newsletter,* 6 Oct. 1780.
33. *Ibid.,* 27 Feb., 17 Aug., 27 Mar. 1781.
34. *Ibid.,* 11, 18, 21 Sept., 2, 9 Oct. 1781; E. H. S. Nugent, 'Down Volunteers', *Ulster Jnl. of Arch.* (ser. 2), x (1904), 143; Ulster Museum, Acc. 19-1947, minute book of the Men of Mourne company.

Thomas Conolly, both strong opponents of 'political' Volunteering, were chosen to conduct summer reviews in different districts.[35] Companies began to talk of their duty to protect the country efficiently, and started to obtain camping equipment to enable them to undertake service away from home.[36] Even at the Belfast review the moderates carried the day against the radicals on the subject of political declarations.[37] Just before the beginning of the new session of parliament in October, Carlisle commented with satisfaction on the Volunteer situation: for the time being, the companies were not objects of apprehension.[38]

The opening months of the new session seemed to justify the lord lieutenant's optimism. In the Commons the patriots were routed on every proposal they made, and outside the Volunteers remained silent, apparently gagged by their new-found respectability and by the vote of thanks for their services which each House of parliament had again deigned to bestow.[39] For the patriots the situation was desperate, and they were tempted into a move which, had it failed, could itself have had desperate consequences.

This move was the calling of the Dungannon Convention of February 1782. Towards the end of 1781 one of the County Armagh units, of which Lord Charlemont was colonel and Francis Dobbs — of *Letter to Lord North* fame — was major, called on every Volunteer company in Ulster to send elected delegates to Dungannon on 15 February 1782, 'then and there to deliberate on the present alarming situation of public affairs'.[40] There could be no pretence that this was anything but direct interference in politics, and Dobbs himself afterwards confessed that the whole idea had been recognized at the time by its promoters as a tremendous gamble. Either a large and unruly meeting or a small and insignificant one could have done profound damage to the patriot cause; and even the spectre of civil war was raised: what if the Volunteers in other provinces chose to ignore, or worse, oppose

35. *Belfast Newsletter,* 17 July, 10 Aug. 1781.
36. *Ibid.,* 14 Sept. 1781; 5 Feb., 2, 12, 26 Mar. 1782.
37. P.R.O.N.I., D.668/24/1/3 (Hezlett Mss.), [John O'Neill] to [Richard Jackson], 23 July 1781.
38. Carlisle to Hillsborough, 24 Sept. 1781, quoted in M. R. O'Connell, *Irish Politics and Social Conflict in the Age of the American Revolution* (Philadelphia, [1965]), p. 307.
39. *C.J.I.,* xx, 101, 174, 196, 260, 263. According to one estimate the effective opposition had been reduced as low as 39 by the beginning of the session (*Life ... of ... Grattan,* ii, 184).
40. *Belfast Newsletter,* 11 Jan. 1782.

the Dungannon example?[41] Controversies were sparked off in the public prints by the idea of armed men interfering in the workings of the free constitution, unwarrantable actions by men who were not freeholders and electors, and so on. The defenders of the idea wisely did not try to argue the ethics of the meeting, for that would have been impossible for them, and instead concentrated on showing how necessary the meeting was at this time.[42].

The Convention was duly held, and, in an impressive display of strength combined with moderation, passed the resolutions which were to provide the necessary lead for national opinion.[43] By no means all the Volunteer companies agreed to send delegates,[44] and not all the delegates who did attend were entirely happy with the proceedings.[45] A phrase used at the time aptly summed up the mixed feelings which armed politics provoked: the Volunteers at

41.   Francis Dobbs, *A History of Irish Affairs from the 12th October, 1779, to the 15th September, 1782* (Dublin, 1782), pp 50-1.
42.   *Belfast Newsletter*, 5, 12 Feb. 1782.
43.   These resolutions are printed in [Henry Joy], *Historical Collections Relative to the Town of Belfast* (Belfast, 1817), pp 180-184.
44.   The representatives of 143 companies attended the meeting. Henry Joy in his 'List of Volunteer Corps in the Province of Ulster, as they Stood about the Year 1783' (P.R.O.N.I., T.D. 2777 [Joy Mss.], iv) gives over 320 companies. T. G. F. Paterson, *'The Volunteer Companies of Ulster'* and *'The County Armagh Volunteers'*, gives a total of over 400 in existence at around the same time.
45.   The instructions given to the delegates were apparently of a rather vague nature. The delegate of one of the Belfast companies was dispatched with orders 'to unite the wise moderation of the citzen with the patriotic firmness of the Volunteer' (P.R.O.N.I., T.965/6, notes and memoranda on the Volunteers). The Rathfriland, Co. Down, delegate was instructed to 'give his most strenuous support to every constitutional question that shall be agitated' (Ulster Museum, Acc. 603-1914, minute book of the Rathfriland Volunteers, meeting on 13 Feb. 1782). The delegates of the Armagh 1st Company were empowered 'to act for us in every matter that may be agitated' (Armagh Public Library, collection of Volunteer papers). Using the discretion instructions like those seemed to give, a few delegates mounted opposition against a number of resolutions at the meeting, especially one which pledged the Volunteers to support at forthcoming elections only those men who had previously demonstrated their support for the great patriotic objectives ([Joy], *Historical Collections*, pp 180-4). The 2nd Armagh Company, part of the battalion which had called the meeting, felt so strongly on the subject that they issued a public declaration of their sentiments: 'neither do we think any such proceedings can tend to the advantage of this kingdom, or the Volunteer corps therein, for we conceive any motion to force, or intention thereof, must be to subvert the necessary freedom of parliament and injurious to Irish Volunteers. We wish, at all times as freemen, freeholders, and

Dungannon were, in the words of one commentator, 'conspirators for the common good'.46

The Dungannon meeting itself probably had a mixed effect on the feelings of parliament. In the following weeks both Grattan and Flood were heavily defeated when they tried to bring the Commons to make an unequivocal statement of its own constitutional rights, and Flood was even forced to make the soothing statement that it was parliament and not the Dungannon meeting which truly represented the people.47 What eventually did bring parliament to respond positively to the Dungannon resolutions was not so much the threat implied by the Convention itself, as the fact that numerous meetings of county grand juries and assemblies of constituents adopted the resolutions as their own and threatened electoral revenge on M.P.s who did not act up to them.48 That, together with the fall of North's ministry in England, left the Irish parliament with no reason not to demand legislative independence. The end result, by whatever means it had been achieved, was the same as in 1779: the voices of people and parliament were united, and Britain had no option but to meet their demand, this time in granting the Constitution of 1782. Grattan looked back on the Dungannon Convention with satisfaction and compared it in importance with — among other memorable events — the coming of Christianity and the signing of Magna Carta.49 Whatever objections may have been raised as to the validity of the first comparison, in terms of armed intervention gaining results there could have been fewer

Irishmen, and think it our right, to canvass the conduct of public men and parliament, but not to compel or endeavour to intimidate with an armed force' (declaration issued 4 May 1782, among the Volunteer papers in Armagh Public Library).
46. *Belfast Newsletter*, 22 Feb. 1782.
47. *C.J.I.*, xx, 311-313; *Belfast Newsletter*, 1 Mar. 1782. The rumour had been circulating in Dublin circles that the object of the Dungannon meeting was to elect three kings for Ireland.
48. See C. H. Wilson, *A Compleat Collection of the Resolutions of the Volunteers, Grand Juries, etc., of Ireland* (Dublin, 1782), pp 38-170. During March and April meetings of the grand juries or the freeholders at large had been held in 29 counties. While only a handful of counties — Armagh the only Ulster one — approved of the Dungannon resolutions *in toto*, the rest found no difficulty in approving the sentiments which had given rise to them. It is important to notice that the majority of these meetings had either taken place or been called before the news came through of the fall of North's ministry at the end of March: the meetings therefore were a response to Dungannon, and not to events in Britain. See also Carlisle to Hillsborough, 19 Mar. 1782, advising that Britain should concede legislative independence before public sentiment gets out of control, quoted in Lecky, ii, 292-3.
49. *Belfast Newsletter*, 23 Apr. 1782.

quibbles about the justness of the second. Meanwhile, the arguments over the propriety of the meeting could be conveniently forgotten, a blaze of glory blinding men to the wider implications of the Volunteers' behaviour.

Grattan, as the architect of the new constitution, and the man who had most exploited the strength of the Volunteer movement for political purposes, was certainly not blind to the consequences to be expected. In order to stimulate national support for legislative independence, he had frankly used and encouraged the Volunteers to act as a political machine. However, once legislative independence had been won, he desired there to be a period of political tranquillity in which the new relationship with Britain might become established and develop; and that meant persuading the Volunteers to relinquish political activity. The struggle which then ensued crystallized around the personalities of Flood and Grattan, the former urging the Volunteers to retain their political involvement, and the latter making equally strenuous pleas for them to beat their swords into ploughshares. Both men of course swore to have only the Volunteers' best interests at heart.

There was a central irony in the 'renunciation' dispute, in that it was an issue which probably need never have arisen. It came about because Grattan and his supporters were over-anxious to end political agitation in Ireland, and tried to stampede the Volunteers – and hence the public – into a similar state of mind. On 18 June 1782 a hand-picked[50] group of Volunteer delegates met in a National Committee, and after a brief debate issued a declaration that the Volunteers of Ireland found the simple repeal of 6 Geo. I, as advocated by Grattan, a sufficient guarantee of Ireland's constitutional security.[51] In the next few days carefully arranged provincial assemblies of delegates dutifully repeated the formula, without being encouraged to question whether such a statement did justice to their feelings.[52] The Belfast Volunteer companies took umbrage at this stage-management, and during July adopted a high moral stand, declaring that the sufficiency of 'simple repeal' was a matter of such great importance that the Volunteers of Ireland would have to make up their own minds about it, without

50. *Ibid.,* 23 Aug. 1782. The accusation of selection came from the earl of Aldborough, one of the Leinster delegates, who had not even been informed that there was a National Committee meeting.
51. *Ibid.,* 28 June 1782.
52. *Ibid.* See also *H.M.C. Charlemont*, i, 411, Francis Bernard to Charlemont, 9 July 1782.

prompting from Grattan and his friends.[53] Left to themselves, the Volunteers might well have found 'simple repeal' perfectly adequate, but the action of the Belfast companies gave Flood the chance to re-open the question and influence Volunteer opinion from his side. The Belfast review in the first week of August produced a large amount of verbal smoke without a really convincing show of renunciatory fire, but the issue of renunciation had been drawn to public attention and from then on developed its own momentum.[54] It is a reflection of the essential irony in the dispute that even the Volunteer companies which had been most radical tended to lose interest in the campaign once the fight to initiate it had been won; and when in April 1783 the British parliament passed an act renouncing all right to legislate for Ireland, the news was received in Ireland with apparent indifference.[55]

This lack of a grand climax tends to conceal the fact that in the renunciation dispute there was a paradox in the attitude of the Volunteers towards parliament. On one level, the dispute demonstrated the Volunteers' continuing faith in the virtues of statute and parliamentary rule, because most of the arguments revolved around the question of Britain giving statutory expression to verbal promises; and yet the dispute also showed that the Volunteers were contemptuous of parliament's views when those views did not suit their own purpose, for the whole issue of renunciation had been raised by the Volunteers in direct defiance of parliamentary edict.

A preoccupation with statutory guarantees was the basis of the arguments in favour of renunciation. A committee of members of the Dublin Lawyers Volunteer Company solemnly reported after weeks of investigation that, although they were convinced of

53. P.R.O.N.I., D.553/2, 3 (Drennan-Bruce Mss.), William Drennan to William Bruce, 6, 27 July 1782; *Belfast Newsletter*, 28 June, 2, 19, 23 July 1782. The argument was not initially about simple repeal at all, but centred round the Belfast claim that the three Ulster delegates at the National Committee meeting — Francis Dobbs, Mervyn Archdall and Joseph Pollock — had been given no mandate to take any decisions which would be binding on the province they represented. Dobbs took this as an affront and in a series of angry clashes with the Belfast companies brought the constitutional dispute down to the level of a personal confrontation. One of the arguments he used was that, while the Volunteers he and his colleagues had represented were undoubtedly well-informed they were not capable on their own of making such 'nice decisions' as those involved in supporting simple repeal.
54. P.R.O.N.I., D.553/4 (Drennan-Bruce Mss.), Drennan to Bruce [4/5 Aug. 1782]; *Belfast Newsletter*, 9, 16 Aug. 1782.
55. 23 Geo. III, c. 33.

Britain's sincerity in promising to give up all right to legislate for Ireland, there had been no statutory safeguards placed around the settlement of May and June, and that these should be sought in an Act of Renunciation.[56] In July, Flood introduced into the Irish Commons his proposals for an Irish Bill of Rights: a measure which would have removed from the King his claim to the crown of Ireland if he gave his consent, even inadvertently, to a British measure which included Ireland within its legislative scope.[57] The Commons summarily rejected the idea, but the Volunteers seized upon it with acclaim, and in the latter months of 1782 placed this Bill of Rights above even an Act of Renunciation in their order of priorities.[58]   The supporters of simple repeal recognized their opponents' thirst for a statutory settlement and in fact turned the argument on its head:

> Were England dispos'd, howe'er we should flounce,
> To renounce a repeal, she'd repeal a renounce.[59]

In other words, if Britain granted a statutory title then Britain by exercising the same powers could annul that title. The logic of this was so strong that the renunciators took care to ignore it. Flood was a lawyer by profession, and his following soon included many enthusiastic amateurs, eager to show their grasp of the subtleties of statute law.

But the renunciators could also turn a blind eye to parliament and parliamentary utterances when it suited them. Twice (in May and July 1782) the Commons declared, almost unanimously, their opinion that Ireland's constitution was in need of no further adjustment.[60] This the Volunteers deliberately ignored, in effect setting themselves up as the new guardians of the constitution. And, if this were not enough, in the autumn of 1782 there arose an issue which brought relations between the Volunteers and parliament to the level of personal animosity.

In the closing weeks of the parliamentary session of 1782 the Commons accepted the government's proposals for raising fencible

56.   O'Connell, *Irish Politics and Social Conflict*, p. 337; *Belfast Newsletter,* 22 Nov. 1782.
57.   There is a copy in P.R.O.N.I., D.562/9321 (Foster/Massereene Mss.).
58.   *C.J.I.*, xx, 422; *Parliamentary Register*, i, 454-67; *Belfast Newsletter,* 13, 23, 30 Aug., 3, 10, 13, 17, 24, 27 Sept., 1, 8, 22 Oct., 8, 15 Nov., 10 Dec. 1782.
59.   *Ibid.*, 2 Aug. 1780.
60.   *C.J.I.*, xx, 378, 422. The opposition in both cases was provided by Flood and one or two supporters.

regiments (a kind of full-time militia) to bring the defence of the country back into official hands. Several of the leading positions in the new force were offered to, and accepted by, prominent Volunteers.[61] The scheme was in fact a direct threat to the existence of the Volunteers, and was received as such. Much verbal ingenuity went into the manufacture of the epithets which Volunteer companies bestowed on the proposed fencibles. As the raising of the fencibles was proceeded with, opinion became divided as to who had committed the more serious crime — those Volunteers weak enough to be seduced into the force by thoughts of money, or the evil-minded M.P.s who had permitted the measure to pass in the first place. Calls were raised for the public humiliation of the former, and the impeachment of the latter.[62] Continued public detestation of the fencibles eventually led to the scheme being abandoned in the autumn of 1783, but despite this triumph the whole episode showed the Volunteers up in a very poor light.[63] Having spent the summer of 1782 in asserting the right of every man to make up his own mind on the subject of renunciation, they spent the autumn and winter denying men the same privilege with regard to the fencibles.

The events of 1782-3 showed that cracks were at last beginning to appear in the facade of Volunteer unity. The separation into Floodite and Grattanite camps on the renunciation issue created deep divisions not merely on the relative merits of simple repeal and renunciation, but on the whole question of continued involvement in politics. Moderate men had begun to resign from the Volunteers at this point, and the government had been able to exploit this by introducing the fencible scheme with its appeal to moderate opinion. The open defiance of parliament, and the vituperation which the fencible issue provoked, soured the reputation of the Volunteers with many men. The fate of both simple repeal and the fencibles had been decided, not in parliament, but on Volunteer parading-grounds, and that was a situation fraught with such

61. *H.M.C. Charlemont,* i, 71; *Belfast Newsletter,* 30 Aug., 3 Sept., 1782. Charlemont, the commander-in-chief of the Volunteers, was offered the command of the fencibles, but refused (*H.M.C. Charlemont,* i, 71).
62. *Belfast Newsletter,* 10, 13, 20, 24, 27 Sept., 8, 11, 15, 22, 29 Oct., 1, 5, 8, 12, 15, 26 Nov., 3, 10, 13 Dec. 1782. On one occasion a confrontation between a fencible recruiting party and local Volunteers in Drogheda lasted two days and resulted in four deaths. See meetings of the Ennis Volunteers on 13 Oct. and 8 Dec. 1782 (N.L.I., Ms. 838), and of the Doneraile Rangers on 13 Oct. 1782 (N.L.I., Ms. 12,155) on this subject, as examples of two companies which had, until then, avoided meetings on political subjects.
63. *Belfast Newsletter,* 16 Sept., 7, 10 Oct. 1783.

dangerous possibilities that responsible men could not permit it to continue.

1783 saw the beginning of the last phase in the relationship between the Volunteers and parliament. Even on its own the general election of that year would probably have brought matters between the two bodies to a head, but following as it did on the heels of the renunciation wrangle feelings were intensified. Even before the Dungannon meeting in February 1782, radical Volunteer companies had been threatening wayward M.P.s with their electoral displeasure, and in many cases the election probably represented a personal showdown.[64]

The results of the election in Ulster — a mixture of success and failure for the Volunteers and their supporters — probably reflected the trend throughout the country. In County Armagh the ex-Volunteer Thomas Dawson was turned out, more or less on the strength of his having accepted a fencible commission; in County Antrim two high-ranking Volunteer officers, John O'Neill and Hercules Langford Rowley, were elected unopposed; and in the borough of Lisburn two Volunteer officers decisively defeated the candidates put forward by the borough owner, Lord Hertford.[65] There were also setbacks. In Fermanagh Mervyn Archdall was returned for one of the county seats despite being a lapsed Volunteer and a fencible officer;[66] in County Londonderry Thomas Conolly had no difficulty in retaining his seat, despite having long since abandoned any attempt to win popular support; and in County Down came the bitterest blow of all, when Robert Stewart, the well-known and respected Volunteer colonel, lost his seat despite the best efforts of the popular interest.[67] Overall, there

64. P.R.O.N.I., T.2541/I.A.1/13/34 (Abercorn Mss.), James Hamilton to Abercorn, 28 May 1780. A resolution passed at the Newry review on 22 Aug. 1780 reprobated the Mutiny Bill and the tax on imported sugar, and bound those present to oppose the re-election of the members who had agreed to those measures (P.R.O.N.I., D.562/9324 [Foster/Massereene Mss.]).
65. *H.M.C. Charlemont*, i, 150; *Belfast Newsletter*, 16 Sept. 1783. Many of the public notices of support for Rowley and O'Neill (*Belfast Newsletter*, 18, 22, 25 July, 8, 12, 15 Aug. 1783) were directed to them as Volunteer officers, not as private individuals.
66. Archdall had also been involved in the simple repeal dispute of the previous year (see above n. 53). One County Fermanagh company felt moved to declare publicly that Archdall by his actions had 'degraded himself beneath our resentment' (*Belfast Newsletter*, 5 Nov. 1782).
67. P.R.O.N.I., T.756/93, 94, 96, 97 (Drennan Mss.), Mrs McTier to William Drennan [Aug. 1783]; W. S. Dickson, *A Narrative of the Confinement and Exile of William Steel Dickson, D.D.* (Dublin, 1812), pp 9-10.

seems to have been no overt attempts by the Volunteers in their armed capacity to influence proceedings; if there had been any such attempts, defeated candidates at least would in all probability have drawn attention to the fact.

From quite early on, it was apparent that the new House of Commons which was due to assemble in October would be scarcely more responsive to Volunteer opinion than the old one had been. But even before the complexion of the new parliament became obvious, the Volunteers — especially in Ulster — were interesting themselves in the reform of the electoral process. Various reviews in June and July declared in favour of reform,[68] and soon a Volunteer Committee of Correspondence was established in Lisburn to act as a focus for the best advice which could be obtained from reformers in Ireland and Britain,[69] and even, it was rumoured, in France and America.[70] During August and early September replies to the Committee's queries were returned to Lisburn,[71] and by the second week in September a specific plan of reform had been formulated for the approval of a provincial assembly of Volunteer delegates at Dungannon.[72]

It was a noticeable feature of this plan, as revealed at Dungannon, that it drew heavily on the advice of the British radical reformers — Jebb, Cartwright, Richmond and Wyvill among them. Perhaps for that reason the constituent parts of the plan did not number moderation among their many virtues, and annual parliaments, elections by secret ballot, the total disfranchisement of rotten boroughs and a generous extension of the franchise were discussed with abandon. The meeting appeared to dismiss entirely the practical difficulties which might arise in securing public support for such a radical scheme and, as if it was intended to emphasize to parliament just how strongly its position was being threatened, the meeting agreed that a national convention of

68. [Joy], *Historical Collections,* pp 234, 237-8, 238-9; *Belfast Newsletter,* 25 July 1783.
69. A circular letter with queries on eight specific aspects of reform was sent, with the assurance that 'what the Volunteers ... shall determine on, people in general ... will adopt and support by every means in their power' (*Proceedings Relative to the Ulster Assembly of Volunteer Delegates in September 1783* (Belfast, 1783), pp 21-6).
70. P.R.O.N.I., T.765/96 (Drennan Mss.), Mrs McTier to Drennan [Sept. 1783].
71. The correspondence survives in P.R.O.N.I., T.D. 2777 (Joy Mss.), xi, 'Letters sent to Lt. Col. William Sharman, Chairman and to Henry Joy, Secretary to the Lisburn Committee of Correspondence'.
72. *Proceedings Relative to the Ulster Assembly,* pp 8-9.

Volunteer delegates (five from each county and large town) should meet in Dublin to co-ordinate Volunteer activity in attaining the desired ends.[73]

Discontent was evident at the Dungannon meeting, however. By no means all the Ulster counties showed themselves to be enthusiastic about the idea of a reforming assembly,[74] and among the delegates who did attend there was clearly some uneasiness at the course events were taking. A resolution stating that, since reform of parliament was the great object, 'the interference of the people was informal and unnecessary', was only given up to preserve unanimity; while the unbridled enthusiasm of the earl-bishop of Derry caused uneasiness to many observers.[75]

The same uneasiness was also manifested throughout the country in the weeks and months before the proposed National Convention was due to meet in October. The inclusion of Catholic relief in the proposed reforms contributed to this, but more fundamental appeared to be the whole question of the propriety of the Volunteers interfering in a matter which was ultimately the concern of parliament itself. The delegates of 40 Connaught companies, at their provincial assembly, unanimously adopted the resolutions of the Dungannon meeting, but neither of the other two provinces followed suit. The Munster assembly passed fairly restrained resolutions in favour of reform and omitted all mention of including the Catholics; while the Leinster meeting had a long debate on the desirability of Volunteer interference, before passing

73. *History of the Proceedings and Debates of the Volunteer Delegates on the Subject of a Parliamentary Reform* (Dublin, 1783), pp 8-12.
74. The meeting was attended by delegates of 272 companies, probably less than two thirds of the total in Ulster (see n. 44 above). More interesting is an analysis of where the companies came from. Counties Antrim and Londonderry sent delegates from 59 and 50 companies respectively, which represented a high proportion of their total number of companies — both had around 60. Tyrone, with 35 companies represented, demonstrated a fairly high level of enthusiasm, but Down, with 42, and Armagh, with only 23, had sent delegates from less than half their total strength. Donegal (24) and Monaghan (23) were enthusiastic but weak on actual numbers; Fermanagh (8) and Cavan (4) simply weak. The four leading counties in Ulster had shown themselves to be divided on the great question. The returns to the meeting are from P.R.O.N.I., T.D. 2777 (Joy Mss.), iv, 223.
75. *History of the Proceedings ... on ... Reform*, p. 8. The earl-bishop was concerned to assure the Volunteers that they were superior to parliament itself: 'he defied the most spirited among them [the delegates] to point out a length ... to which he would not lead or follow' (*History of the Proceedings ... on ... Reform*, p. 8). See also P.R.O.N.I., T.755 (Pelham Mss.), i, 199-201, R. J[ackson] to [Thomas Pelham], 20 Sept. 1783.

a resolution that parliamentary reform could best and most constitutionally come through parliament itself — they too refused to make any declarations in favour of the Catholics.[76]

The Volunteers were now faced with two major problems. Firstly, they were devoid of effective leadership. With Grattan alienated, and Flood becoming increasingly preoccupied with English politics, the battle for dominance in the movement was fought between the cautious Charlemont and the abrasively radical earl-bishop of Derry: neither of the two was a political mastermind, and neither had the ability effectively to unite the movement again. Secondly, the Volunteers were becoming increasingly deprived of the support of men of influence. Both Houses of parliament had once more begun the session by expressing their thanks to the Volunteers for their services,[77] but this was merely a gesture. Chief Secretary Pelham wrote in October that the Volunteers still had too great a hold on men of influence for effective action to be taken against them, but, he added, if the fears of moderate men could be played upon much support could be won from the Volunteers and gained for the government side.[78] One anxious contemporary referred to the autumn of 1783 as 'a period when civil authority seems to be in very great peril from the overbearing power of the sword, when the constitution of parliament ... is threatened under the pretence of securing liberty, and the religion and property of the kingdom [are] to be laid at the feet of the Roman Catholics'.[79] With their own ranks dividing, and the forces of the opposition rallying against them, there was little reason in the weeks before the National Convention for the Volunteers to feel sanguine as to their chances of success.

There is no need to describe in this paper the debates in the Convention, nor the scheme which it produced, except to say that both were a great deal more moderate than might have been expected.[80] On 28 November, while the Convention was still

76. *History of the Proceedings ... on ... Reform*, pp 16-26.
77. *C.J.I.*, xxi, 17; *Parliamentary Register*, iii, 21.
78. P.R.O.N.I., T.755 (Pelham Mss.), i, 226-32, [Pelham] to Portland, 24 Oct. 1783. See also *ibid.*, 247-59, Portland to Pelham, 27 Oct. 1783.
79. *H.M.C. Emily*, i, 180, W. Ellis to E. S. Pery, 23 Oct. 1783. Ellis, although English, had extensive Irish interests.
80. *History of the Proceedings ... on ... Reform* gives a full account of the Convention, including the debate on the 18-point plan of reform which was eventually adopted. The *Belfast Newsletter,* printing reports directly from Henry Joy (who was one of the delegates), differs in certain details from the *History*, but agrees in fundamentals.

sitting, Chief Secretary Pelham and some of the leading supporters of the government met to discuss the situation and to work out a plan of opposition. They agreed that if the Convention were to bring forward a scheme of reform efforts should be made to prevent it being introduced into the Commons, the objections to be grounded on the fact of the scheme having originated in an armed assembly, and resolutions should subsequently be proposed declaring parliament's determination to uphold its own rights and support the present constitution.[81] On the morning of 29 November about 50 members from both Houses met to approve this plan, and in the early hours of the following day the Convention's scheme of reform was refused even the briefest of airings in a House of Commons almost hysterical with fear and indignation.[82]

The National Convention took its defeat quietly, and it was tacitly agreed that the best chance of bringing about reform now lay in moderate action.[83] To have followed the rantings of the earl-bishop and forced reform on parliament at bayonet point would have gone against the political instincts of most of the delegates.[84] The bishop of Cloyne put it rather more cruelly: 'to talk nonsense costs nothing to fools, but to act ... will make even fools consider.'[85] From the very beginning of their involvement in politics, there had been an uneasy awareness among thinking Volunteers that there should be a distinction between the Volunteer as a private citizen instructing parliament, and the Volunteer as an armed citizen threatening parliament. Success had always blurred the issue before, but the campaign for parliamentary reform brought into stark focus the fact that the Volunteers had been led into a position where they seemed prepared to take upon themselves the representative and legislative functions in the constitution. When that realization dawned, the Volunteers could only retreat.

The Volunteer delegates returned from the Convention with only a few fulminations from the earl-bishop on the need to show

81. P.R.O.N.I., T.755 (Pelham Mss.), i, 289-97, [Pelham] to Portland, 30 Nov. 1783.
82. *Ibid.; Belfast Newsletter,* 5 Dec. 1783; *C.J.I.,* xxi, 358.
83. *History of the Proceedings ... on ... Reform,* pp 126-7, 134-5.
84. 'The reformer of 83 had been taught from his infancy to reprobate certain disorders in the constitution of his country ... [and] when it appeared that a reform could not be effected but at the point of the bayonet ... the Convention closed.' (P.R.O.N.I., T.D. 2777 (Joy Mss.), v, 93-5.)
85. *H.M.C. Lothian,* p. 425, Bishop Richard Woodward to Buckinghamshire, 9 Nov. 1783.

the Commons that they could not intimidate Volunteers.[86] Few companies bothered to pay attention. The Connaught Volunteers, in a provincial assembly in January 1784, resolved to continue supporting reform, but only by means of freeholders' meetings and not Volunteer assemblies.[87] No other substantial body appears to have expressed any opinion. Charlemont even began to feel brave enough to begin urging that the Belfast companies be restrained from further political intervention.[88]

The following months saw popular politics degenerate into confusion, without the organization and direction which the Volunteers, even in decline, had been able to provide. A welter of unco-ordinated and misconceived ideas for forcing parliamentary reform were aired: the withholding of taxes; an organized campaign of petitions direct to the King; a scheme for all patriotic members to withdraw from the present corrupt parliament and set up an alternative assembly at Athlone; the procuring of French assistance to enforce reform, and so on.[89] Very much a part of this chaotic scene was the notion that the Volunteers should set about recovering their strength and influence by inviting all ranks of men, of whatever religion, to join them.[90] This was a counsel of despair. The new recruits — variously described as 'stout fellows', 'clever fellows', 'the scum of the people', and men who, if not learning the use of arms, would spend their time 'drinking and debauching' — represented an increase in numbers only, and not a regaining of influence. Their presence lent the venom to Grattan's jibe that the Volunteers had degenerated into the armed beggary of the nation, and the bishop of Cloyne could remark with satisfaction that

86. *Belfast Newsletter,* 16 Dec. 1783, 13, 23 Jan. 1784. A collection of the earl-bishop's speeches and public utterances at this time was kept by Secretary Pelham, who was seeking grounds for legal action against him (P.R.O.N.I., T.755 (Pelham Mss.), i, 271, 330).
87. *Belfast Newsletter,* 9 Jan. 1784.
88. P.R.O.N.I., T.765/135 (Drennan Mss.), Mrs McTier to Drennan [Feb. 1784].
89. *Belfast Newsletter,* 9 Mar., 4, 25 May 1784; *The Voice of the People, in a Letter to the Secretary of His Grace the Duke of Rutland* (Dublin, 1784); *H.M.C. Rutland,* iii, 107-8, W. N. Miles to Sir Edward Newenham [16 June 1784].
90. Patrick Rogers, *The Irish Volunteers and Catholic Emancipation* (London, 1934), pp 144-56.
91. *Belfast Newsletter,* 9, 13, 23, 27 Jan., 6, 27 Feb., 2, 27, 30 Apr., 7, 11, 14, 18, 21, 25, 28 May, 4, 8, 11, 22, 29 June 1784.

'the Volunteer spirit had at last worn out among people of rank and fortune'.[92]

The reviews in Ulster during the summer of 1784 proved to be the last twitchings of the corpse of political Volunteering. At Belfast on 13 July, with a show of spirit, the assembled companies presented Charlemont with an address pledging continued support for parliamentary reform, with Catholic assistance and participation. Charlemont poured cold water on it, and at the Newry review a few days later caused a fiery address to be abandoned in favour of a colourless declaration much more in line with his own wishes.[93] Even at Londonderry, in the heart of the earl-bishop's territory, Charlemont was able to impose comparative moderation.[94] In sum, he ensured that the Volunteers would provide no lead for national opinion. Even the King, who had taken a personal interest in the outcome of the Ulster reviews that year, could not have hoped for a more satisfactory result.[95] The Volunteer presence had finally been removed from politics.

There was one postscript. Shortly after the opening of the new session in 1784 the lord lieutenant, Rutland, had concluded that the best way of getting rid of the Volunteers was to pass a new militia act: he had even toyed with the idea of accompanying it with a measure which would have made treasonable any armed service outside government control.[96] By early in 1785 he was ready to bring forward this militia legislation and on 14 February Luke Gardiner moved in the Commons that £20,000 should be granted towards the formation of a new militia.[97] In the course of his speech Gardineer referred to the Volunteers — 'their existence now

92. *H.M.C. Lothian*, p. 428, Bishop Richard Woodward to Buckinghamshire, 16 May 1784.
93. [Joy], *Historical Collections*, pp 307-11; *Belfast Newsletter*, 23, 27 July 1784; P.R.O.N.I., T.765/158 (Drennan Mss.), William Drennan to Mrs McTier [July/Aug. 1784]. The abandoned address survives in a collection of notes and memoranda on the Volunteers, in Drennan's handwriting (P.R.O.N.I., T.965/6). Its burden was that the Volunteers should refuse to lay down their arms. 'They are dear to us ... for what they have gained, dear for what they will gain ... should our enemies ever express a desire of wresting [them] out of our hands ... we can but answer ... Try.'
94. *Belfast Newsletter*, 3 Aug. 1784; P.R.O.N.I., T.D. 2777 (Joy Mss.), iv, 269; *H.M.C. Charlemont*, ii, 5-6, Charlemont to Dr Haliday, 27 Aug. 1784.
95. George III to Sydney, 26 July 1784, quoted in W. S. Childe-Pemberton, *The Earl-Bishop. The Life of Frederick Hervey, Bishop of Derry, Earl of Bristol* (2 vols., London, [1925]), ii, 346-7.
96. *H.M.C. Rutland*, iii, 145, Rutland to Sydney, 25 Oct. 1784; *ibid.*, 148, same to Pitt, 14 Nov. 1784.
97. *Ibid.*, 182, Rutland to Sydney, 20 Feb. 1785.

was unconstitutional, and not of the least use to support the civil power and keep the peace' — and this motion was accepted by 139 votes to 63.[98] On 18 February William Brownlow of County Armagh moved that the Volunteers should be thanked once more for their services to the country, although even he spoke in the past tense: 'the Volunteers had been eminently useful to their country by the protection they had afforded against the foreign enemy ...'[99] This vote of thanks was only accepted when a contemptuous amendment of Gardiner's had been added, to the effect that the House was even more thankful to those who had left the Volunteer ranks. It was a sad and undignified end to what had been a unique relationship. The fact that the new militia act was not passed until 1793 was an indication of how far the Volunteers were from parliament's mind in the following years.

The later years of the eighteenth century saw profound changes taking place in Irish society, especially in Ulster, and to a lesser extent throughout the rest of the country. New ideas were thrown up; wider horizons were explored in many different areas of life. The Volunteers were very much a part of this new wave, yet they could never entirely free themselves from the old order. Men in Volunteer uniform found themselves continually beset by divided loyalties. Their pride in freedom and desire for political equality ran counter to their accustomed and inescapable deference to social rank; their desire to bring about complete legislative free-dom for Ireland was at variance with their feeling for and depen-dence upon a close connection with Britain; and above all, their immediate experience of successful political intervention conflicted with basic and long-held beliefs that armed interference in politics was wrong. The period from 1779 to 1784, therefore, was one which might be described in terms of new wine and old bottles, and what it produced proved in the main to be ephemeral. One feature of the period was destined to have a lasting significance however. When all is said and done, Volunteering represented the first successful example of the bringing cf the gun into Irish politics, and the implications of that philosophy are with us even today.

98.   *Ibid.*, 181, Rutland to Sydney, 18 Feb. 1785; *Belfast Newsletter*, 18 Feb. 1785.
99.   *Life ... of ... Grattan*, iii, 226-7.

'THE PARLIAMENTARY TRAFFIC OF THIS COUNTRY'

A. P. W. Malcomson

In 1799 Colonel George Napier, a Scot resident in Ireland, remarked priggishly: 'I contemplate the parliamentary traffic of this country with so much disgust', that when offered a seat at the previous general election 'my answer ... was that my ambition as a gentleman and a soldier had always been to keep respectable company and to serve my King and country, and that ... I was unable to discover how a seat in the Irish parliament would conduce to either of these purposes ...'[1] The seat which Napier claimed to have been offered was for a county, Kildare; writing about the seats for a borough, Enniscorthy, at about the same time, John Colclough, the brother of Enniscorthy's 'patron', used even stronger language:

> 'I think you are more respectable out of parliament than in it', he admonished his brother. 'For myself, I would just as lief go into gaol as amongst such a pack. No, no. Sell your seats, and lay out the money for the good of your tenantry ... Indeed, if you would take my advice, you would sell the borough out and out ...'[2]

Historians have been little more charitable in their strictures on the Irish parliament, and particularly on that element of it on which the 'parliamentary traffic' was focused, the borough constituencies.

The Irish parliament was described by Grattan in 1797 as 'a borough parliament'.[3] Of the 300 seats which it contained, between 1692, when it reached its full complement, and the Union in 1800, 234 – or more than 75% of the whole – were for boroughs. This was only a little higher than the contemporary percentage for England and Wales (Scotland must be left out of the reckoning, as the Scottish boroughs were on the whole more 'popular' and open constituencies than the Scottish counties). However, these percentages do not tell the whole story. Old Sarum and Gatton notwithstanding, fairly wide borough franchises and fairly large borough electorates were more common in Britain than in Ireland. For

1.   P.R.O.N.I., D.3030/456 (Castlereagh Mss.), Napier to [Cornwallis?], 6 Jan. 1799.
2.   P.R.O.N.I., T.3048/C/18 (McPeake [Colclough] Mss.), John Colclough to Caesar Colclough, 5 July 1795.
3.   Quoted in *The Speech of the ... Earl of Clare ... [on the Union] on Monday, February 10, 1800* (Dublin, 1800), p. 42.

example, the biggest single element in the borough representation of late eighteenth-century Britain was the 101 freeman boroughs, where, as the name implies, freemen enjoyed the vote;[4] the biggest single element in the borough representation of Ireland in the same period (though perhaps not at the beginning of the century) was the 56 or so corporation boroughs, where the vote was confined to members of the corporation, usually no more than 13 in number. This distinction was more important on paper than in reality. A more important fact, and this time one redounding to the credit of the borough representation of Ireland, was that by 1690 no Irish town of any size or significance remained unenfranchised. Lurgan, which its improving landlords, the Brownlows, vainly tried to get incorporated and thus enfranchised, in the early eighteenth century,[5] had stronger claims than uninhabited Bannow and Clonmines, but its claims were not as strong as Manchester's. The chief defect of the borough representation of Ireland was not that places of size and significance were excluded, but that far too many places were *included* that were of no size or significance whatever. Some had originally been incorporated in the unfulfilled hope that incorporation would stimulate urban development, while others had been incorporated for much less laudable purposes, notably to provide a Protestant majority in James I's parliament of 1613.[6]

An examination of the different types of boroughs constituting the borough representation of Ireland shows that width of franchise and size of electorate had some, but by no means a decisive, bearing on the 'closeness' or 'openness' of the borough concerned. The eight county boroughs must be classed as 'open', or else it would be necessary to class some counties as 'close', and all had reasonably wide franchises and large electorates; one of them, Carrickfergus, actually boasted the incredibly large electorate of 2,000 in 1739.[7] Of the remaining 109 boroughs (all of them, be it

4.   P. J. Jupp, *British and Irish Elections, 1784-1831* (Newton Abbot, 1973), pp 13, 78-9.
5.   *C.S.P. Dom.*, 1703-4, pp 232-3.   The last borough actually to be incorporated was Dunleer in 1683.
6.   The primary printed sources for the study of the borough representation of Ireland are *C.J.I.* and *Municipal Corporations (Ireland), Appendix to the First Report of the Commissioners, parts i-iii*, 1835. The major secondary sources, besides Jupp, *British and Irish Elections*, are E. and A. G. Porritt, *The Unreformed House of Commons* (2 vols., Cambridge, 1903); J. L. McCracken, 'Irish Parliamentary Elections, 1727-68', *I.H.S.*, v (1942); and E. M. Johnston, *Great Britain and Ireland, 1760-1800* (Edinburgh, 1963).
7.   P.R.O.N.I., D.162/33 (Dobbs Mss.), Arthur Dobbs's answer to the charges brought against him as Lord Conway's agent, [1739?].

remembered, double-member constituencies), only Londonderry and Swords, both boroughs with fairly large electorates, can be described as really and consistently 'open'. The rest must be written off as 'close', in the sense that at any one time their representation was controlled by one or two individuals or by a small clique. Some had deceptively large electorates: among the 36 or so freeman boroughs, the eleven potwalloping boroughs (where mere inhabitancy was the qualification until 1795) and the six manor boroughs (seven after 1783), electorates of several hundred were not uncommon.[8] Yet, among these boroughs, the existence of a large electorate cannot be regarded as a proof of democracy – or as a protection of democracy either. Patrons and would-be patrons often tried to narrow the franchise or otherwise reduce the electorate; but it is significant that, in the two spectacular instances of Tory, patron reaction in the age of reform, the Beresfords in Coleraine and the Handcocks in Athlone, increasing the electorate, not reducing it, was the device the patrons used.[9] The frequent concomitant of large electorates was voters who were economically vulnerable or plain venal. For this reason, large electorates were a complication and an expense rather than a serious bar to patron control. In the freeman boroughs, the oligarchic, self-electing corporation was generally able to regulate the composition of the freeman body, while in the potwalloping and manor boroughs, the power of the landlord was generally effective in keeping the numerous but dependent tenant-electors in check.[10] From one point of view, that of the government in 1799, some of these constituencies with large electorates were 'practically the very worst species of representation – potwalloping boroughs and open elections by the mob, where neither property, nor family connections, nor the good opinion of neighbourhood nor any other good species of influence would weigh against adventurers ... with large purses or backed by any temporary clamour'.[11] In reality, how-

8. This categorization of the Irish boroughs is Professor Johnston's (*Great Britain and Ireland*, pp 144-78). I have deliberately used the expression '36 or so' freeman boroughs, because the distinction between a freeman borough and a corporation borough is sometimes fine.
9. See the Municipal Corporations Commissioners' *Report* on Belturbet, Coleraine and Athlone.
10. See A. P. W. Malcomson, 'The Struggle for Control of Dundalk Borough, 1782-92', *County Louth Archaeological Journal*, xvii, no. 1 (1969); 'The Foster Family and the Parliamentary Borough of Dunleer, 1683-1800', *ibid.*, no. 3 (1971); and 'Election Politics in the Borough of Antrim, 1750-1800', *I.H.S.*, xvii (1970).
11. Anonymous memorandum, dated Cleveland Row, 8 Oct. 1799, printed in *Memoirs and Correspondence of Viscount Castlereagh* ed. Londonderry (4 vols., London, 1848), iii, 60-61.

ever, Swords was probably the only constituency which consistently answered this description; its electors, conforming to the Tammany definition of a dishonest man, resolutely declined to 'stay bought', and it was once described as being often contested at enormous expense and with some effusion of blood. With the exception of Swords, and of Londonderry and the county boroughs (where the 'good species of influence' was also present), all the Irish boroughs can be deemed 'close'.

The hard arithmetic of this conclusion — that 107 constituencies out of 150 were 'close' — requires considerable interpretative softening before a true picture of the eighteenth-century Irish parliament can emerge. For one thing, the very scarcity of open constituencies greatly enhanced the attractiveness of representing them. Government control of the Irish House of Commons depended on the 107 close boroughs, and could have been maintained through the medium of the close boroughs alone. But this by no means damped the government's enthusiasm for winning the representatives of the open constituencies over to its side, or for assisting supporters to contest the open constituencies. This is to be seen most clearly at the time of the Union crisis. The government could have carried the Union, and in practical terms did carry the Union, through manipulation of the borough representation under the terms of the Place Act of 1793, but this in no way diverted its attention from the open constituencies, and it was still labouring to procure popular demonstrations of support for the Union in the country long after its majority in the House was secure.[12] The Union crisis is, however, only the most striking example of a recurrent theme in eighteenth-century parliamentary history. Governments were always tolerant of trimming and unsteadiness on the part of supporters who sat for open constituencies. In 1775, for example, a Castle list of the Irish House of Commons noted indulgently that John Foster, M.P. for County Louth and the future Speaker, was 'very often with government, but being a member for a county sometimes, though very seldom, quits it on popular questions'.[13] Counties and close boroughs carried the same weight in arithmetical terms only: in terms of prestige there was a world of difference between them.

The attractiveness of open constituencies is confirmed by the merest glance at the kind of constituencies for which many of the

12. See G. C. Bolton, *The Passing of the Irish Act of Union* (Oxford, 1963), *passim*.
13. *The Irish Parliament in 1775* ed. W. Hunt (Dublin, 1907), p. 22.

men of ability in the Irish House of Commons sat. It is a common-place that, in late eighteenth-century Britain, the most open constituencies returned the dullest members: the men of ability and political ambition usually sat for close constituencies, where they could be re-elected without trouble or much expense if they attained their ambition -- office -- or were involved in a ministerial reshuffle. In Ireland there was no Place Act until 1793 and consequently no compulsion for members to vacate their seats on acceptance or change of office. This undoubtedly contributed to the attractiveness of the open constituencies. The contrast between English and Irish attitudes in this respect is brought out strikingly in the first Earl Camden's advice to his young Irish *protege,* Robert Stewart, soon to become Lord Castlereagh, about Stewart's relationship with his County Down constituents. Camden's cynical and worldly-wise counsel (in which, incidentally, it is hard to recognize the glorious Pratt of General Warrants fame) was that Stewart should on no account be 'as assiduous in preserving your interest as you was to acquire it'. Surely, he asked, Stewart did not intend to return to County Down at the end of every session to get drunk with his constituents? This would be slavery, and might well do no good, 'for men oftentimes lessen themselves by too general a familiarity. Besides, the Irish are captious and quarrelsome, especially when they are in liquor'. If Stewart's constituents expected him to live among them all the time, 'they expect too much and ought not to be indulged. But they will not vote for you at the next election? Then you save your money and come in for Lisburn [a borough controlled by Stewart's grandfather]'.14 Significantly, Stewart never did fall back on Lisburn; and it was not he who rejected County Down, but County Down which rejected him, at a by-election in 1805 made necessary by his acceptance of office. Like him, several other prominent office-holders and govern-ment supporters, whose official situations identified them with many unpopular causes, continued to struggle (successfully) with popular and open constituencies: John Foster with County Louth, John Beresford with County Waterford, Sir John Parnell with Queen's County, and so on. All but one of the eighteenth-century Speakers of the Irish House of Commons -- and in the eighteenth century the Speaker was always one of the most able and influential members of the House -- sat for open constitu-encies.15 Dublin University, the open constituency which enjoyed perhaps more prestige than any other, until contaminated by the

14. P.R.O.N.I., D.3030/F/5, Camden to Stewart, 16 Oct. 1790.
15. A. P. W. Malcomson, 'John Foster and the Speakership of the Irish House of Commons', *Proceedings of the R.I.A.,* lxxii, Section C, no. 11 (1972), 290-91 n.

Hely-Hutchinsons, sent an amazing bevy of talent to the Commons. Of the many people of distinguished ability who sat in the Irish parliament of the eighteenth century, Grattan and Flood are among the few who sat for close boroughs; and Grattan later sat for Dublin city, and Flood had earlier sat for County Kilkenny. In 1760, when Anthony Malone was forced to give up the open constituency he had represented for over 30 years a contemporary commented: 'Would you believe that Anthony Malone, meeting with a universal repulse in the Co. Westmeath, has been reduced to supplicate Lord Shannon for a seat in parliament, and is to come in for Castle-martyr.'[16]

The attractiveness of the open constituencies meant that the close ones were often used as bargaining counters for them. In 1727 Thomas Carter, the future Master of the Rolls, observed – in language which suggests that this was a standard practice: 'I have secured so many freeholders' votes in the county of Meath [that] I shall, I fancy, force into a borough (Navan) or throw one [of the other candidates] out of the county.'[17] In 1761 a contest was averted in County Louth because two candidates promised to find a borough seat for the third; and in 1768 a contest was protracted in County Tyrone because one candidate made a contingent promise of a borough seat to his running-mate in order to persuade him to carry on.[18] In County Sligo peace was for many years preserved by an arrangement whereby the Wynne family, who controlled Sligo borough but liked to sit for the county, bought the acquiescence of a county rival by returning him for the borough free of charge.[19] Like Sligo, County Monaghan was a one-borough county, where competition for the local seats was at its maximum; and the one borough in the county, Monaghan town, seems to have been used by its successive patrons in much the same way as the Wynnes used Sligo.[20] The same phenomenon is, however, to be observed in

16. N.L.I., Talbot-Crosbie Mss. (P.C. 188), Robert FitzGerald to Hon. William Crosbie, 15 Nov. 1760. For a fuller discussion of the prestige attached to the open constituencies and their representatives, see A. P. W. Malcomson, *John Foster: The Politics of the Anglo-Irish Ascendancy* (Oxford, 1978), chapter five, *passim.*
17. P.R.O.N.I., D.2707/A/2/14 (Shannon Mss.), Carter to Henry Boyle, 27 June 1727.
18. A. P. W. Malcomson, 'The Earl of Clermont: A Forgotten Co. Monaghan Magnate of the Eighteenth Century', *Clogher Record,* viii, no. 1 (1973), 33; P.R.O.N.I., T.2541/I.K.8/2/44 (Abercorn Mss.), Abercorn to Claudius Hamilton, 5 Sept. 1768.
19. W. G. Wood-Martin, *A History of Sligo, County and Town* (3 vols., Dublin, 1892), iii, 37-8.
20. Malcomson, *'Earl of Clermont',* 35-6.

counties much more generously endowed with boroughs, provided of course that the borough patrons had ambitions in the county: in County Kerry, for example, the patrons of the three boroughs were very active in county politics and represented the county when they could, cheerfully horse-trading with their borough seats when this helped to accomplish their main object.[21] The absence of hard evidence is not to be taken as an indication that such horse-trading was not also taking place elsewhere: arrangements over the disposal of seats in parliament were not lightly committed to paper, and since they were not capable of enforcement at law, being in their nature outside the law, if not actually illegal, they were often not committed to paper at all. On the whole, it is remarkable that so much hard evidence has survived. The practice of using borough seats as bargaining counters in county elections is one with which historians have for a long time been familiar, although they have underrated its extent. It has hitherto been adduced as an illustration of how the county representation could be closed, but it can equally well be adduced as an illustration of how the borough representation could be opened. There was a considerable element of 'virtual representation' in the Irish parliament; and the small and influenced electorates of the close boroughs were often, indirectly, the vehicle for a genuinely popular election.

The Irish parliament was, therefore, less of a borough parliament than the mere arithmetic of its composition would suggest. The 86 members who sat for the counties and open boroughs carried much greater weight than their numbers alone entitled them to; and in any parliament there are likely to have been many more who owed their presence in the House of Commons, at least indirectly, to a popular election. Moreover, the Namierian argument that the Cornish boroughs can be justified on the ground that they rectified the under-representation of London, applies to some extent to Ireland. In a parliament of landlords, where no town or city, no matter how large or prosperous, was represented by more than two members, commercial interests could only find adequate representation through the medium of the close boroughs. Thus Sir Nicholas Lawless, a Dublin merchant, twice bought himself into parliament for the close borough of Lifford; William Hare, a fabulously wealthy provisions merchant in Cork, bought for himself

21. T.C.D., Ms. 3821/175 (Crosbie Mss.), copy of an 'agreement tripartite' between Sir Maurice Crosbie, Arthur Denny and John Blennerhassett over the representation of County Kerry and the boroughs of Ardfert and Tralee, 6 July 1727; FitzGerald Mss. (Mr Adrian FitzGerald, 16 Clareville St., London, S.W. 7), 1/48, Launcelot Crosbie to Arthur Crosbie, 3 Jan. 1761; 11/11, Lord Ventry to Maurice FitzGerald, 8 Sept. 1817.

and his connections no less than four seats in the parliament of 1797; and John Bagwell, a miller of Clonmel, purchased the patronage of that borough and also bought seats for his connections elsewhere. Unfortunately, the Namierite argument begins to wear thin at this point, as these three men were all trying to extricate themselves from 'trade' as fast as they could, and to establish themselves as 'county families' and (Lawless apart) as county M.P.s; they did not enter the House of Commons in order to give it the benefit of their commercial experience, but in the hope of being translated to the Lords. (Only in Bagwell's case was this hope unfulfilled: because of his milling interests he laboured under the devastating nicknames of 'old Bags' and 'Marshal Sacks', and no government, no matter how unscrupulous or hard pressed for votes, dared ennoble him.) One M.P. who remained active in commerce after having entered the Commons was Sir Thomas Lighton, a prominent Dublin banker, who was returned for Carlingford in 1798; 'his only object', however, was 'to receive the bank letters free and have the honour of walking in and out of the House.' With such a limited object, Lighton was presumably an ineffective spokesman for the commercial life of the country.[22] Arguably, the only effective spokesmen for that interest were the distinguished banking family of Latouche, who in the main sat for purchased borough seats. It was not the bankers and merchants, but the lawyers, who were the chief beneficiaries of 'the trade of parliament';[23] had they not been able to purchase their way in for close boroughs, they would have had no other easy way of entering; and parliament would have been much the poorer without them.

The arguments put forward so far, all of them in effect variations on the theme of 'virtual representation', suffer from one major distortion of view: they are inspired by hindsight and a dim feeling that the unreformed electoral system has to be apologized for in terms which are meaningful in the context of twentieth-century democracy. An apology in such terms requires a highly eclectic singling-out of supposedly democratic elements in the 107 close boroughs (and even then the criteria of twentieth-century democracy are far from being satisfied, because of the

22. W. Playfair, *British Family Antiquity* (9 vols., London, 1809-11), v, 288-91; P.R.O.N.I., T.2451/I.A.5/1/14, 16, 17 (Abercorn Mss.), James Galbraith to Abercorn, 26 Sept., 2 Nov., 15 Dec. 1797; P. J. Jupp, 'Irish Parliamentary Representation, 1800-20' (Reading Univ. Ph.D. thesis 1967), entries under Bagwell, Clonmel, *etc.*
23. P.R.O.N.I., T.3319/60 (Pitt/Pretyman Mss.), anonymous memo on the union, [July/Aug. 1798].

sweeping denominational restrictions against Roman Catholics and Dissenters, which of course applied in open and close constituencies alike). While it is right that attention should be drawn to the element of 'virtual representation' in the returns for the close boroughs, the principal object of this paper is to examine their *actual* representation — how people were returned for them and who returned these people — and to judge the actual representation according to eighteenth-, not twentieth-, century criteria.

When the 107 close boroughs are put under the microscope several interesting things are observable. The first is that these boroughs were 'close' only in the sense already given to the word — they lay at any one time effectively under the control of one or two individuals or of a small knot of individuals. This, however, does not mean that abnormal circumstances could not arise to shake or break patron control, or that boroughs did not change hands politically as a result of take-over bids or treachery. Only exceptionally were these contests for control inspired by a genuine desire to widen the franchise or open the borough — as in the potwalloping boroughs of Antrim and Lisburn and the freeman borough of Dundalk, during the Volunteer period. But even if these contests were only power-struggles among rival patrons, they still lent an element of unpredictability to elections even in the closest of boroughs. The supreme example is the borough of Baltinglass, which was furiously contested from the 1770s to the 1790s among members of the same family, the Stratfords, earls of Aldborough, and which was a corporation borough with an electorate of only thirteen. A few other examples must suffice as an illustration of a widespread phenomenon. The corporation borough of Belfast, again with an electorate of only thirteen and often cited as a symbol of the 'closeness' of the borough representation of Ireland, was the scene of three petitions in the period 1707-15 and was very nearly lost to the patron family, the earls of Donegall; while the corporation borough of Coleraine, with a larger corporation and electorate (36 people), was the scene of the most violent disputes from 1707 to 1727, and did not settle down under defined patron control until 1751.[24] The freeman borough of Cashel, with an electorate of uncertain size, was wrested from the

24.   *C.J.I.*, ii, 536, 746; iii, 26; P.R.O.N.I., T.974, Maxwell Given's notes on the Privy Council approbation books for Coleraine, made prior to their destruction in 1922; P.R.O.N.I., D.2092/1/3/93 (Castle Ward Mss.), Richard Jackson to [Michael Ward?] , 4 Dec. 1727; P.R.O.N.I., D.2977/5, part (Antrim Estate Mss.), Lord Tyrone to Lord Antrim or R. Magill, 19 Jan., 6 and 23 Feb. 1739, John McNaghten to Lord Antrim, 14 May 1751; *Aspects of Irish Social History, 1750-1800* eds. W. H. Crawford and B. Trainor (Belfast, 1969), pp 134-5.

archbishop of Cashel by the Pennefather family in the 1730s.[25]
In the first half of the century the boroughs of the absentee earl of
Burlington in Counties Cork and Waterford were in constant
dispute; in the end Burlington lost Bandon and Youghal, and
though he held on to Dungarvan, Lismore and Tallow, his successors' interests there went on being challenged up to the end of the
century.[26] In 1740 Burlington's kinsman, Lord Orrery, was reminded that 'without much application, good words and kind
promises, few people have success in elections'; yet this reminder
related, not to an open constituency, but to the thirteen-man
corporation borough of Charleville, from which Orrery was almost
ousted by a *coup de main*.[27]

The index to the Irish *Commons' Journals* makes it possible to
quantify the number of election petitions to the Irish House of
Commons and the constituencies they came from. Over the period
1692-1800 there were 313 petitions in all; of these, 97 related to
counties, three to Dublin University, and 43 to the eight county
boroughs plus Londonderry and Swords; this leaves no less than
170 petitions to the credit of the 107 supposedly close boroughs.[28]
170 petitions is an impressive total in itself. But it must be remembered that the number of election petitions is not necessarily an
indication of the number of contests for control of boroughs,
since the impartiality of the procedure for trying such petitions
prior to the Irish Grenville Act of 1771 was, to say the least,
suspect, and the expense of the procedure thereafter still almost
prohibitive. In any case, there were alternative arenas for contests
over incorporated boroughs – the Irish Privy Council in particular.
Since 1672 this body had been charged with the supervision of all
the corporations; and in the case of 21 specified corporations (the
county boroughs and Londonderry among them, but the rest
'close') this supervision was exercised through the 'approbation' or
rejection, by the Privy Council, of the annually elected chief magistrates (and of other borough officials elected as and when

25. Municipal Corporations Commissioners' *Report* on Cashel; *H.M.C.
Var. Coll.*, vi, 60, the bishop of Kilmore to George Dodington, 4 Mar. 1734.
26. The evidence for these disputes is so voluminous that I can only refer the
reader to the Chatsworth Mss. (Chatsworth House, Derbyshire – P.R.O.N.I.,
T.3158); N.L.I., Lismore Mss.; and P.R.O.N.I., D.2707 (Shannon Mss.).
Burlington's successors lost, in effect, one seat for Dungarvan, but more than
compensated for this by regaining one each for Bandon and Tallow.
27. N.L.I., Orrery Mss. 7/24, p. 789, Richard Purcell to Orrery, 27 June
1740. The Orrery family later had to cede one seat to their kinsmen and
rivals, the Boyles, earls of Shannon.
28. I am indebted for these figures to Mrs Geraldine Wylie.

vacancies occurred).[29] Not only were these annual municipal elections much more frequent than parliamentary elections; they were also more important. Municipal elections determined the balance of power within a corporation, and once the balance of power was determined, parliamentary elections — even in the freeman boroughs — usually resembled a deed of registration. This point is illustrated by the case of the freeman borough of Kinsale. Between the 1720s and the 1760s Kinsale was in dispute between the absentee Southwell family, hitherto its patrons, and the resident Meades. The dispute vented itself in both municipal and parliamentary elections, and in 1731 Edward Southwell was as anxious about the outcome of the annual election for chief magistrate, due at the end of June, as he was about the outcome of a parliamentary by-election in the autumn. In the end, Southwell got his man elected and approved as chief magistrate, but lost the parliamentary by-election. This however proved to be only a temporary setback, as he again got his man elected and approved as chief magistrate in the municipal election of the following year. So long as his control of the corporation held firm, he could survive reverses in parliamentary elections; and he was ultimately successful in the contest over Kinsale. Although Kinsale was one of the 21 specified boroughs of 1672, the evidence about its municipal elections comes from family papers:[30] disastrously, the official records of the Irish Privy Council were destroyed in the Four Courts in 1922. Transcripts made before 1922 by an antiquarian concerned only with the municipal history of Coleraine, give a striking impression of the quality of these records, and the seriousness of the loss.[31]

A borough which resembles Kinsale in being one of the 21 specified boroughs of 1672, and also in the excellence of the available documentation, is the corporation borough of Strabane. Here again the documentation comes from the papers of the patron

29.   'New Rules' of 1672, promulgated under 17 and 18 Car. II, c. 2, s. 82 (the Act of Explanation): the 'close' boroughs specified were Athlone, Cashel, Charlemont, Clonmel, Coleraine, Dundalk, Kinsale, New Ross, Strabane, Trim, Wexford and Youghal. The other extra-parliamentary arena for contests over incorporated boroughs, was the court of King's Bench; for comment on the relationship between the King's Bench and the Privy Council in this sphere, see B.L., Add. Mss. 47,028, fos 30-31, Philip Perceval to Lord Perceval 3 July 1715, and for comment on the more general role of the King's Bench in election contests see Malcomson, *John Foster*, pp 125-6.
30.   The two main blocs of Southwell papers are B.L., Add. Mss. 21,122-3 and N.L.I., Mss. 875-6; there are also some significant letters in P.R.O.N.I., T.2534/2.
31.   P.R.O.N.I., T.974, Given's notes.

family, the earls of Abercorn.[32] The Abercorn papers show that, although Strabane had been incorporated virtually for the benefit of the Abercorns, although they owned the soil on which it stood and although it had an electorate of only thirteen, yet they were very far from having it in their pocket. Between the 1690s and 1733 they controlled only one seat, and between 1733 and 1764 they controlled neither but were supplanted by two local men whom eventually they were able to buy off. It is an interesting exercise to consider for a moment what picture of the representation of Strabane would emerge if it were not for the Abercorn papers and if the only sources of information on the borough were the standard printed ones. For all the report of the commissioners appointed to enquire into the state of the municipal corporations of Ireland in 1833 says to the contrary, Strabane might have lain under the unchallenged control of the Abercorns for the whole of the eighteenth century. (Not surprisingly, the Whig/Liberal appointees who composed the commission sought and received little private information from the Tory patrons of the Irish boroughs; the commissioners' evidence is particularly defective and biased when it comes to the parliamentary representation of Strabane and the 84 other boroughs which had ceased to be represented in parliament over 30 years previously.) The *Commons' Journals* are capable of the same interpretation — unchallenged Abercorn control — and for the very good reason that there was never an election petition over Strabane, nor as far as can be ascertained even a contested parliamentary election. The report of the commissioners appointed to award compensation for boroughs disfranchised by the Act of Union mentions a rival claim to the Abercorns', but gives no details. The identity of those recorded in the 1877 return to the House of Lords at Westminster as sitting for Strabane in the Irish parliament of the eighteenth century is not incompatible with the idea of unchallenged Abercorn control; and the many printed Castle lists of the Irish parliament are unhelpful, since they start in 1769, after the Abercorn family had regained control. The only suspicious circumstance recorded in the printed sources — in this case in the printed division-list on the money bill issue of 17 December 1753 — is that the one Strabane M.P. present in the House, William Hamilton, voted on the opposite side to the one member of the Abercorn family present. If the records of the Irish Privy Council had survived, they would of course provide evidence — certainly for the period 1732-33 — of the

32.   For the information on Strabane in this and the succeeding paragraph see A. P. W. Malcomson, 'The Politics of "Natural Right": The Abercorn Family and Strabane Borough, 1692-1800', *Historical Studies*, x (Dublin, 1976), 43-90.

dispute then raging over control of Strabane corporation, since Strabane was one of the many boroughs where political activity manifested itself in municipal rather than in parliamentary elections. However, in the absence of the Irish Privy Council records, and, in the case of many boroughs besides Strabane, of information from the standard printed sources, the assumption is usually made that the boroughs concerned were not disturbed by so much as a political tremor. The example of Strabane, with its exceptionally rich documentation from private sources, casts doubt on this facile assumption, and to some extent shifts the onus of proof.

The first feature of the close boroughs that shows up under the microscope is, therefore, that the word 'close' has to be used with care, and does not necessarily imply the dead weight of a static, unchanging and unchallenged control. The next is that the government view, already quoted, that there was both a good and a bad species of influence, was not pure cant. Swords is the classic example of the bad species. One of the recurrent themes of electioneering in the open boroughs, or in close boroughs in dispute, is the enthusiasm of at least the lower class of voters for being bribed. As one borough patron, Lord Newtownbutler, observed sadly in 1727, 'we can hardly expect poor people can refuse £50 or more for a vote, which is the case in some places amongst us'.[33] In this limited sense, narrow franchises and patron control were only saving people from themselves. In Londonderry it seems to have been expected, in the first half of the century at any rate, that intending candidates should donate money to various municipal improvements,[34] and this convention seems to have prevailed in some of the Burlington boroughs as well. Elsewhere, however, where hard cash was an element in electioneering, it was apt to be spent not on improvements but on votes. And although eighteenth-century political man saw no objection (within limits which will be discussed) to buying seats or even the patronage of whole boroughs, he had a horror of buying votes. In most instances the patrons of close boroughs did not have to buy votes; they had what the earls of Abercorn were described as having in Strabane, a 'natural right' in their boroughs, by virtue of owning all or part of the soil. When the Abercorns were ousted from control of Strabane borough in 1733, the then head of the family considered it an 'indignity' that anyone should 'endeavour supplanting us in a borough which must belong to me and my family'; and the Abercorn who regained

33. P.R.O.N.I., T.659/8 (transcripts from State Papers in the P.R.O.), Newtownbutler to Charles Delafaye, 30 Sept. 1727.
34. P.R.O.N.I., D.1449/12/51 (Lenox-Conyngham Mss.), William Lenox to George Vaughan, 25 Nov. 1746.

control of Strabane borough in 1764 was by no means politically-minded and wanted control of the corporation mainly because, without it, he could not administer his estate in the town effectively. The prosperity of his estate was inseparable from the prosperity of the town, and no one but he had the capital or the motive for advancing the prosperity of both. Significantly, the inhabitants of Strabane who did not belong to the corporation and so had no vote, seem to have welcomed the return of the Abercorns in 1764.[35] Some patrons of course had little capital, and some boroughs were incapable of urban growth regardless of whether their patrons fostered it or not. But in general the patron's role was not exclusively political — although the tendency for political and economic history to be studied as things apart obscures this important point: as well as political boss of the borough, the patron was usually ground landlord, town planner, promoter of trade and industry and source of whatever social security there was. Significantly, there was no dominant landlord influence in Swords.

The fact that most borough patrons were not just borough patrons, but ground landlords as well, and that borough patronage descended by inheritance along with the estates on which the boroughs stood, is illustrated by the existence of a few reluctant patrons, for whom control of seats in parliament was not a 'jewel of great price'. This remark was made by Edward Southwell. During the struggle over Kinsale, Southwell was always looking for opportunities to 'slip my neck out of this noose', and carried on mainly because of a 'nicety' about leaving the more economically-vulnerable of his supporters to the mercy of his opponents.[36] This matter of the economic vulnerability of voters is significant: just as there were patrons who would have been glad to be rid of their boroughs, so there were voters who would have been glad to have had no vote. A case in point was a Youghal freeman, who

35. For a discussion of the sale of borough patronage, and of the extent to which borough patronage was divorced from landownership, see A. P. W. Malcomson, 'The Newtown Act of 1748: Revision and Reconstruction', *I.H.S.*, xvii (1973), 335-6. The list of sales given on pp 340-2 needs to be expanded and, in one instance, corrected: the Barrington family sold Ballynakill to Lord Drogheda between 1761 and 1768; the Jephson family sold Mallow to Richard Longfield in 1790; Lord Westmeath sold Fore to Lord Downshire in 1793, not 1797, and for £13,000, not £14,000-£16,000; Lord Mount Cashell sold Clonmel to John Bagwell, the miller, in 1799; William Handcock, the co patron of Athlone, bought out the other co-patron in 1800; and the Colclough family sold Enniscorthy to Lord Lismore in the same year. These transactions though they lengthen the list of sales, do not affect the arguments about sales there advanced.
36. N.L.I., Ms. 875 (Southwell Mss.), Southwell to Marmaduke Coghill, 2: Apr. 1735, 14 Feb., 11 Mar., 1736.

wanted to stay neutral in an election in 1719, but was bluntly told that he could not: 'the like hard usage as they give to such as vote for Mr Rugge, the same we will return to those who don't.'[37] 'They' in this instance were the supporters of the patron, 'we' were his opponents in the borough; and each side presumably had to indemnify its supporters against economic reprisals by the other. At this time, Burlington was the greatest borough-patron in Ireland. Yet the Lismore papers — the papers of his Irish agents — emanate the spirit of Sisyphus, not that of a political leviathan. While there is much talk of protecting the rights of the 'noble family' from invasion and of showing favour to those who have deserved well of the 'noble family', toughness and assertiveness are largely lacking, which no doubt explains why two of the Burlington boroughs, Youghal one of them, were captured by other patrons. Southwell and Burlington may of course be untypical of patrons, in that they were absentees who thought of themselves primarily as Englishmen: Lord Egmont, for example, another magnate in the same category, took the view that there was 'neither advantage nor honour ... in being a member of parliament in Ireland, except to obtain a collectorship or a low post in the army, for which the ministry there must be sued to and their feet kissed'.[38] Yet, before the 1750s — and Egmont's remark was made in 1745 — seats in parliament were not the object of intense competition, particularly borough seats, and certainly borough patronage was not financially attractive, as it later became. In these circumstances, it is not fanciful to suggest that many patrons looked after their borough interests in the same spirit as they attended to the running of their estates. A sense of duty, above all a sense of honour, forbade them to neglect anything which had been transmitted from their ancestors and which they were bound, if at all possible, to transmit to their posterity.

Honour is in fact the dominant theme in the good species of influence. Often the members of the corporation of a close borough were gentlemen of similar social standing to the patron, bound to him by a common gentlemanly code of behaviour. In 1760 a burgess of Killyleagh replied thus to a canvassing letter:

> I had the compliment paid me of being burgess thirty or forty years ago by those of the other side of the question,

37. N.L.I., Ms. 13,154 (Lismore Mss.), Thomas Croker to Thomas Boyce, 16 July 1719.
38. P.R.O.N.I., T.1839 (Moira Mss.), pp 70-71, Egmont to Sir John Rawdon, 3 May 1745.

who confided in me as their friend; and I am sure you would not desire or expect that I should break the confidence reposed in me, which would be attended by the black crime of ingratitude.[39]

What it is important to remember is that being asked to be a burgess of even the closest borough was received as a great compliment, almost equivalent to being asked to stand godfather to a man's child.   Indeed, godfatherhood was the metaphor which Francis Leigh, a quaint eighteenth-century survival into the age of reform, employed to describe the agreement subsisting between his and the Tottenham family over the municipal and parliamentary patronage of New Ross:

> The burgesses and freemen of Ross are all honourable men. They know upon what terms they have obtained their freedom, and I have no doubt will most honourably perform their contract ... I look upon us both [Leigh and Charles Tottenham of Ballycurry, County Wicklow] to be in some degree the godfathers of these freemen − [we] recommend and are answerable to each other for them. You are not only the father, but on this occasion the godfather, of your son, and should be answerable to my family for his support of them.   I am godfather to my grandson, and if he does not follow the honourable part I shall point out to him (as I am certain he will), I shall be the first to oppose him.[40]

In many boroughs, of course, patron control was exercised through dependent tenants and occasionally even menial servants; but in most the courtesies were always observed, and votes were 'desired', not demanded.   In 1812 the earl of Shannon, the then patron of ever-contentious Youghal, wrote to Burlington's representative, the duke of Devonshire:

> Your Grace ... seems to consider the borough of Youghal as properly belonging to you. In this opinion I am sorry that I never can agree, for in my mind no person can claim a right to the borough of Youghal but by the good wishes of the majority of the respectable part of the corporation. Such wishes it has been the fortune of my family to have long

39.   Edward Baillie to Gavin Hamilton, 15 Dec. 1760, printed in *Letters from the Burgesses of Killyleagh to Gavin Hamilton Esq. Declining to Vote for him in 1760* (Dublin, 1833), p. 28. I am indebted for this reference to Professor J. L. McCracken.
40.   N.L.I., p. 4937 (Tottenham Mss.), Leigh to Tottenham, 6 Dec. 1830.

enjoyed. And so long as I am thought deserving of the same
flattering distinction, I must feel myself bound to support the
political connection that subsists between us ...[41]

Obviously, the circumstances in which this letter was written were
special: Shannon was anxious to say nothing which could be used
against him, and to put Devonshire in the wrong. Nevertheless, the
language is that of the good species of influence. Horace Walpole
once described an encounter with a highwayman who nearly blew
his head off, as an affair conducted with the utmost good breeding
on both sides: to the unenfranchised inhabitants of a close borough
the good breeding observed among members of the corporation was
as much comfort as the good breeding of the highwayman would
have been to Walpole if his head had in fact been blown off. Yet, it
is a not unimportant consideration that the members of a corporation generally regarded borough patronage as a trust, not an
expropriation, and behaved accordingly.

Another sphere in which, surprisingly, a sense of honour can
be seen as a major factor is the apparently dishonourable matter of
the sale of seats and indeed the sale of the patronage of whole
boroughs. The first and fundamental point about such transactions
is that they were not flagrant or overt. An agreement whereby a
seat or a vote was bartered for money, if its existence could be
proved, would be a sufficient ground for making void an election;
and at least two election petitions (one for Baltinglass in 1777 and
one for Enniscorthy in 1783) adduced such an agreement as a
ground for voiding the election.[42] The most striking feature of the
first marquess of Abercorn's purchase of the patronage of Augher in
1790 was the hugger-mugger with which he shrouded the transaction; in 1791 an opposition peer, Lord Arran, was the object of
distrust and dislike because it was suspected that he had divulged to
the opposition the details of his sale of two seats for his borough of
Donegal at the previous general election, in order to give them
ammunition for a motion in the House of Commons; in 1798
Lord Portarlington, writing to a fellow borough-patron and a
friend, about the sale of the seats for Portarlington, would not
even use the word 'seats', but instead referred to them darkly as
'certain commodities I have to dispose of'; and in 1800, the
incredibly late date at which the Colclough family at last sold the

41. Chatsworth Mss., Shannon to Devonshire, 27 Aug. 1812 (transcripts
made by the late Professor A. Aspinall and placed at my disposal by Dr P. J.
Jupp).
42. *C.J.I.,* ix, 383; xi, 176. I am indebted for these references to Mrs
Geraldine Wylie.

patronage of Enniscorthy, they resorted to a phoney mortgage 'to screen the *illicit agreement* of the sale of the borough'.[43]   Again, the sale of seats (or for that matter of borough patronage), which became a common practice after 1760, and particularly after the passing of the Octennial Act in 1768, was an extremely uncommon practice earlier in the century. The earliest offer of money for a seat, which has so far come to light, was made in 1714 for the borough of Dingle, the sum being a mere £100; and the earliest sale on record, for the same borough, occurred in 1731, the price being a mere £500 − after 1768 it was to stand at roughly £2,500.[44]   The usual practice in the first 60 years of the century seems to have been that the member was returned free, except that he paid his own election expenses. Until 1768 there was no predictable limitation on the duration of parliaments, and therefore no method of assessing the value of seats. In these circumstances only the most short-sighted patrons, or those in the most desperate financial difficulties, would ever have made an outright sale, which would have left the member for their borough free of their control for an indefinite period. It is important that the circumstances obtaining in the later eighteenth century should not be foisted on the earlier.

Even in the later eighteenth century there were a great many niceties and delicacies in the matter of buying and selling seats. At the beginning of the period, in 1760, a prospective candidate, William Talbot, wrote: 'I believe you would not recommend it to me to come into parliament upon pecuniary terms, as I hope I shall never descend so low as to think of reimbursing myself by turning my voice (if I had one) to private advantages.'[45]   The borough patrons who were less well-off financially did sell seats on a pure cash basis: cases in point are the Rams, who at one time controlled both Gorey and Duleek; the Ruxtons, who controlled Ardee; the Hores, who controlled Taghmon; and so on. These were the people whom John Beresford described, not without a sneer,

43.   P.R.O.N.I., T.2541/I.B.1/1/9, 11, Thomas Knox to Abercorn, 28 Apr., 15 May 1790; T.2541/I.B.1/2/6, Knox to Abercorn, 22 Feb. 1791; N.L.I., Talbot-Crosbie Mss., Portarlington to Glandore, 10 Jan. 1798; P.R.O.N.I., T.3048/C/84, Caesar Colclough to Messrs. Reeves, 14 June 1839.
44.   T.C.D., Ms. 3821/160, Maurice FitzGerald to David Crosbie, 14 Aug. 1714; entry in Lord Egmont's diary, 24 Feb. 1731, printed in *Journal of the Cork Historical and Archaeological Society* (ser. 2), xxviii (1921), 21. See also B.L., Add. Mss. 47032, ff 27-8 (Egmont Mss.), Philip Perceval to Lord Perceval, 11 July 1727.
45.   N.L.I., Wicklow Mss. (P.C. 226-7), William Talbot to William Forward, 20 Nov. 1760.

as poor men who lived by the sale of their seats.[46] Richer men acted differently. The great borough-owning magnates — Lords Shannon, Downshire, Ely, Abercorn and the dukes of Leinster and Devonshire — never sold. This was partly a matter of pride and principle (in 1790 two lesser borough patrons explicitly stated that they considered it wrong in principle to sell[47]), and partly a matter of common prudence. In the long term it conduced much more to a great man's influence (and often to his pecuniary advantage) if he returned political *proteges* free of charge and then negotiated with the government over the rewards for their support as and when ticklish measures came before the House. Even the dukes of Leinster, frequently in opposition, went in for negotiations of this kind. Then, in the 1790s, the second duke, under pressure of financial difficulties, departed from the practice of the great borough-owners and sold, not only seats, but the entire patronage of one borough. He was at pains, however, to allege motives other than financial. In 1799, for example, he explained that, 'being disgusted with Irish politics, I was determined to withdraw myself totally, by which I am deprived of given [*sic*] the ... [Union] any opposition but my own vote in the House of Lords'.[48]

The newest arrival among the great borough-owners of the 1790s was the first marquess of Abercorn. His frank, sometimes naive, pronouncements illustrate the contradictions and complexities of the borough-owning mentality, and the dangers of generalization on the part of twentieth-century historians. Like the other great borough-owners, Abercorn was usually in the market for a spare seat for somebody else's borough. But he had his own ideas on this subject, which he outlined in a letter to the chief secretary which is not only unblushingly candid, but smacks of the broker rather than the *grand seigneur*:

My way of considering the subject is this. If I pay an annuity [*i.e.* an annual rent] during the sitting of the members brought in, I am prepared for all casualties. If the King dies, if a regency occurs, if a dissolution takes place (all which God forbid) or if my member dies, in all these cases my annuity ceases and I am *fresh* and *flush* to begin again. But suppose all these contingencies after I have paid down large sums of money, and what of the result? I have spent my money while

46. Quoted in Bolton, *Union*, p. 33.
47. Malcomson, *'Newtown Act'*, 337.
48. N.L.I., Ms. 13,840 (Rosse Mss.), Leinster to Sir Laurence Parsons, 16 Jan. 1799.

we are strong, and upon such emergencies I am (so far at least) drained at the time my exertions are most wanted. I had rather therefore at once purchase the perpetuity of some borough, if I can light upon any in my part of the world. The boroughs of which you have the disposal by peerages or other jobs, you probably have chaps enough for ... But if you had rather trust to men of mine than others you can less depend on, I am very ready to produce two (or three) men with £1,000 apiece ...[49]

At the same time, Abercorn was capable of being, as he said himself, 'too romantic upon the subject'; writing only a month later to his member for Strabane (who cannot have read the letter with much satisfaction), he said:

as I never had or will have a job or any interested view of my own to promote, the object of my ambition is that no man shall embark with me who will not be honourable, firm and steady in the storm as well as in the sunshine, and hold out a contrast to other Irish parliamentary connections of a band of gentlemen immovable in every danger, unvarying in every fortune.[50]

What he had in mind, and elsewhere stated bluntly, was that people whom he returned free of charge should not expect him to obtain for them jobs from the government as well.

Abercorn was unique in his *naivete*, and his political connection was soon on the rocks. All the same, he illustrates dramatically the odd mixture of lucre and honour which characterized the parliamentary traffic of Ireland. The relationship between a patron and the member for his borough, expressed at its simplest, was that either the patron returned the member free and so bound him in honour to vote as the patron wished, or that the member paid the patron money for the seat and so made himself his own boss. An example of the former relationship is Grattan's with Lord Charlemont; of the latter the type of straight sale usually made by the poorer patrons. However, there was a wide intermediate zone. Patrons at all sensitive about their own honour and dignity, and not desperate for ready money, usually tried to return, at a reduced price of course, relations, friends or political associates. This meant

49. P.R.O.N.I., T.2541/I.K./11/9, Abercorn to Robert Hobart, [late Dec.-early Jan. 1790].
50. *Ibid.*, T.2541/I.K./11/12, Abercorn to Henry Pomeroy, 19 Feb. 1790.

that, because the price was reduced, they could claim some say in the member's political conduct, or, if the member and they were politically in tune, that it would not be obvious that a cash transaction had in fact taken place. For example, in 1787 the financially embarrassed earl of Glandore was advised that 'no distress could justify' his selling a seat to a stranger; in 1790 the financially embarrassed earl of Granard sold two of his seats, but to fellow members of the opposition and at £500 each below the market price; and in 1795 Viscount Midleton, who was not financially embarrassed but wanted promotion in the Church for his brother, was prepared to give a seat free to the government provided it nominated a member known personally to his family and not someone 'ludicrous' like Sir Boyle Roche.[51]   Not surprisingly, the attitude of many buyers of seats was the converse of that of these patrons: such buyers, unlike William Talbot, did not think it dishonourable to buy seats, provided it was a straight cash transaction which left them independent of patron control.   In 1775 John Forbes, the future M.P. for Drogheda, was advised: 'you will not go into parliament with views of venality — I am sure I know your principles — and [if] you purchase a seat, rely upon it, you are more independent in the senate (though chosen in so unconstitutional a manner) than the member chosen for the city of Dublin'; and Flood consistently declined to 'render either his seat or conduct dependent on the approbation or disapprobation of another', failed in advance of the 1790 parliament to find a borough patron who would make an outright sale, and in the end did not sit in that parliament at all.[52]

More surprisingly, the government too — although the fount of corruption, the biggest single intermediary in sales of seats and the bogy of the parliamentary reformers — displayed considerable delicacy in transactions of this kind.   Because management of the House of Commons was relatively a much more important function of the government in Ireland than it was in Great Britain, the Irish government probably fell below the standards of the contemporary British one in this respect; for instance, British borough patrons

51. N.L.I., Talbot-Crosbie Mss., Dean Thomas Graves to Glandore, 1 Mar. 1787; Lamport House, Fitzwilliam Mss., T. L. O'Beirne to Fitzwilliam, 25 Nov. 1794 (Aspinall transcripts, once again placed at my disposal by Dr P. J. Jupp); N.L.I., Ms. 889/15 (Midleton Mss.), Midleton to Bishop Brodrick, 13 Nov., 6 Nov. 1795.
52. N.L.I., Ms. 10,713/iv (Forbes Mss.), William Glascock to Forbes, 29 Mar. 1775; *Original Letters ... to the Rt. Hon. Henry Flood* (London, 1820), p. 143, Flood to Chandos, 15 Apr. 1784; pp 174-5, Charlemont to Flood, 24 Nov., 19 Dec., 1788.

who gave the government the nomination to their seats seem to have received the full market value for them from the government's nominees, while Irish patrons often gave the nomination for nothing or at a much reduced price. The consequence was that in Ireland the government was much more deeply in the patrons' debt, a debt it repaid so regularly in peerages that the convention became established that when a man left the Irish House of Commons for the Lords he gave the unexpired term of his seat to the government for nothing. In Britain, by contrast, possession of borough patronage was a very minor ground for ennoblement and some of the greatest patrons had to wait a long time for their titles. Yet, whatever practices the Irish government resorted to, it never seems to have given cash for a seat: it gave peerages and jobs; its nominees often gave cash — but the government itself did not. In 1768 for example, Lord Baltinglass's terms for returning a government nominee for Baltinglass were a reduced price of 1,000 guineas from the nominee and a living in the Church for Baltinglass's son (although it was hoped that a step in the peerage might suffice, as Lord Baltinglass's 'vanity exceeds even his avarice'); and in 1790 two commoners who had bought two seats each for government nominees (at a cost to one of the commoners of £4,700) were in reward created Lords Glentworth and Kilmaine.[53] In all such transactions, the government must have been fully aware that money had changed hands, but at least the money was not its own. Indeed, after the passing of the Place Act in 1793, it even adopted the hypocritical rule of refusing to grant escheatorships (the Irish equivalent of the Chiltern Hundreds) unless the vacating member gave an assurance that no cash transaction was involved. One might suspect that this was only an excuse to keep political undesirables out of the House, but a private letter in September 1798 from a recently departed lord lieutenant shows that the rule was genuine.[54] It did not long survive that date, being forgotten amid the large-scale turnover of members at the start of the session of 1800.

The general effect of the Union crisis, and of the provisions of the Act of Union, was to undermine rules, conventions and niceties of this kind — to undermine, but not entirely to demolish

53. N.L.I., Ms. 394/41-2 (Townshend Mss.), Godfrey Lill to Townshend, 9, 10 July 1768 (three letters); Kilmaine Mss. (the late Lord Kilmaine, The Mount House, Brasted, Kent), copy of an agreement between Sir John Browne and Lord Arran for the purchase of the Donegal seats, 10 July 1789.
54. S.P.O., 511/49/7, draft reply from Castlereagh to William Tighe, *post* 4 May 1798; P.R.O.N.I., D.3030/277, Camden to Castlereagh, 16 Sept. 1798.

them. Even during the Union crisis, the government still baulked at directly purchasing seats, and the opposition's practice of buying 'seats in parliament by subscription' was sincerely regarded by government supporters as 'incorrect'.[55]   The government also baulked at what it called 'the embarrassing principle of avowed compensation' for boroughs disfranchised by the Union. The plan of Union envisaged in 1799 did not include compensation, and the government began by questioning whether compensation could be paid except in cases where the patron could prove that he was the heir or assign of a patron actually named in the charter. In the end, of course, compensation was awarded on much less rigid grounds than these, and the commissioners appointed to award it were able to place a monetary value on the respective interests (if there was more than one) in all the 85 boroughs disfranchised, except for Swords. Yet this extension of the principle of compensation was not solely inspired by a desire to buy off the borough patrons; there were two other motives as well, both laudable. The government genuinely wanted to adopt a plan of disfranchisement which would dispose only of close boroughs and retain the more open ones, provided that this aim was not avowed and the hands of the English parliamentary reformers strengthened accordingly. Again, the government wanted to disfranchise boroughs outright rather than form them into a rota system, on the Scottish model, which would mean paying partial compensation and thus admitting that boroughs which were still to be represented in every second or third parliament were a species of private property.[56]   All the same, although the government acted with greater delicacy and from purer motives than is usually recognized, the effect of the Union crisis and of Union compensation on contemporary attitudes to borough representation was not uplifting. In March 1800 the patron of Athenry wrote openly and vulgarly of the value of what he called 'borough stock'.[57] The commissioners of compensation were inundated with written agreements over the sale of seats and of borough patronage — the type of document which had hitherto been most sedulously concealed — and awarded sums of money, not just to borough patrons, but to a few individuals who had

55.   Keele University Library, Sneyd Mss. (P.R.O.N.I., T.3229/2/51), Under-Secretary Edward Cooke to Lord Auckland, 18 Jan. 1800.
56.   Anonymous memorandum cited in n. 11; P.R.O.N.I., D.3030/656, notes by Cooke on boroughs incorporated for the benefit of individuals, [1799?]; *Memoirs and Correspondence of Castlereagh*, iii, 56-61, 'Project for the Representation of Ireland in the Imperial Parliament', [1799?]; 68-9, 'Suggestions of the Lord Lieutenant relative to the Representation', [1799?].
57.   S.P.O., 515/85/7, Theophilus Blakeney to James Ormsby, 22 Mar. 1800.

purchased seats at the general election of 1797 (probably to the few who had stipulated in 1797 that the seat was to be for a certain number of years). Above all the post-Union government of the United Kingdom did not observe the convention of the Irish government, and entered directly into the market for Irish borough seats, for example purchasing four for a total of £18,000 at the general election of 1806.[58]

At one level the niceties and nuances which have been discussed are as irrelevant as the good breeding of Horace Walpole's highwayman; at another they are significant. The analogy of the highwayman is perhaps unhappy, since what has been argued is not that there was honour among thieves, but that thieves was the very last thing that borough patrons and their burgesses and members would have thought of themselves as being. The co-existence of lucre with honour is the facet of eighteenth-century political life, and particularly of borough representation, which twentieth-century man finds hardest to grasp. Yet it is axiomatic that total corruption is an impossibility, since corruption is effective only when there is a bond of trust between corrupter and corrupted (if indeed it is possible to distinguish between the two in the case of the spontaneous corruption of the eighteenth century). Honour bound the burgesses of a corporation to the patron who had appointed them, bound the member to the patron who had returned him free or at a reduced price, and in turn bound the patron and member to the administration which had conferred favours on them. Yet, because the members of the Irish House of Commons were men of honour, they were sensitive, when popular measures were in agitation, to the charge of being government hacks and hirelings, 'uniform drudges of administration'. In these circumstances, their sense of honour, which normally underwrote their sense of obligation to the government, pulled them in the opposite direction; and popular measures were accordingly carried. To counteract the pull of such measures, the government could attempt stepped-up exertions of patronage. But exertions of patronage were self-defeating in two respects. First, patronage once given was, by and large, gone for ever: the government could dismiss great men from their offices and emoluments if they were politically disobedient; but they could not dismiss the great men's numerous dependants from minor jobs theoretically outside the political sphere, notably in the revenue. Again, the more patronage

58. National Library of Scotland, Edinburgh, Elliot of Wells Mss., William Fremantle to William Elliot, 16 Oct. 1806. I should like to express my thanks to Mr Iain Maciver, for all the help he gave me in exploring this collection.

was given, the more was needed. Borough patrons were not content to remain barons for the good reason that earldoms were going, and their support was not to be bought by one outright purchase but by ever larger instalments. The Irish government depreciated the currency of its patronage, and was the main victim of the ensuing inflation.

This is an utterly cynical line of argument. But does any other line of argument satisfactorily explain the all-important fact that the patrons and the representatives of the close boroughs did not prevent, as numerically they could have done, the winning of Free Trade in 1779 and the Constitution of 1782, did not prevent the passing of many popular measures, above all, did not prevent successful opposition being given to the Union in 1799? Grattan called the Irish parliament of the late eighteenth century, 'a borough parliament'; but it is as 'Grattan's Parliament' that it is rightly remembered today.[59]

59.   In addition to the owners and depositors of papers, record offices and various individuals mentioned in the footnotes, I should like to make an especial acknowledgement to the Deputy Keeper of the Records, P.R.O.N.I., under whom Mrs Geraldine Wylie and I have been engaged on research for a *History of the Irish Parliament, 1690-1800.* This paper is a by-product of our research.

MIDDLEMEN

David Dickson[1]

Recent work in Irish agrarian history has considerably modified historians' attitudes towards some of its central characters,
notably the nineteenth-century landlord[2] and the eighteenth-
century absentee,[3] and from this a more credible view of the
development of the Irish 'land system' is emerging.[4] In the future,
research may concentrate more on the nature of agricultural
production than on institutional factors surrounding tenurial
arrangements. However, for eighteenth-century Ireland it is difficult at present to turn aside from questions of landlord and tenant
relations, firstly because estate records are our main source of
information and are chiefly concerned with these; and secondly,
because a less ambiguous and more regionally-defined picture of
tenurial conditions is a necessary prerequisite to fuller analysis of
agricultural change itself. The semantic problems surrounding such
terms as cottier, *scullóg, gneever,*[5] yeoman, peasant and, as this
paper will argue, middleman, must at least be made explicit and
debated, if not resolved.

1.   I should like to thank Mr W. H. Crawford, Professor L. M. Cullen,
Dr A. P. W. Malcomson and the editors for very constructive comments on an
earlier draft. And of those who have stimulated my thoughts on middlemen,
I would particularly like to thank Professor J. S. Donnelly.
2.   For the most complete exercise to date in revisionism, see W. E.
Vaughan, 'Landlord and Tenant Relations in Ireland 1850-78' (Dublin Univ.
Ph.D. thesis 1974, abstracted in *Irish Economic and Social History*, i (1974),
62-3).
3.   A. P. W. Malcomson, 'Absenteeism in Eighteenth-Century Ireland', *Ir.
Econ. and Soc. Hist.,* i (1974), 15-35.
4.   Cf. W. H. Crawford, 'Landlord-Tenant Relations in Ulster 1609-1820',
ibid., ii (1975), 5-21; R. Crotty, *Irish Agricultural Production* (Cork, 1966);
L. M. Cullen, *An Economic History of Ireland Since 1660* (London, 1972);
J. S. Donnelly, *The Land and the People of Nineteenth-Century Cork*
(London, 1975); W. A. Maguire, *The Downshire Estates in Ireland, 1801-1845*
(Oxford, 1972); B. L. Solow, *The Land Question and the Irish Economy
1870-1903* (Cambridge, Mass., 1971).
5.   *Scullóg* and *gneever* were words used in the course of the eighteenth
century to distinguish the small working farmer from those above and below
him. There was a measure of independence associated with the *scullóg* which
was not so obviously the case with the *gneever.* However, use of the two
terms together has not been found by this writer, so that the precise nuances
of the terms — as well as their currency — remains unclear.

2

The term middleman can be defined in a strict sense fairly easily: the recipient of a lease who himself relets all or part of the land demised to him. Such a phenomenon has not been uniquely Irish; the Scottish tacksman of the early modern period is an obvious parallel, and nineteenth-century Europe had a number of regions where reletting was extensive and the subject of comment — Spain, for instance, and Sicily, where the *gabellotto* flourished. Yet the prominence of the so-called middleman system in public debate has been unique to Ireland, as Edward Wakefield suggested:

> Middlemen are abused by the editor of every newspaper in Ireland; they are reviled, and even loaded with maledictions by the lower orders in all parts of the country; and they are treated by the gentry with that sovereign contempt which is usually shown to the most worthless and abandoned in the human race. Writers in general from Mr Young downwards, have inveighed bitterly against them; and no class of man, I believe, in the empire, have been attacked with more virulence from every quarter.[6]

Wakefield was right to point to Arthur Young as the first major polemicist against the middleman. Indeed, Young seems to have coined the term, in the aftermath of his tour: it replaced such descriptions as petty or 'petit' landlord, the Irish *tiarna beag* (anglicized as terny beg).[7] Young's views, set out in the chapter on tenantry appended to his *Tour in Ireland,* were to be constantly re-echoed in the literature of Irish political economy until at least the 1820s — in the Dublin Society's statistical surveys, in travellers' tours, in the pamphlet ephemera — and at first sight there would seem to have been a consensus denouncing 'the baneful influence of the middleman system', a consensus of view that has been taken as firm evidence by those historians who have relied too heavily on the printed source.

6.   Edward Wakefield, *An Account of Ireland, Statistical and Political* (2 vols., London, 1812), i, 286.
7.   Young uses the term 'terny beg' on several occasions (see Arthur Young, *A Tour in Ireland ... Made in the Years 1776, 1777 and 1778* (2 vols., Dublin, 1780), i, 261, 284, 362). For petty/'petit' landlords, see N.L.I., Ms. 2,786, 'Rental and Observations on the Estate of Sir Thomas Dundas', 1783; L. Marron, 'Documents from the Bath Papers', *Clogher Record,* vi, no. 1 (1966), 119-20. For an unusually early, if loosely formulated, attack on intermediate tenure, which used a variety of terms to describe the middleman (landjobber, subgentry, tenant-landlord and vice-landlord), see *The Tribune* (Dublin), 9 Dec. 1729.

However, even if one goes no further than the contemporary literature, it is possible to detect certain problems in defining and assessing the category 'middleman'. Firstly, the opponents of the system betrayed on occasions an uncertainty as to what they meant by the word; secondly, they contradicted themselves in their claims of the results and indeed incidence of middlemen; thirdly, and most importantly, one must take notice of a significant literature defending the existence of middlemen. As an example of the first problem, Young's own references to middlemen are ambiguous; generally he seems to have had in mind tenants, usually non-resident, who relet at a profit rent, but what is one to make of his reference to the situation in County Clare? 'Middlemen [are] not common, but much land [is] re-let, arising from the long tenures which are given of three lives &c.'[8] Are only outside speculators in short-term leases to be covered by the term? As an instance of the second problem, one can find anomalies in the evidence concerning the effects of middlemen engrossing leases in a district. On the one hand, William Tighe, in writing of County Kilkenny in 1802, believed that 'in consequence of letting to these land-jobbers some grounds have been depopulated, tenants preferring to become cottiers on other lands or vagabonds', yet the objection of many landlords to middlemen, particularly after 1815, was their irresponsible subletting.[9] Another contradiction concerned the effect of the Revolutionary and Napoleonic wars on the survival of middlemen. Some sources claimed that land-jobbing and lease speculation reached an all-time peak in the heady years of war inflation, while others pointed to the 1793 act enfranchising the Catholic forty-shilling freeholder, and its effects — the multiplication by land-owners of small direct lettings on one-life leases, created in order to maximize their political weight electorally, and the consequent elimination of middlemen.[10]

The greatest mistake in accepting at face value the hostile evidence about middlemen is that by so doing one overlooks the literature dissenting from Young's critique. Young himself recognized that the intermediate tenant was an object of controversy in the 1770s: 'it is in Ireland a question greatly agitated, whether

8.   Young, *Tour in Ireland,* i, 411.
9.   William Tighe, *Statistical Observations Relative to the County of Kilkenny* (Dublin, 1802), p. 424.
10.   Compare the statements of William Parker, *Observations on the Intended Amendment of the Irish Grand Jury Laws* ... (Cork, 1816), p. 134, and [Horatio Townsend], *A View of the Agricultural State of Ireland* ... (Cork, 1815), p. 21, with the views of the earl of Rosse, in a letter to Baron Redesdale, 3 May 1822 (P.R.O.N.I., T.3030/13/3 [Redesdale Mss.]).

the system has or has not advantages, which may yet induce a landlord to continue in it.'[11] The two arguments for the defence which he believed worth considering were firstly, that landowners, especially absentees, found it far more convenient 'to let a large farm to some intermediate person of substance, at a lower rent ... [where] profit may be his inducement ... for becoming a collector from the immediate tenants' than accept the risk of direct letting to the poor occupier with the likelihood of greater arrears and bankruptcy, or 'the drudgery of such a minute attention' that management of such a vast array of small tenants would entail; secondly, that the substantial tenant was more likely to improve than 'the mere cottar', at least around his own residence. Young dismissed these possibilities in several ways: he pointed to the moral degeneracy and, in some cases, absenteeism of middlemen as a group, 'your fellows with round hats edged with gold, who hunt in the morning, get drunk in the evening and fight the next morning'; further, he challenged the assumption that undertenants were less capable of paying the rent regularly than their lessors. But his central argument was that 'intermedate tenants make no improvements; if non-resident they cannot, and if resident they do not; but they oppress the occupiers, and render them as incapable as they are themselves unwilling'. Young by implication accepted that there might be a historical or theoretical defence of middlemen, but the propagandist in him scorned and ridiculed it: all landowners must accept one simple maxim, 'to let their estates to none but the occupying tenantry'.[12] Young's bitterness against middlemen and his black-and-white verdict on their worth were probably not unrelated to his experience as agent to Lord Kingsborough, the young owner of a very large property centred on north-east Cork, where Young was employed after his tour in 1777-8 in a general reletting of the estate, nine-tenths of which, he later stated, were in the hands of middlemen. He pursued a policy (that Kingsborough had apparently commenced) of direct letting, and in so doing alienated a relation of Lady Kingsborough, who was a substantial leaseholder on the estate. By intriguing against Young the threatened party successfully engineered his dismissal.[13]

A defence of middlemen, albeit often grudging and some of it only retrospective, developed. It can be found both in the pamphlet literature and in private correspondence. There appear to have been two main arguments, one broadly socio-political, the

11. Young, *Tour in Ireland,* ii, part ii, p. 17.
12. *Ibid.,* pp 17-21.
13. *Ibid.,* pp 276-7; *The Autobiography of Arthur Young ...* ed. M. Betham-Edwards (London, 1898), pp 76, 78-80.

other economic. The private observations of the second earl of Rosse in the troubled year of 1822 represented an explicit statement of the the former:

> The lower orders are much more formidable now than they ever were in this island, from their great increase in numbers, from fewer gentlemen residing, from the extinction of the great farmers who were Protestants and the descendants of the English, and from the habit of organization and the taste they have got for it; also from the number of disbanded soldiers and militia.

> Forty years ago, the lands of Ireland were let in farms of 500 or a 1,000 or 1,500 acres: now landlords, finding that they can get higher rents and have more voters, let them to Catholics in portions of 20, 30, or 40 acres, and these, as they multiply fast, again subdivide them among their sons and daughters, as they marry. Therefore, the old modes of preserving order and enforcing obedience to law will not do now.[14]

The threat to the existence of the local Protestant interest, the 'yeoman' farmers, and the short-circuiting of their income that the setting of direct leases to former under-tenants implied, was one theme. The other was put by a south Cork landowner, James Kearney, when making a more oblique defence of middle tenures in a pamphlet of 1790:

> It is the want of capitals, which gave rise to what are generally called here middlemen, or landjobbers, men of some property, who take large tracts of ground, to let it at advanced rents to dairymen, and to poor farmers. The dairymen they generally supply with the entire stock for the land, and the farmers with a great part of their stock. There can be no doubt, that it would be more for the interest of the farmer, to hold from the landowner, than from the intermediate tenant; provided that he was able to receive the same assistance from him, but landowners are in general not fond of trusting them with money to buy stock. For this reason, and because there is so large a proportion of Ireland under dairies, I fear that there is a necessity of middlemen at present. Few landowners, even residents, would pay that degree of attention, which is

14. P.R.O.N.I., T.3030/13/1 (Redesdale Mss.), Rosse to Redesdale, 30 Mar. 1822.

requisite, to prevent being imposed on by dairymen. As for absentee landlords, they must have a *stake* for their rents.[15]

In other words, even if Young's assertion about the failure of middlemen to invest in improvements was valid, Kearney could see an essential function for middlemen in the south: the provision not of fixed capital but of working capital, if investment in livestock for the under-tenants can be so described.

It is possible to see aspects of this debate over middlemen in the 23 county statistical surveys published between 1801 and 1834, with some authors following Young, and others accepting in varying degrees the case for the defence. Hely Dutton, in his 1808 survey of Clare, in denouncing middlemen, expressed his pride at being able to be thus associated with Young, 'who has so ably detailed the abuses of middlemen, and their oppressions to the lower classes of society', and, in his 1824 survey of Galway, commented that

It is really astonishing that landed proprietors do not perceive the losses they sustain by letting to any but occupants. Formerly the great reputed wealth those land-jobbers possessed blinded the judgment of proprietors ...[16]

Horatio Townsend, writing of County Cork in 1810, also condemned middlemen on the grounds of their behaviour towards under-tenants, the latter resembling 'more the slaves of a West India planter, than the subjects of a free government'.[17] Townsend recognized that there were exceptions to the general run of middlemen, but it was the Englishman, Robert Fraser, who wrote the survey of County Wicklow in 1801, that explicitly criticized the conventional wisdom about giving leases to middlemen:

It has been the fashion of late years to decry this mode of letting lands, and some non-residents in this county have refused to renew to those principal tenants, and have parcelled out their lands in small tenements, expecting from this arrangement to receive a considerable addition to their rents;

15. 'A Country Gentleman' [James Kearney], *Essays on Agriculture and Planting* (Dublin, 1790), pp xiv-xv.
16. Hely Dutton, *Statistical Survey of the County of Clare ...* (Dublin, 1808), p. xv; *idem, A Statistical and Agricultural Survey of the County of Galway ...* (Dublin, 1824), p. 148.
17. Horatio Townsend, *Statistical Survey of the County of Cork* (Dublin, 1810), p. 184.

and I do believe, being also led into a persuasion of thereby ameliorating the circumstances, and adding to the prosperity of the immediate occupant of the soil.[18]

But this, Fraser believed, was a mere prejudice, for land could only be improved with capital investment, and the small man, however secure his tenure, would never be an improver. He admitted that head tenants in other areas had earned some of the criticism they had received, but that in County Wicklow the primary tenants, the yeomen, were being mistakenly uprooted, and he questioned 'whether it is better for a non-resident to let his estate in large farms to men of sufficient capital, who can be made accountable for the rents, or let it in small tenements to poor tenants'. His answer was that, 'with regard to this county at least, the experiments made by letting farms in small parcels to occupying tenants, and taking away the intermediate and primary tenants, have not answered the intended effect ... where this has taken place, there is greater poverty and actual distress than in any other part of the country'.[19]

As late as the 1820s a defence of middlemen was still being reiterated, notably by Whitley Stokes in 1821.

The middleman is necessary to Ireland, as the shopkeeper is necessary to London. The London consumer cannot deal conveniently with the merchant, nor the Irish small farmer with the nobleman or gentleman who possesses a large estate ... if you impede the appointment of a middleman, there will be fewer small farms and higher prices given for them, and if you deter respectable men from undertaking this valuable mediation, you will throw it into a few inferior hands, who will gain by the monopoly you confer upon them.[20]

On the whole, however, by the end of the Napoleonic wars there seems to have been a greater readiness to see a compromise between the two positions on middlemen. Wakefield in 1812 pulled his punches in his own criticisms, contrasting the *rentier* intervening on an estate where agriculture was already developed, with the improving farmer with capital who extended cultivation by colon-

18. Robert Fraser, *General View of the Agriculture of the County of Wicklow* (Dublin, 1801), p. 213.
19. *Ibid.*, pp 214-215.
20. Whitley Stokes, *Observations on the Population and Resources of Ireland* (Dublin, 1821), pp 30-1.

izing wasteland with cottiers, and created underholdings on virgin or previously marginal land.[21] This view that middle tenure was a complex phenomenon was further developed by William Parker, a Cork pamphleteer, several years later:

> In middlemen there are great shades of discrimination. Those that take farms and relet them without previous occupation, at rack rents, to a poor tenantry, often ruin them and rob the inheritors of the fee of the value of the soil; this has been frequently the case, and these kind of middlemen, have not been improperly called land sharks, or pirates. And in these, Ireland has abounded by the late fatal advance in lands, which was quite unnatural, and which caused the hordes of semi-squires in the country, who became a multitude of upstart gentry, without manners or education, oppressive to the poor ...
>
> But many respectable gentlemen of family, character, and property, have become middlemen in Ireland, from an anxiety to possess landed property, and to secure an interest in the soil for their families. Under this idea, they have taken farms, laid out considerable sums, and in many cases have acquired a handsome property, though not possessing the fee; so that from occupation, residence, industry, and money expanded, they justly become participators in the actual revenue of the estate, to which they have as just, though secondary, a claim, as the head landlords.[22]

Parker thus shared the belief that a great extension in land-jobbing had recently taken place. That this phenomenon — as opposed to mere subdivision — really did occur has yet to be confirmed by evidence from estate papers. But whatever its dimensions, the post-war developments are less controversial. In the context of agricultural depression, it is clear that middleman tenants became increasingly embarrassed financially, being unable to adjust their rent obligations to the falling incomes of their own tenants. Parallel to this, congestion and subdivision became more visible, and exposed middle tenants to the charges of damaging the interest of an estate and neglecting lease covenants against sub-letting. For these reasons the case for the defence became far less tenable, and the 1826 act against subletting (in all lease contracts from that date) underlined the existence of a general consensus

21. Wakefield, *Account of Ireland,* i, 286-9.
22. Parker, *Observations,* pp 134-5.

against reletting.[23] The continuous erosion of intermediate tenures in the pre-Famine decades led official investigations such as the Poor Inquiry and the Devon Commission to concentrate on agrarian problems other than middlemen as such, although their demise was generally noted with satisfaction.[24]

3

If a survey of the printed literature on middlemen demonstrates a greater diversity than historians have assumed, how far is this confirmed by unprinted sources, in particular estate records? To what extent is the dichotomy between the *rentier/jobber* in farms and the gentleman/improver historically clearcut? Indeed, how far were the middlemen of Young's day the product of fundamental changes in early and mid-eighteenth-century Ireland, notably of the expanding economy and the demographic revolution? Is it possible to observe the phenomenon at the beginning of the eighteenth century, in a significantly more backward economy, with a smaller population, when the term 'middleman' did not exist and the problem of intermediate tenure was seldom raised? The argument of this paper is that at that stage various types of tenant could indeed be found with some of the future attributes of middlemen, but that structural changes in the economy were to alter their functions drastically, bringing them collectively into greater public prominence in later years. These tenant-types can be treated under four headings: (a) the Protestant chief tenant (b) the Catholic ex-freeholder (c) the lease speculator (d) the perpetuity tenant. These categories can be set against an alternative classification, based more simply on scale and function: the multi-townland farmer (holding more than, say, 400 statute acres), subletting in part; the multi-townland *rentier* not engaged in farming operations; the farmer of a townland or less, subletting in part; and the townland *rentier*, probably non-resident.

(a) *The Protestant chief tenant.* The seventeenth-century inheritance is clearest here and in (b), the Catholic ex-freeholder group. The existence of large Protestant tenants, especially in areas that had experienced formal plantations, derived in large measure from the legal obligations of the original planters, under their patents, to settle English and Scottish tenants on their new property. Indeed, the Ulster and particularly the Munster plantations

23. R. D. C. Black, *Economic Thought and the Irish Question, 1817-1870* (Cambridge, 1960), pp 6, 209, 211.
24. Quoted in George O'Brien, *The Economic History of Ireland from the Union to the Famine* (London, 1921), p. 93.

implied a hierarchical structure on an estate from the beginning, with the larger tenants covenanting to organize the enclosure and improvement of land based on the townland unit, *i.e.* in farms of approximately 300-400 statute acres.[25] If in much of Ulster, and in parts of Leinster and Munster, the Protestant chief tenant was common enough by 1700, that very year almost marks the end of a century of English and Scottish immigration, the end of a supply which had greatly fluctuated.[26] As a rule, the demand of landowners for potential tenants of some substance had sufficiently outstripped supply to lead to the creation of distinctly favourable leases, granted to English and Scottish tenants for terms of 31 or 61 years, three lives or even three lives renewable. The level of rents, lower than that sought from Irish tenants, reflected both the general preference for the Protestant tenant and the greater security of rent payment expected. The motives behind the seventeenth-century landlord's preference for the non-Irish tenant extended beyond questions of legal obligation or regularity of rent payment, for the basic assumption of the British interest was that the Protestant tenant, all other things being equal, was more likely to attempt the range of agricultural and land-use changes that a landlord sought in order to raise the value of his estate. Such could not to be expected of the Irish gentry; thus the agent of the Petty property in Kerry in the 1690s, observing the low rental of the estate, wondered 'what the same would yield had their natures allowed the Irish gentlemen to build good houses, plant orchards, set out fields with double ditch and quick and other improvements as by their leases they [were] bound to do'.[27] Even without allowing for early population growth it can be assumed that the Protestant chief tenant was a middleman, in so far as part of his holding would be sublet in a variety of ways, depending on the location and agriculture of the district, and the point in time considered.

(b) *The Catholic ex-freeholder.* In many non-plantation areas the old Catholic families, best described as ex-freeholders or ex-proprietors, continued as 31-year leaseholders, or, through 'protection', on longer *de facto* agreements. This group can be seen most clearly in Munster; how far they survived elsewhere is problem-

25.   The initial plantation arrangements envisaged a variety of tenant classes, all holding directly from the undertaker, but the low level of subsequent immigration defeated such intentions: see 'Ulster Plantation Papers' ed. T. W. Moody, *Analecta Hibernica,* viii (1938), 196-7; and Robert Dunlop, 'The Plantation in Munster, 1584-1589', *E.H.R.*, iii (1888), 257.
26.   L. M. Cullen, 'Population Trends in Seventeenth-Century Ireland', *Economic and Social Review,* vi (1975), 151-8.
27.   R.I.A., Ms. 12.L.2 (Orpen Mss.), p. 59.

atical, although even in Ulster examples (such as the MacDonnells of Antrim) can be found. Some families of course were to conform in religion and become socially indistinguishable from (a), but in the poorer and more backward areas there were many equivalents of the famous Mahonys of Dunloe and the O'Connells of Derrynane. Commenting on this group, Sir Robert Southwell wrote in 1681: 'there is not among them one in twenty that turns their minds to any industrious course, but expect to be regarded as unfortunate gentlemen, who yesterday lost an estate and were to be restored tomorrow.'[28] Eighteenth-century criticism of them, less extreme than this, was not unlike that directed towards the Highland tacksmen, but they continued to survive because, given the slower economic development of the districts where they were commonest, it was they alone who could make a cash rent, and having residual authority in their localities they controlled law and order.[29] With the general rise in land values in the course of the eighteenth century the position of this group, at least in Munster, was weakened by the incursions of the grazier and the lease speculator.[30]

(c) *The lease speculator.* The lease speculator (or land-jobber) covers the category of tenant who took a lease purely as an investment, having perhaps bid against the occupiers, or against a previous resident tenant who had gradually become a subletter, like O'Hara's gentlemen farmers of the 1750s who, having 'thriven, are setting their land and lessening their farms'.[31] A lease speculator, where an ongoing rise in land values was anticipated, might seek no initial profit from subletting if short under-leases were given, but would bid high in the confidence of a future return.[32] This phenomenon of the non-farming tenant, jobbing in leases, seems to have been a distinctly eighteenth-century one, being particularly associated with periods of rapid inflation in land values; certainly the printed evidence suggests that the 1750s and 1760s, together with the period of the Revolutionary and Napoleonic wars, saw the most pronounced stages of this development, when the *rentier*/lease-jobber seems to have been a major force determin-

28.   *H.M.C. Egmont,* ii, 115, Sir Robert Southwell to Sir John Perceval, 16 May 1682.
29.   Cf. E. R. Cregeen, 'The Tacksmen and Their Successors', *Scottish Studies,* xiii (1969), 93-144.
30.   This is implied, for instance, in Bishop Moylan's remarks on Kerry in K. O'Shea, 'Bishop Moylan's Relatio Status, 1785', *Journal of the Kerry Archaeological and Historical Society,* vii (1974), 24-5.
31.   P.R.O.N.I., T.2812/19 (O'Hara Mss.), Charles O'Hara, 'Account of Sligo in the Eighteenth Century', *sub* 1758.
32.   Townsend, *Survey of Cork,* p. 185.

ing rent levels.[33] Any survey of eighteenth-century newspaper
advertisements highlights the openness of the lease market, even in
fairly short tenures. Indeed, the penal legislation against Catholic
investment in fee simple land and in mortgages probably diverted
investment into short leasehold interests.[34]

The contrast here with contemporary England lay not in the
Penal Laws and their effects, or indeed in the rapid rise in land
values, but in the flexibility of the lease instrument itself. Aspects
of the differences in leasing practice are well known; they were
summed up by a King's County agent when briefing his employer
in 1714:

> You are to observe that tenants will not hold land in Ireland
> from year to year as in England but expect leases of 21
> years, sometime 40 years or three lives. For in Ireland the
> tenants make all repairs and improvements at their own
> charge, consequently lands there must be leased out or lie
> waste.[35]

The lease in fact developed precociously in Ireland as the mode of
estate management from the early seventeenth century, being both
in plantation and non-plantation districts the normal mode of
letting land. The discontinuity of land ownership in the seventeenth century, and the management problems of the new owners,
created a need for an explicit contractual relationship with a tenant.
The large size of some estates, the fragmented nature of many
grants of land and the partial absenteeism of the new owners ruled
out the possibility of developing some quasi-manorial structure.
Direct large-scale farming by landowners, although apparent in some
counties during the seventeenth century, was in the long run quite
eclipsed by the practice of renting out, usually to those who could
make a payment in cash rather than in kind. Because leasing in
many areas was imposed on a pattern of traditional, overwhelmingly
subsistence farming, ill-suited to the rigidity of a formal legal
contract, and because landowners, at least up to the early eighteenth century, were predisposed to let to British tenants where
possible, extensive leases were granted to larger tenants on favour-

33. Young, *Tour in Ireland,* i, 97; ii, 8; [Townsend], *View of Agriculture,*
p. 21; Parker, *Observations,* p. 134; Isaac Weld, *Statistical Survey of the
County of Roscommon* (Dublin, 1832), p. 667.
34. Cf. B.L., Add. Mss. 46,968, fos. 10-11, Berkeley Taylor to Sir John
Perceval, 11 Mar. 1716-17.
35. P.R.O.N.I., D.607/A/11 (Downshire Mss.), abstract of Mr Meredyth's
letter, 16 July 1714.

able terms; the relative length of leases and tenants' security for the duration gave rise to the market in leases, thanks to one vital factor, the *de facto* toleration by landowners of lease alienation. The consequent market in unexpired lease terms was a vital dimension for the lease speculator, both facilitating entry into lease investment and permitting the realization of such assets if required.[36]

(d) *The perpetuity tenant.* This type of tenant was generally the holder of what was a legal innovation of seventeenth-century Ireland, a lease for three lives, renewable for ever. This approached the absolute security of a fee farm interest but for the obligation on the tenant to enter a new name in the lease on the payment of a fine every time a named life died. The fine, which could vary from a certain quantity of claret to the equivalent of one year's rent, was fixed, as of course was the rent itself. Such leaseholders were tenants — and middlemen — in a legal sense only, but they had close affinities in origin with Protestant chief tenants on determinable tenures. In the 1840s the Devon Commission believed that one seventh of all land in the country was held under this form of tenure,[37] and larger, more improbable, estimates of its extent had been made in 1780, when the Tenantry Bill was being debated in the Irish parliament. This piece of legislation, designed to protect the position of a lives-renewable lessee who had omitted to renew on the 'falling in' of a life, was made necessary after a ruling by the British House of Lords upholding the right of a head landlord to repossess in such a situation. The broad-based — and hardly disinterested — support that the bill received is a measure of the importance of renewable tenure to many parliament-men, even if its proponents suggested that it would help 'the peasantry of Ireland.'[38]

Commentators at the end of the eighteenth century often expressed surprise at the folly of their ancestors who had set such leases, thereby losing control of their estates and failing to derive any benefit from the enhanced value of lands. But such opinion overlooked the recentness of the assumption that land was a continually appreciating asset (as it seemed in 1800), and the importance that landlords a century before had attached to retaining a group of substantial British tenants on an estate, who could be relied on to maintain a regular payment of rent. It is true

36. Cf. Crawford, *'Landlord-Tenant Relations in Ulster'*, 10.
37. Quoted in Maguire, *Downshire Estates*, p. 110.
38. M. R. O'Connell, *Irish Politics and Social Conflict in the Age of the American Revolution* (Philadelphia, [1965], pp 266-81.

that in the course of the eighteenth century such tenures were usually granted because of the short-term financial needs of the landowner, who would grant perpetuities at a reduced rent in return for fining off the amount reduced at the going rate of interest. Absentees in particular appear to have used this device, sometimes to raise funds for the purchase of lands in England, or alternatively to finance their conspicuous consumption, as the history of the last and famous earl of Cork and Burlington demonstrates: he was forced by the debts arising from his architectural extravagance to sell and to fine off in perpetuity tenures between 1728 and 1738 some £300,000-worth of property in Counties Waterford and Cork.[39]

The experience on institutional estates was not strikingly different. Head tenants on such estates, *i.e.* churchlands, the estates of Trinity College, of the London companies and of various smaller institutions, were often in very similar circumstances to the tenants of perpetual absentees. The eighteenth-century development of the London companies' estates awaits definitive study but it seems that the practice was to grant relatively long determinable leases, such as the 61 years/three lives formula used on the Drapers' and Fishmongers' estates, to large Protestant chief tenants.[40] Here the convenience factor in such an arrangement was probably uppermost. On the huge but highly fragmented Trinity College estates, embracing over one per cent of the whole country, leases were restricted by law to 21 years, but were renewed every year at the same rent, although with an adjustable fine. By the eighteenth century it seems to have been exceptionally rare for a College tenant not to get a renewal; generally tenants appear to have been large, usually men who combined College tenancies with other leasehold or fee simple property.[41] Churchland — or at least its major component, bishop-land — was normally let on a similar system of 21-year tenures, normally renewable with flexible fining, although the comments on the poverty of churchland subtenants

39.   For a comment on part of this sale, see *H.M.C. Egmont Diary*, ii, 452. For an example from the early nineteenth century of a resident, but indebted, peer acting in a similar way, see also W. A. Maguire, 'The 1822 Settlement of the Donegall Estates', *Ir. Econ. and Soc. Hist.*, iii (1976), 21-32.
40.   Olive Robinson, 'The London Companies as Progressive Landlords in Nineteenth-Century Ireland', *Economic History Review* (ser. 2), xv (1962-3), 104-5.
41.   F. J. Carney, 'Pre-Famine Irish Population: The Evidence from the Trinity College Estates', *Ir. Econ. and Soc. Hist.*, ii (1975), 38; W. J. Lowe, 'Landlord and Tenant on the Estate of Trinity College, Dublin 1851-1903', *Hermathena*, cxx (1976), 5-7.

would imply that renewal was less automatic than on College land.[42]

Tenants in this and the previous category were to survive on the whole until the nineteenth-century Land Acts, long after most intermediate tenures had been swept away.

Many paths could lead, therefore, to a situation in which middlemen became prevalent on an estate or in a district by the late eighteenth century. Yet some who found themselves classed as middlemen by that time had only comparatively recently become subletters of land, because of changes in relative agricultural prices. The main example of this was the grazier (*i.e.* the fatstock producer). Graziers as a class had been the main target in pamphleteers' criticism of rural society for much of the century, until they were replaced by what seemed a new set of malefactors, middlemen. Reacting to harvest failures and the apparent sharp decline in tillage, the polemical writers, particularly of the 1720s and 1730s, had attacked the grazier as a depopulator and an agent of famine, in terms quite as bitter as those directed against the sheep-master and engrosser in Tudor England. However, the significance of the grazier has been exaggerated,[43] for the rise of great bullock farms and sheep-walks displaced small tenants and village settlement only on the better grazing lands, notably in central Leinster, Roscommon, east Galway, Limerick and of course Tipperary, where complaints against the sheepmaster can be traced back to the seventeenth century.[44] The relatively favourable prices for beef and dairy products in the 1750s and 1760s accentuated a pattern of block leasing to graziers that in general had begun to emerge in the first quarter of the century.[45] The image of the grazier as a depopulator might suggest that he was the antithesis of the middleman; as Charles O'Hara in his survey of eighteenth-century Sligo wrote:

By the year [17]20 the demands for store cattle for the south had reached us and the breeding business grew more profit-

42.   W. D. Killen, *The Ecclesiastical History of Ireland* ... (2 vols., London, 1875), ii, 312n.; J. McEvoy, *Statistical Survey of the County of Tyrone* (Dublin, 1802), p. 101. For evidence that suggests greater security of tenure on churchland, see D. J. Dickson, 'The Barony of Inishowen in the Century before the Famine' (Dublin Univ. B.A. thesis 1969), p. 9.
43.   L. M. Cullen, 'Problems in the Interpretation and Revision of Eighteenth-Century Irish Economic History', *Transactions of the Royal Historical Society* (ser. 5), xvii (1967), 10, 18-19.
44.   Cf. B.L., Add. Mss. 21,127, fo. 54, Richard Cox's notes on Sir William Petty's *Political Anatomy*.
45.   Cf. 'Mallow District in 1773', *Journal of the Cork Historical and Archaeological Society* (ser. 2), xxi (1915), 22-23.

able. Many villagers were turned off and the lands which they had occupied stocked with cattle. Some of these village tenants took mountain farms but many more went off ... [about] 1726 the graziers, encouraged by the markets, first raised the price of land in order to cast the cottagers out of their farms.[46]

However by the 1750s domestic industry, he believed, was allowing the village tenants to re-establish themselves.[47] And with the rise of land prices in the mid-1760s, O'Hara noted that 'even the regular farmers bid high [for leases], well knowing that if they can't make their rent by stock, they can set to the lower people who make their rent by labour and industry'.[48] Thus when cattle prices fell in 1772 he observed that 'the graziers and jobbers have been so great losers by the fall of cattle that they are all intent on setting their land'.[49] In effect, therefore, graziers, in an environment where the small-holders had increased bidding power, could easily become in part middlemen. Thus in neighbouring Mayo, Arthur Young found that 'farms are very extensive ... all stock ones, with portions re-let to cottars who are the principal arable men here'; 'most of the tillage of the country is performed by little fellows, cottars and tenants to these large farmers'.[50] And in much of the secondary grazing areas, and in lands close to markets for grain, the expansion of tillage in the following half-century effected the transformation of many graziers into non-farming middlemen.[51]

4

Such a typology as suggested above ignores the degree of regional differentiation that economic development was helping to create. But eighteenth-century regional research is very patchy; our knowledge, for instance, of the agricultural structure of the greater Dublin hinterland is very limited. However, by taking specifically south Munster and parts of Ulster it is possible to make some regional observations.

In the former area — the greater Cork region — middlemen of categories (a) and (b), members of substantial Protestant and old Catholic families, were the normal head tenants in the earlier part of the eighteenth century. They combined a degree of mixed

46. P.R.O.N.I., T.2812/19, Charles O'Hara, 'Account of Sligo ...'
47. *Ibid., sub* 1758, 1762.
48. *Ibid., sub* 1765.
49. *Ibid., sub* 1772.
50. Young, *Tour in Ireland,* i, 367, 351.
51. Cf. Wakefield, *Account of Ireland,* i, 267.

farming with subletting, mainly to partnership farmers. In the environment of a low, yet under-employed population, labour was the resource that the chief tenantry could harness, both by their sub-leasing to small farmers who could bring in marginal land, by po-tato cultivation, and by their employing labourers in extensive farming operations – in planting, enclosure and building (and the degree to which this type of improvement occurred before 1750 should not be underrated). They were also involved heavily in the dominant regional specialization, butter production, as master-dairymen letting out milch cattle (as Kearney was to point out).[52]

Landowners, while not opposing this state of things, sought to prevent the accumulation of leases in the hands of one man: a single townland was the desirable farm unit.[53] Where leases fell – or were surrendered – at a time of heavy arrears, as in the 1740s, it is possible to find a foretaste of late eighteenth-century arguments concerning intermediate tenure. Thus the first earl of Egmont, when faced with arreared tenants on his north-west Cork estate in 1743, observed of undertenants,

> My land seems more exposed to be injured by 'em whilst under a head tenant, as than if they possessed their portions in their own right, and I am almost as great a sufferer by more of my head tenants when any of the others breaks, as I should by these under ones, for my head tenants made that pretence to run in arrear ... whereas when undertenants have land of their own it is an encouragement for them to be industrious, all the profit they make being their own, and enabling them to pay their rent with ease and pleasure. But this is supposing they have some stock of their own to put on their small farms, which I believe they generally have not: yet some may be found. I acknowledge this may be some more pains to my steward to look after them, yet the bailiffs whom I have appointed for boundkeepers might ease him, if they did their duty ...[54]

52. This section is based on the author's research in progress on the Cork region in the eighteenth century.
53. The townland seems in practice to have been the denomination most used, although different rules-of-thumb could be employed: in 1713 Sir John Perceval resolved to make 500 acres the ceiling to be let to one man (B.L., Add. Mss. 46,965, fo. 148, Perceval to Berkeley Taylor, 17 July 1713); by 1726, with the rise in land values, he informed his agent, 'I should be ... well pleased that a less quantity were given to each particular one, and a tenant of a hundred pound is I think the best on several accounts' (B.L., Add. Mss. 46,977, fo. 30, Perceval to Taylor, 23 July 1726).
54. B.L., Add. Mss. 46,994, fo. 86, Egmont (formerly Sir John Perceval) to Richard Purcell, 29 Dec. 1743.

Egmont's agent resisted such a policy. When his employer proposed to divide up some lands out of lease several years later, the
man on the spot countered:

> I doubt not but they may be set for more by dividing them to
> different tenants, than by setting them to one; but I am of
> opinion that the loss by the death, elopement or failure of low
> tenants will always far exceed any advantage which may be
> had by setting land to them; and in general they hurt land, by
> burning and harassing it, and making a number of useless
> ditches; so that if I had an estate of my own to let, I would
> always choose to set to a wealthy man, who could bear the
> shock of bad prices for a year or two, or the loss of part of his
> stock by diseases or severe weather ...[55]

The key issue here, made explicit by both correspondents, was that
of 'substance', the wealth of undertenants. Sometimes the criterion
used to determine whether a potential tenant was sufficiently solvent was ownership of assets equivalent to one year's rent: below
that, the risk was considered too great. This was usually related, as
Egmont suggested, to cattle ownership. The evolution of a stock-
owning tenantry who could challenge the economic arguments used
here by the agent was a gradual process in Munster, but it accel-
erated after 1750. However, this trend is less visible in restrospect
because it was accompanied by a general demographic expansion,
with a particular growth in cottierization under the farmers. In
other words, undertenants of the 1740s, solvent enough to be
direct tenants by, say, the 1770s, were themselves increasingly
tempted to sublet portions of their farms because of the growing
demand of cottiers for holdings.

When one turns to Ulster it is clear that in the central and
eastern parts of the province the disappearance of the old-style
chief tenant came much earlier than in south Munster and that the
grazier and the lease speculator were not prominent (if one overlooks such grand exceptions as Thomas Gregg and Waddell
Cunningham). The chief explanation for this situation, as the work
of W. H. Crawford has shown, was the greater bidding power of
resident occupiers, benefiting directly or indirectly from the growing rural linen industry.[56] The process was most pronounced in the
districts that specialized in the weaving of fine linens, through
which Dean Henry passed in 1739 and commented on 'the happy

55. B.L., Add. Mss. 46,997, fo. 74, Purcell to Egmont, 2 Sept. 1746.
56. Crawford, *'Landlord-Tenant Relations in Ulster'*, 13-14.

success which this method of dividing the land into small partitions
and encouraging the cottager and the manufacturer has had in
enriching both landlord and tenant'.[57] Smallholder-weavers were
able to gain this direct relationship with their landlord because
of their sufficient substance, and because what they sought were
accommodation holdings, not viable farm units.

The linen industry was diffused over the greater part of the
province by the time of Young's tour, yet he noticed the existence
of middlemen on the earl of Antrim's estate; also in County
Donegal and in Fermanagh. And it would seem from other evidence
that in parts of Counties Monaghan and Tyrone, even where linen
manufacture had developed considerably, the small men had less
success in their attempts to become direct tenants.[58] The earl of
Donegall's Inishowen estate in north-east Donegal, the largest individual grant of land in the Ulster plantation, is a well documented
illustration of this.[59] Prior to a general reletting of the estate in the
late 1760s there were 48 tenants, each holding on average over
four townlands. The reletting took place against the background of
Donegall's indebtedness, so that fines equivalent to about four
years' rent were sought from prospective tenants, thus weakening
the poorer undertenants' chances of obtaining direct leases. In the
event some 140 tenants received leases, but although about three
quarters of these lived on their holdings they must all have been
middlemen in part, for few of the leases were for less than 100
statute acres. There was a constraint in the degree to which direct
letting was possible: the Donegall family adhered to the principle
of letting to Protestants only, as a Catholic undertenant observed in
1765 in a letter to one of the O'Connells of Kerry:

> The original Irish are very happy in your part of the [country]
> ... here are few else except hewers of wood and drawers of
> water; in short, we are in the most abject slavery in this

57. P.R.O.N.I., Mic. 196, Dean Henry, 'Hints towards a Natural and Topo-
graphical History of the Counties Sligo, Donegal, Fermanagh and Lough
Erne', p. 69.
58. Young, *Tour in Ireland*, i, 215, 238, 261, 290; for the Bath estate, see
L. Marron, 'The Bath Estate, 1700-77', *Clogher Record*, vi, no. 2 (1967),
334-5; and 'The Bath Estate, 1777-1800', *ibid.*, no. 3 (1968), 554-64; for the
Abercorn estate, W. H. Crawford, 'Landlord and Tenant in Ulster in the
Eighteenth Century' (unpub. paper).
59. The following is based on Dickson, 'The Barony of Inishowen', pp 2-13.

barony of Inishowen especially, and not a foot of land to be renewed to any as prime tenant to our landlord the earl of Donegall, that is of the old stamp.[60]

A contrasting sentiment was expressed a few years later by a Protestant neighbour who had secured a number of 61-year leases in the reletting, when writing to his son: 'never let it slip from your mind that what we have now is of short duration, that we must and ought to make a fortune out of our Donegal leases equal to what we now have ...'[61] By the 1820s there were over 210 head tenants on this estate, yet this does not indicate the eclipse of middlemen, given the parellel growth of population and sub-division in the barony.[62]

5

Developments in other regions are much less clear and to a considerable extent the arguments of this paper are drawn from the evidence of Munster and Ulster. However, if one returns to Arthur Young, over 30 references to aspects of middle tenure around the country can be found in his *Tour in Ireland,* some of baffling ambiguity.[63] The general impression that he appears to have gained can be summarized thus: that the system was in decline or had disappeared in east Leinster and much of Ulster; that it survived to a degree on the Ulster periphery; that reletting was an intrinsic part of the stock-farming of Connaught; that in the parts of the south midlands and north Munster which he visited large-scale farming with extensive cottier labour varied with zones of partnership tenure; that in south Munster middlemen mainly took the form of master-dairymen or jobbers in leases, and that both phenomena were beginning to decline in importance.

What Young would seem to have been witnessing over most of the country was the early phase of the dissolution of multi-townland middle tenure. With agricultural change and population growth the multi-townland farmer was becoming the multi-

60. N.L.I., Reports on Mss. in Private Collections, ed. J. F. Ainsworth, no. 361, O'Connell Fitzsimon Mss., John Dougherty to Morgan O'Connell, 22 Mar. 1765.
61. Harvey Mss. (Mr Ian Harvey, Ballymena, Co. Antrim), George Harvey to John Harvey, 1 Dec. 1770.
62. Dickson, 'The Barony of Inishowen', p. 25.
63. Young, *Tour in Ireland,* i, 29, 47, 60, 88, 97, 106, 118-9, 152, 206, 215, 226, 238, 255, 261, 284, 290, 295, 302, 332-3, 351, 362, 365, 367, 392, 404, 407, 411; ii, 8, 27, 122, 124-5, 221, 270, 276.

---

townland *rentier*, and even for the medium-sized lessee in non-grazing districts the relative profits of direct farming and subletting were changing. The head tenant who at the beginning of a three-lives lease would have been a farmer-employer likely to improve, was leaving heirs who at the end of the lease had turned profit-renters and could be regarded as middlemen. There was also a political factor: the value of the Protestant tenant on a lives lease to a landowner involved in county politics fell sharply with the new political situation after 1793, and on the estates of some of the political landlords there was a systematic creation of small one-life freeholds in order to enfranchise the Catholic tenantry.

If it is at least understandable why late eighteenth-century landowners could regard their middle tenants as parasites – in so far as they were living on an inflating profit-rent to which it seemed they contributed nothing – how much was the other charge, that they had become tyrants, also justifiable? Because of the polemical nature of the attack one can assume a degree of hyperbole. The issue centres on the question of leasing: to what extent did the various types of middlemen have a contractual relationship with undertenants and under what conditions? On this answer hangs much else, the degree for instance to which the majority of the population of Ireland enjoyed the benefits of the secular upward movement of agricultural prices. Writers on middlemen were rather careless in observing this problem, some assuming no leases, others emphasizing the element of duty-work.[64] One can be certain that variations in practice were great in different farming systems and over time. Without the survival in any quantity of farming records, it is very difficult to go beyond what is hinted at in landed estate records; from the latter it would seem that for the greater part of the century subleasing on terms ranging from seven to 31 years was common enough, except in the more backward districts where informal arrangements probably operated, and in those regions where cottier subtenants were more strictly farm labourers, holding from year to year.[65] As long as there was a relative under-supply of

64. For explicit references to leasing by middlemen, see Sir R. C. Hoare, *Journal of a Tour in Ireland, A.D. 1806* (London, 1807), p. 307 n.; M.G. Moyles and Padraig de Brún, 'Charles O'Brien's Survey of Kerry, 1800', *Jnl. Kerry Arch. and Hist. Soc.*, ii (1969), 108; Townsend, *Survey of Cork*, p. 184.
65. For Inishowen subleasing, see Dickson, 'The Barony of Inishowen', pp 9-13; for confirmation of subleasing in north Cork, B.L., Add. Mss. 46,968, fo. 52, Berkeley Taylor to Sir John Perceval, 18 June 1717; B.L., Add. Mss. 46,995, fo. 9, Richard Purcell to Egmont, 27 Jan. 1743-4. It was part of the argument against middlemen that occupiers receiving leases directly from

would-be farmers in the choppy economic conditions of the first half of the century, the lease would be a stabilizing force. The extent to which undertenants gained as leaseholders depended of course on the conditions and length of tenure, but probably the greatest variation in experience came from the actual timing of the setting of the lease: where a contract was negotiated in a period of depressed prices or economic uncertainty, there was a prospect of gain for the lessee in the ensuing upturn, whereas those entering farms at periods of high prices stood a greater chance of encountering difficulties.

One practice that seems to have been restricted to those parts of Ulster where reletting continued in the late eighteenth century was that of 'protection leasing'. This apparently took the form of a direct contract between head landlord and undertenant, guaranteeing the lease held by the undertenant from the middleman in the event of any change in the status of the latter's relationship with the head landlord, such as would follow the sale of the main lease during its term.[66] It would seem that the undertenant was also protected from any liability for arrears of rent owed by the head tenant. Where such a guarantee did not operate, conflict sometimes occurred between undertenants and the head landlord when the former's stock was distrained to cover a head tenant's arrears. This manifestly inequitable procedure could trigger agrarian disturbance.[67]

6

If there was such a multiplicity of conditions and categories associated with the phenomenon of middlemen, how far can one generalize about their demise? Failure to specify what type of middlemen are being referred to has caused some of the recent dispute among historians. To some extent it must have been a two-way process. *Multi-townland* tenants were failing to have leases renewed from the 1760s — a result of the great rise in land values and the relative improvement in undertenants' circumstances — but, as lives leases set before this period did not run out until the early decades of the nineteenth century, it was a long-drawn out process. Yet the speculation in *townland* leases obviously continued, and it

landlords would enjoy longer terms: cf. Surrey R.O., Guildford Muniment Room, Midleton Mss., letterbook 1782-4, p. 20, Midleton to Michael McCarthy, 19 Nov. 1782.
66. Dickson, 'The Barony of Inishowen', p. 13.
67. B.L., Add. Mss. 46,997, fo. 100, Richard Purcell to Egmont, 8 Dec. 1746.

G

was the jobbers in these who contributed in some districts to the pushing up of rent levels during the French wars. But after the extended growth in population and cottierization by the 1820s, the position of subletters of even townland units was being challenged.

The role of absentees in this process is complex. When John Foster, speaking of Louth, told Arthur Young 'that the system of letting farms to be relet to lower tenants was going out very much: it is principally upon the estates of absentees, whose agents think only of the most rent from the most solvent tenant', he was asserting a belief that would still be current in the 1820s.[68] Absentees were generally among the larger property owners, where the management problems of a huge tenantry would be greatest. Yet it was on absentee estates that some of the more determined removals of middlemen occured, from the early case of the Holroyd estate in Meath in the 1760s to the London companies in Derry in the 1820s.[69] Perhaps it was easier for an outsider to break through the web of vested interest that seems to have defeated a resident such as Lord Kingsborough. With the greater wealth and social prestige of the absentee peer went a greater social distance from his gentleman tenants, permitting a greater freedom of movement; the bonds of blood and social intercourse were probably constraints on the actions of the small resident landlord.

The prejudice against middlemen, associated with the period of their decline, must to some extent have been consolidated by its very impact on the behaviour of the objects of attack. It seems reasonable to suppose that a middleman, fearing non-renewal, was more likely to become the stereotyped non-improver. And on some estates middlemen carried out evictions (or systematically refused to renew subleases) in order to appear at the end of a head lease as the sole occupying tenants.[70] Such behaviour may have obscured the issue but did little to alter the process of direct letting.

With the arrival of the post-war depression, exemplified on many estates by an arreared middle tenantry and increasing congestion, direct leasing to undertenants as such was no longer an answer to the problems of estate management. For, as the old-style middlemen were cleared away, the cottier population multiplied beneath the farming class, or alternatively the subdivision of farms themselves continued beyond the control of landlords. Consolidations seemed the rational solution, yet as recent work has shown, it

68. Young, *Tour in Ireland,* i, 152.
69. *Ibid.,* 47; Robinson, *'London Companies', passim.*
70. *E.g.* Marron, *'Bath Estate, 1770-1800',* 559-60.

was seldom achieved in the pre-Famine decades.[71] The scale of this problem is illustrated by the tenural position on the Trinity College estates in three counties in 1843: in County Armagh, under the eight near-perpetuity College tenants, there were 1,086 tenants, subletting to 1,160 labourers, some of them in turn letting out land to 765 families. In Kerry, in very different economic circumstances, the College tenants were leasing farms to 840 families who sublet to 1,790, who in turn relet to 1,248. In a less congested county, Fermanagh, there were 597 tenants to the College lessees, and 193 presumably labouring families under them.[72] Such a multiplicity of sub-townland letting – a consequence of demography, and one in which *bona fide* farmers were the beneficiaries – was not, it should be emphasized, what the eighteenth-century debate over middlemen was all about.[73]

71. Cf. J. S. Donnelly, *Nineteenth-Century Cork*, pp 52-72; Maguire, *Downshire Estates*, pp 151-3, 250.
72. T.C.D., Ms. V/Mun./78/61.
73. I should like to thank the following for permission to draw on their material: Mr Ian Harvey and Lord Redesdale; also the British Library Board, the Trustees of the National Library of Ireland and the Deputy Keeper of the of the Records, Public Record Office of Northern Ireland, and the Librarian of the Royal Irish Academy.

CHANGE IN ULSTER IN THE LATE EIGHTEENTH CENTURY

W. H. Crawford

Many historians have speculated on the nature of political events in Ulster in the late eighteenth century and have assessed their influence on Irish history. Although they have not considered whether these events were reflecting fundamental changes in the economy and society of the province, there are good grounds for such an assumption. Contemporaries commented on the growing prosperity of the province and the great increase in its population. The chief source of this prosperity was the linen industry, but it was supplemented in the last quarter of the century by the rising tide of exports of farm products, mainly cattle on the hoof, pork and butter. What contemporaries did not remark was the impact on Ulster of the revolution taking place in the British economy. In economic terms Ulster's earnings from linen and agriculture enabled the province to pay for manufactured goods. The growing volume of imports and exports stimulated the Ulster ports and began to shift the centre of economic activity in the province away from the 'linen triangle' (the area enclosed between Dungannon, Lisburn and Newry) into Belfast. In social terms the British industrial revolution helped to alter the balance between the forces of the establishment and its opponents while it excited several major interests, especially the presbyterians and the merchants, to agitate for political and social reform.

The economic and social structure of Ulster in the middle of the eighteenth century reflected the character of its colonization during the seventeenth century and its subsequent exploitation. Although in the early seventeenth century landlords had been granted extensive powers under royal patents, they were able to realize the value of their estates only by leasing land for rents to tenants, since they themselves did not command the capital to develop these resources on their own. Until the Restoration they found it difficult to obtain British colonists and when the colonists did appear landlords had first to attract them to settle on their estates by the offer of leases on good terms and then to encourage them to stay by treating them well and nursing them through years of bad harvests or other agricultural disasters.[1] Many thousands of English and Scots entered the province in the half-century between 1660 and 1710 but the slowness of the colonization and the ability

1.   See W. H. Crawford, 'Landlord-Tenant Relations in Ulster 1609-1820', *Ir. Econ. and Soc. Hist.*, ii (1975), 7-9.

of the Irish to maintain some sort of position, especially in the remoter areas, reflected the relative strength of the natives and newcomers. In the early eighteenth century landlords were compelled by the necessity of securing some return on their lands to lease large tracts to substantial British tenants. Where this class of men was absent they were inclined to let to partnership groups of lesser individuals who were bound jointly for the rents: these lessees included Irishmen.[2] Land was leased by the townland: in the poorer and remoter areas by individual townlands, but in the more improved and cultivated districts by fractions of townlands when landlords were in a position to select tenants.

The settlement and development of the land required a substantial and increasing population. From the 1690s until about 1745 the population of Ulster fluctuated with attacks of disease and famine, and then, as elsewhere in Europe generally, it began to increase, at first steadily and then rapidly over the remainder of the century.[3] In Ulster population increase led to widespread land reclamation from the waste. The family unit reclaimed marginal land with the potato and the children of the tenant farmer were rewarded by their father with portions of the original holding.[4] The practice of the subdivision of holdings was permitted by landlords who themselves often granted leases direct to the subtenants on the expiry of the main lease. A lease confirmed security of tenure for the period of the lease and so a tenant was able to enjoy the value of the improvements he had made: that was the reason for the existence of so many three-life leases in Ulster in the late eighteenth century. As the agent for the Abercorn estate explained to his master in 1749: 'I have found the tenants complain of the short tenure they had, and seemed always to hold twenty-one years leases in great contempt, which they said hindered them improving their farms.'[5] The lease was often used as security to raise capital. Native Irish tenants benefited as well as the British, although their thirty-one year leases might be shorter in practice than the usual Protestant lease for three lives. The subletting of holdings by

2.   See W. Macafee, 'The Colonisation of the Maghera Area in South Derry during the Seventeenth and Eighteenth Centuries', *Ulster Folklife*, 23 (1977).
3.   D. Dickson, 'Irish Population in the Eighteenth Century: Some Reconsiderations', *Bulletin of the Irish Committee of Historical Sciences* (ser. 3), no. 1 (1974); V. Morgan, 'Mortality in Magherafelt, County Londonderry, in the Early Eighteenth Century', *I.H.S.*, xix (1974), 125-35.
4.   C. Coote, *Statistical Survey of the County of Armagh* (Dublin, 1804), pp 136-7.
5.   P.R.O.N.I., T.2541/IA1/1D/44 (Abercorn Mss.), Nathaniel Nisbitt to Abercorn, 24 Feb. 1749.

farmers to subtenants and of patches of potato ground to cottiers was also encouraged by the absence of good foreign markets for agricultural produce in the mid-eighteenth century: thus farmers found it more profitable to sublet rather than farm the land, especially where dense population created a strong demand for land.

It is probable that agriculture would have remained mainly subsistence in character because Ulster was less well placed than the provinces of Leinster and Munster, which served the expanding economy of Dublin and the Atlantic victualling trade respectively. In fact, it is likely that it was this competitive weakness that had caused the English colonists in the Lagan valley to concentrate their resources on the linen industry after the Cattle Acts of 1667 and 1681 restricted the cattle trade (which had been an important Ulster export in the early seventeenth century).[6] It is certain, however, that the linen industry succeeded because it was able to produce an increasing quantity of good quality linens for the growing British and colonial markets throughout the eighteenth century.[7] Contemporaries commented as early as 1740 on the impact which the domestic linen industry had made on the linen counties: their population had increased so much that they were no longer able to feed themselves but had to draw supplies of cattle and oatmeal as well as their yarn from counties as far away as Sligo.[8] The industry encouraged the employment of young children, and the opportunities it provided for young people to establish and maintain homes stimulated subdivision on a remarkable scale, so that in the linen triangle substantial farmers disappeared in the flood of weavers. The late 1740s saw a further

6. See W. H. Crawford, 'The Origins of the Linen Industry in North Armagh and the Lagan Valley', *Ulster Folklife*, xvii (1971), 42-51. For the importance of the cattle trade in seventeenth-century Ireland, see D. Woodward, 'The Anglo-Irish Livestock Trade in the Seventeenth Century', *I.H.S.*, xviii (1973), 489-523.
7. N. B. Harte, 'The Rise of Protection and the English Linen Trade, 1690-1780', *Textile History and Economic History* eds. N. B. Harte and K. G. Ponting (Manchester, 1974), pp 74-112.
8. P.R.O.N.I., T.2812/19/1 (O'Hara Mss.), Charles O'Hara, 'Account of Sligo in the Eighteenth Century', *sub* 1735; Armagh Public Library, Lodge Mss., 'County Monaghan by Archdeacon Cranston and Mr Lucas, January 8th., 1738-9', answers to queries 10 and 11; *The Distressed State of Ireland Considered, More Particularly with Regard to the North in a Letter to a Friend* (Dublin, 1740), pp 4, 39; R. Barton, *A Dialogue concerning Some Things of Importance to Ireland, Particularly to the County of Armagh* (Dublin, 1751), p. 14; [C. Smith and W. Harris], *The Antient and Present State of the County of Down* (Dublin, 1744), p. 108.

rise in output as bounties were given for linens for export. The industry spread rapidly from its original home in the Lagan valley and north Armagh into all the neighbouring counties, except the corn-growing areas of east Down and the pastoral farms of Fermanagh. Developments in the technology of bleaching in the mid-1730s led to much investment in the construction of bleach-yards with their beetling engines along the most suitable stretches of certain rivers: the Callan near Armagh city, the Bann and Lagan in County Down, the Sixmilewater and Maine in County Antrim, the Agivey and the Roe in County Londonderry and the Mourne in County Tyrone.[9]

In its turn this industrial development required an improved system of communications. It was to owe much of its success to the Newry canal, which was opened in 1742 as the first major inland navigation in the British Isles and was constructed with the original intention of providing Dublin with cheap coal from Coalisland in County Tyrone. The expansion of the road network was equally impressive and several of the main roads became turn-pikes.[10] These new lines of communication opened up central and southern Ulster to the energetic Dublin merchants and bankers and led to the rise of the port of Newry and to substantial urban development both in County Down and in the Lough Neagh basin, as reflected in small towns like Cookstown, Moy, Coagh and Aughna-cloy.[11] Belfast's influence then extended no further than its immediate hinterland, from Antrim and Carrickfergus in the north to Ballynahinch and Newtownards in the south. Lack of leadership from the Donegall family was blamed for the poor appearance of the town around the middle of the century.[12] Nevertheless, with

9. P.R.O.N.I., D.562/1270, Robert Stevenson's 'View of County Armagh in 1795'; H. D. Gribbon, *The History of Water Power in Ulster* (Newton Abbot, 1969), pp 81-90; E. R. R. Green, *The Industrial Archaeology of County Down* (Belfast, 1963); T. H. Mullin, *Aghadowey: a Parish and its Linen Industry* (Belfast, 1972), chapter 5 and Appendix A.
10. W. H. Crawford, 'Ulster Landowners and the Linen Industry', *Land and Industry* eds. J. T. Ward and R. G. Wilson (Newton Abbot, 1971), pp 127-9. For a fuller treatment of the road development, see J. T. Fulton, 'The Roads of County Down, 1600-1900: the Evolution of the Road System of an Irish County' (Queen's Univ. Belfast, Ph.D. thesis 1972).
11. *The Antient and Present State of Down*, pp 83, 95, 100; R.I.A., Charlemont Mss., i, letter 26, Thomas Adderley to Charlemont, 28 Jan. 1755; P.R.O.N.I., D.1449/12/55 (Lenox-Conyngham Mss.), George Conyngham to John Watt, 7 Feb. 1753; G. Camblin, *The Town in Ulster* (Belfast, 1951), p. 81.
12. *Aspects of Irish Social History, 1750-1800* eds. W. H. Crawford and B. Trainor (Belfast, 1969), p. 86.

the rest of the province it was to share in the prosperity of the 1750s and 1760s engendered by the success of the linen industry.[13]

It might be thought that this period of prosperity would have strengthened the existing structure of society, and on the surface the social structure did remain surprisingly stable until the mid-1770s. There was no real challenge to the domination of the gentry in local government and they retained control in the counties and the boroughs. The Church of Ireland was recognized as the state church and continued to attract social climbers. Presbyterians had been preoccupied with theological differences, while the Catholics wanted to convince the government of their loyalty. The only element which did cause unrest was the class of small tenant farmer-weavers created by the prosperity of the linen industry and emboldened by the security of holding long leases. As 'Hearts of Oak' they agitated against the active enforcement by the local authorities of the traditional annual imposition of six days' road-making, after the government had passed an act to excuse day labourers from their statutory obligations, leaving the main burden to be carried by the farmer-weavers:[14] they were also annoyed by the attempts of Church of Ireland clergy to increase their falling real incomes from tithes.[15] Although parliament abolished the six days' labour in 1765 it had to transfer the cost of road-making to a county cess or rate, and the collection of this rate was opposed: the barony of Oneilland East in the north of County Armagh paid no county cess for more than five years from 1767.[16] A decision to collect it with military aid led to rioting in 1772. This agitation coincided with the 'Hearts of Steel' unrest in south Antrim, where the occupants of lands on the Donegall and Upton estates were protesting against land being let to anyone but themselves.[17] The trouble occurred during an economic depression caused by three years of bad harvests and the simultaneous failure of several London linen merchants.[18] In spite of the disturbances the county cess remained and in Ulster alone it was supplemented in 1772 by the imposition of a parish cess of one penny to twopence per acre, to

13. *Arthur Young's Tour in Ireland (1776-9)* ed. A. W. Hutton (London, 1892), pp 144-6.
14. 33 Geo. II, c.8, s.2; *Aspects of Irish Social History*, pp 34-6.
15. Lecky, ii, 45-6.
16. *Aspects of Irish Social History*, p. 38.
17. *Ibid.*, pp 42-3; Crawford, *'Landlord-Tenant Relations in Ulster'*, 15-16.
18. L. M. Cullen, *An Economic History of Ireland Since 1660* (London, 1972), p. 74; C. Gill, *The Rise of the Irish Linen Industry* (Oxford, 1925), pp 123-6.

maintain the by-roads which did not fall under the 1765 act.[19] These outbursts demonstrated to the authorities that they had to reckon with an effective new social force in the small tenant farmer-weavers, or 'manufacturers' as they were known. They were more independent than small farmers elsewhere in Ireland in the period from 1750 to 1770 because they had a steady income and managed to obtain three-life leases on their small holdings. Their numbers were increasing from subdivision, and they were presenting problems of administration for landlord and agent alike. When the tide of prosperity began to turn against them they were to prove difficult to control by the traditional methods.

And yet it was not this group that was to herald the significant changes in local politics in the last quarter of the century. It was the group above them in the social scale, made up of substantial farmers, a growing body of professional men and the merchants in the ports, a group united by presbyterianism. Their opportunity to engage in political life was provided by the Octennial Act of 1768, which limited the life of an Irish parliament to eight years and made it more responsive to local pressures. The first issue to arise was a quarrel between presbyterians and Church of Ireland clergy in 1774 after a new Vestry Act had barred Dissenters from the parish vestries, because they had been obstructing the administration of the Church of Ireland at a parochial level. Thirty-nine presbyterian congregations organized petitions against the act, and the threat of independent parliamentary candidates sponsored by the presbyterian church in the 1776 election compelled Thomas Conolly, the very influential member for County Londonderry, to introduce a bill to repeal the offending clauses.[20] The passing of this act may have led to some reduction in the presbyterian pressure, but in the 1776 election James Wilson, a half-pay naval captain, won a seat for the independent interest in County Antrim by defeating the establishment family of Massereene. He had, as a contemporary eulogy said, 'offered himself to this county on constitutional grounds, conducted himself by constitutional principles and offered satisfactory assurances as to his future conduct in parliament'.[21] The new character of politics was reflected in the attitudes and conduct of the Volunteers when they appeared in

19. 11 Geo. III, c. 9, s. 1.
20. *Aspects of Irish Social History*, pp 164-5.
21. [H. Joy], *Historical Collections relative to the Town of Belfast from the Earliest Period to the Union with Great Britain* (Belfast, 1817), p. 129. For the significance of this election to the Massereene family see A. P. W. Malcomson, 'Election Politics in the Borough of Antrim, 1750-1800', *I.H.S.*, xvii (1970), 33-5.

1778: the country gentlemen who traditionally provided officers for the militia were upset to find 'that those whom they [the Volunteers] call their officers must obey their orders; they are their constituents and their orders must be observed'.[22] In 1780 the government repealed the sacramental test which had hitherto excluded presbyterians from borough corporations. In Ulster society the presbyterians had seized the strong position that they had been denied from the beginning of the century and were now in a situation to launch a campaign against the establishment, although the failure of the Volunteers to secure parliamentary reform would limit their gains.[23]

The success of the Volunteers' struggle for legislative independence in 1782 has tended to obscure the course of another significant quarrel in that year.[24] The regulating act for the linen industry, which was passed in 1782, had followed a thorough investigation by a parliamentary committee, itself occasioned by the serious blow to the reputation of Irish linens sustained by the rejection of a large number of webs at the Chester fair.[25] The act tried to enforce the authority of the Linen Board over the bleachers, not only by taking bonds for £200 as security from each of the bleachers who acted as their sealmasters, but also by making each of them perfect a warrant of attorney confessing judgement on the bond, which would give the Board the authority to take out of the bond the money for any fines they might impose. The Ulster bleachers (more commonly known as linen drapers although this term included also the buyers in the markets) absolutely opposed the scheme as despotic, and decided at meetings held in Lisburn, Lurgan and Newry and later at Armagh that they would not carry on the purchase of brown linens in the markets until they were dispensed from the requirement to take the new oath or give any other than the usual simple bonds for their conduct. The drapers also secured the support of five local gentlemen who were also trustees of the Board (Lords Hillsborough and Moira, Sir Richard Johnston, William Brownlow and John O'Neill) to enable them to circumvent the act. In consequence, the offending clauses had to be

22. *Aspects of Irish Social History*, p. 166.
23. J. C. Beckett, *Protestant Dissent in Ireland, 1687-1780* (London, 1948), pp 100-105; P.R.O.N.I., D.607/B/31 (Downshire Mss.), Robert Ross to Hillsborough, 7 Sept. 1778.
24. Crawford, *'Ulster Landowners and the Linen Industry'*, 131-3.
25. The webs were damaged by unskilled attempts to bleach with lime instead of the more traditional barilla, cashub or Dantzig [pot] ashes, which were in short supply because of the American War of Independence (P.R.O.N.I., D.2309/4/3 [Armytage-Moore Mss.], John Moore to Annesley, 20 Oct. 1781; Gill, *Rise of the Linen Industry*, pp 211-213).

repealed. The incident had wide repercussions in Ulster. Within three months a meeting of linen drapers at Dungannon discussed the site for a white-linen hall in the heart of the manufacture, and argued that it was unnecessary to sustain the expense and possible damage in transporting cloth to the Dublin white-linen hall when it might be shipped from Belfast or Newry. Neither town would concede to the other the opportunity of building the white-linen hall, and so by 1785 white-linen halls were completed in both towns.[26] Results showed, however, that their construction was more of a gesture of defiance towards Dublin and the Linen Board rather than a new commercial strategy: Newry linen hall soon fell into disuse and was converted into a military barracks, while the Belfast hall was used as a warehouse for storing linens.[27]

The contest between Newry and Belfast for the white-linen hall indicated the strength of the rivalry of their respective groups of merchants. In the 1770s Newry was a worthy rival to Belfast, but fundamental changes in the economy were soon to make Belfast the undisputed capital of the region. The reasons for this shift of commercial power are complex, but they can be appreciated only in the context of that historical process to which we apply the term 'industrial revolution'. It is worthwhile examining the significance for Belfast and Newry of at least three aspects of that process: the rise of the cotton industry in Belfast while Newry continued to service the linen industry; the relative response by Belfast and Newry merchants to the new opportunities for retailing the products of the British industrial revolution; and the growth of the Ulster livestock industry.

The cotton industry came to Belfast in the late 1770s, and by the mid-1780s it had begun to import cotton wool on a significant scale: in 1787, for example, it imported 572 hundred-weight direct from the West Indies and another 262 hundred-weight from

26. *Londonderry Journal*, 17 Dec. 1782, reported that 'at the last meeting of the linen drapers in Armagh, in consequence of the competition between the towns of Newry and Belfast, a disagreement arose between the two parties concerning the situation of the intended new linen market. After the several resolutions relative to the revisal of the linen laws were gone through with the approbation of all present, the first resolution relative to the removal of the white linen market to the North was proposed, which those who were for the Belfast situation opposed, and seeing, as we are told, the weakness of their number, they withdrew from the meeting, when the resolution ... passed almost unanimously. The Belfast party have published their account of the transaction.'
27. Gill, *Rise of the Linen Industry*, pp 189-91.

England. A sudden surge in imports of cotton yarn in the early 1790s indicates that the local spinning industry was not able to supply sufficient yarn to the weavers, of whom there were reckoned to be 8,000 in 1790.[28] By 1800 it was claimed that the industry employed 13,500 persons within a ten-mile radius of Belfast, and that there was £192,000 invested in it.[29] Cotton weaving had attracted many linen weavers because it provided double the wages for less strenuous work, while the fact that cottons required little bleaching and therefore only a small investment in fixed plant encouraged many small manufacturers to take risks to develop their businesses.[30]

Newry's prosperity on the other hand remained tied to the linen industry. By way of the Newry and Coalisland canals its merchants had cheap and easy access to the towns and villages of the Lough Neagh basin and to the heart of the linen country from Banbridge to Dungannon and Monaghan, which they supplied with flaxseed and with potash and other chemicals for bleaching. In the 1770s Newry exported 47.5 million yards of linen cloth as against Belfast's 42.7 million (22% of total Irish exports as against 21%), but in the following decade, in spite of the new linen halls, Newry's share, with 45.5 million yards, slipped to 17% whereas Belfast's share increased to 22%. Newry does seem to have suffered a sudden setback in 1781 and 1782, because within three years after its peak year for linen exports (more than seven million yards in 1778 – twice that of Belfast) its exports plunged to a total of 4.6 millions, little more than half of Belfast's figure. It soon recovered but it never regained its lead over Belfast and in

28. N.L.I., 'Volumes of Dublin Imports and Exports', 1771-1823. These are misleadingly named since they contain the statistics for all the Irish ports: I have used the figures to trace the rivalry between the merchants of Belfast and Newry. I am indebted to Mr Norman Gamble, who is engaged on a thesis about economic and social life in Belfast in the late eighteenth century, for helping me to formulate my ideas on this topic.
29. Gribbon, *Water Power in Ulster,* pp 112-114.
30. J. Dubourdieu, *Statistical Survey of the County of Down* (Dublin, 1802), pp 235-7. In February 1804 Robert Gemmill of Belfast made this point in a letter to McConnel and Kennedy, his yarn suppliers in Manchester: 'you may think and justly that two months [credit] is a great risk in the present state of Ireland, but I wish no Englishman would give longer to Ireland. We would not have such crowds of small manufacturers who do no good to themselves and ruin the trade, and would keep some bigger ones in more bounds. It often surprises me to see with what trifling sums people think they may carry on the cotton manufacture here. For my own part I began with 10,000 British pounds and found the same little enough to carry on in a proper manner ...' (quoted in C. H. Lee, *A Cotton Enterprise, 1795-1840: A History of McConnel and Kennedy, Fine Cotton Spinners* (Manchester, 1972), p. 73).

the 1790s it fell away badly: the reasons have yet to be diagnosed.

There can be no doubt that the textile industries were the chief source of Ulster's prosperity but they do not by themselves account for the growth of Ulster towns. By comparison with Dublin, Cork and Limerick even Belfast was still puny in 1791 with just over 18,000 inhabitants.[31] The majority of textile workers lived in the countryside and even in 1810 it was reckoned that only 2,000 people in Belfast were employed in cotton out of a total population of about 25,000.[32] That the growth of the town was more closely linked with the development of commerce is suggested by a comparison of the rise in both the population figures and the tonnage handled by the port during the first half of the nineteenth century. An analysis of the commodities of trade listed in the customs' returns is required to ascertain how this developing trade affected the occupational structure of the town's population: for example, growing imports of coal would have led to a substantial increase in the carting trade. Even in the middle of the eighteenth century the ports of Belfast and Newry had differed in the nature of their trade, for Newry imported raw materials for the linen industry and bulky goods for the Lough Neagh basin, while Belfast imported most of the tobacco, sugar and rum. The wholesale trade in draperies, hardware and imported groceries (such as dried fruit, spices, *etc.*) had for long been a preserve of Dublin merchants and many newspaper advertisements of the 1760s show that retail merchants in mid-Ulster informed their customers whenever they had purchased new supplies from Dublin.[33] As the standard of living increased in Ulster, Belfast's interest in these wholesale trades livened very noticeably and by the 1780s her merchants were very active. Belfast's imports of hardware increased sixfold and its imports of draperies and stockings fivefold. While the merchants of Newry also showed interest in this development — there was a fivefold increase in hardware — the figures for draperies, stockings and haberdashery reveal a much smaller increase and may represent the slower growth of prosperity among the linen weavers at this time. Account must be taken, however, in the Newry

31. See the analysis of the population of Belfast in 1782 and 1791 published in G. Benn, *A History of the Town of Belfast* (Belfast, 1877), pp 621-3.
32. J. J. Monaghan, 'The Rise and Fall of the Belfast Cotton Industry', *I.H.S.*, iii (1942), 3.
33. For example, *Belfast Newsletter*, 26 June 1767: '[Abraham Wynne's] wife has just returned from Dublin and has laid in on the best terms a large assortment of fine china ware, drinking glasses flowered and plain of different fashions.' See also *ibid.*, 20 Oct. 1761, 11 Mar. 1762, 26 Feb. 1765.

figures, of the impact of competition from Dundalk into the southern section of Newry's traditional hinterland in the counties of Monaghan and Cavan, while Belfast was beginning to penetrate the northern section with the completion of the Lagan canal as far as Lough Neagh in 1794 (although problems with the canal prevented it from becoming a real threat to the Newry merchants until after 1810). Belfast was becoming the most important wholesale distribution centre in the province. As William Drennan noted in 1802, 'Newry, I hear, is growing a poor, pitiful place, but Belfast is become the warehouse of the North, and its Custom House revenue is £240,000 per annum'.34

An important factor in the growth of the Ulster economy at this time, and one which has hitherto been overlooked, is the resurrection of the Ulster livestock industry. After Irish livestock had been excluded from the British market by the Cattle Acts of 1667 and 1681, the southern counties in Ireland developed a provision trade which served the Atlantic economy. Because Ulster was badly placed to compete, her cattle markets stagnated until the ban on the export of live cattle from Ireland to England was lifted in 1759, when the English graziers realized their need for store cattle. Soon cattle were again trekking across the province of Ulster from the Sperrins and from Fermanagh to Donaghadee for the shortest sea crossing. In fact almost all Irish cattle exports were from the northern ports. Over a three-year period in the mid-1780s Ulster exported more than 56,000 cattle, three-quarters of the number through Donaghadee and one-sixth through Newry.35 At the same time there was a very marked increase in the export from Belfast and Newry to Britain of barrels of butter, pork and beef as well as large numbers of untanned hides. This expansion of the British market for Ulster livestock and later for grain, which continued until the end of the Napoleonic Wars, had very important

34. P.R.O.N.I., D.591/1019, Drennan to Mrs M. McTier, [c.Dec 1802].
35. *C.J.I.*, xii, Appendix, cccxc. See also R. Stephenson, *A Letter to the Right Honorable and Honorable the Trustees of the Linen Manufacture and also to the Trustees for Distributing Bounties etc.* (Dublin, 1971), p. 20, on the live cattle trade: 'if this business was thoroughly considered by all parties in Ireland, the poor cotters, the improvers and tillers of coarse lands, the landed interest, and the citizens and merchants would find a mutual interest in promoting the traffic of supplying England fully with lean stores to fatten and heifers to replenish their dairies, which are the only kind of cattle they want from us. It is an indisputable truth, that every lean half-fed beast slaughtered in Ireland, where the beef, hide, and tallow are exported, the beef generally at great disadvantage and hazard, loses to this country forty shillings on every five pounds of what the same beast would produce if exported alive to England for the use of their manufacturers ...'

Table to show changes in the import and export trade with Britain of three Ulster ports 1771-90

IMPORTS	BELFAST		NEWRY		LONDONDERRY	
	1771-80	1781-90	1771-90	1781-90	1771-80	1781-90
Draperies: yds	269,023	1,434,430	636,973	572,616	132,522	261,511
Stockings: pairs	9,306	48,756	5,342	11,658	1,672	11,160
Haberdashery: £	1,772	5,817	2,126	2,768	548	1,297
Coal: tons	78,491	194,624	39,406	92,681	14,493	22,470
Bark: barrels	24,990	58,506	32,425	59,361	22,129	36,756
Lead: cwts	5,311	8,042	3,966	4,629	1,569	3,712
Steel: cwts	359	892	546	853	344	429
Hardware: £	2,971	20,062	3,336	16,341	1,872	18,438
EXPORTS						
Linen cloth: 1000s of yds	42,761	58,447	47,598	45,565	337	4,470
Linen yarn: cwts	1,047	2,804	4,183	229	161,687	137,793
Live cattle	-	387	commenced 1785	16,287	-	-
Live pigs	-	-	5,239	17,491	-	-
Beef: barrels	24,786	39,316	12,220	22,480	1,308	1,796
Pork: barrels	10,689	27,384	12,101	43,773	331	518
Butter: cwts	83,812	128,467	55,969	90,148	1,751	649
Untanned hides	73,578	68,297	41,406	63,510	35,946	23,268
Untanned calf-skins	183,784	245,720	45,648	119,244	not given	16,108

consequences for Ulster society because it helped to reverse certain trends. It strengthened the economic position of the substantial farmers and enabled them to hold off the challenge of the rapidly increasing cottier element in the population. It was becoming more profitable to farm than to sublet. In the heart of the linen country many of the manufacturers would have liked to revert to farming because their income from linen was rising too slowly during a period of inflation, but their holdings were too small for anything but the rearing of pigs and the production of some butter. The success of the potato as a food crop for man and pig was a real asset on the small holding and it enabled families to sub-divide their land still further or use it to pay cottier labour. It gave the farmer more room to manoeuvre in his fight to maintain his standard of living but its benefits could not increase indefinitely. Nevertheless many families pressed it to its utmost, by using the security of a patch of land as a bait to keep their children at home to work for them in order to reduce to a minimum the overhead costs in spinning and weaving.[36]

So far in this paper no mention has been made of the north-west of the province. The reason is that the north-west comprised a distinct and independent economic and social region with its own rhythm of economic activity. It had few dealings with Belfast and looked rather to Dublin. The hinterland of its port, Londonderry, extended as far south as Omagh but, as the Abercorn agent wrote in 1768, 'most of the inhabitants above Omagh go to Newry for their goods'.[37] The region's economic wealth depended on linen but much more on the export of linen yarn for the Lancashire manufacture than on linen cloth itself. Yarn exports reached a figure of almost 19,000 hundred-weight in 1780, but this figure dwindled away steadily as a result of British inventions in cotton spinning which produced cotton fit for the warps on the loom. As if to replace this lost source of income the export of linen cloth rose rapidly to more than 2,000,000 yards annually by 1800. It was not until the nineteenth century that Londonderry became an important exporter of agricultural products. It did, however, increase its imports as the wholesale centre for its region although this increase came later and slower than in the east coast ports.[38] In

36. J. McEvoy, *Statistical Survey of the County of Tyrone* (Dublin, 1802), p. 99; C. Coote, *Statistical Survey of the County of Cavan* (Dublin, 1802), pp 41-2, 218; Coote, *Statistical Survey of Armagh,* pp 136-7.
37. P.R.O.N.I., T.2541/I.A.1/8/105 (Abercorn Mss.), John Hamilton to [Abercorn], 27 Nov. 1768.
38. The Ordnance Survey *Memoir of the City and North-Western Liberties of Londonderry, Parish of Templemore* (Dublin, 1837), pp 254-93, contains the statistics for Londonderry's trade in the period 1770-1823.

this role Londonderry did not have to face the challenge of any other port.

The towns of Belfast, Newry and Londonderry were now substantial enough to breed a new kind of society: urban society. In their attitudes these townsmen differed radically from country-men. In the rural community the churches were almost the only social institutions but in Belfast men of different religions met each other regularly for business and pleasure, whether in the Chamber of Commerce, the Charitable Society, the music or reading societies, clubs, the various lodges of freemasons, in bookshops and libraries, theatres, public and private balls, and weekly coteries.[39]   This society was articulate, because it contained so many educated men, whether from the Scottish universities of Glasgow and Edinburgh or from Trinity College, Dublin, or even from the Belfast Academy (founded in 1785) and the many private schools in the province. These men were alive to events in the outside world and aware of political developments in Britain, America and France, so that among them were writers able to contribute to the *Belfast News-Letter* (founded in 1737), the *Belfast Mercury* or *Freeman's Chronicle* (the organ of the Volunteers from 1783 to 1786) and the *Northern Star* (run by the United Irishmen from 1792 to 1797).

The development of these urban communities soon exposed weaknesses in local administration. Although Belfast was a corpor-ate town the corporation was controlled by the Donegall family, the ground landlords. In the first half of the eighteenth century the practice of securing the election of non-residents as freemen and burgesses of corporations had been used by landlords to retain control over the return of borough representatives to parliament. The legality of this practice had been confirmed by the Newtown Act of 1748 and a subsequent judicial decision in 1758.[40] As a result there were in Belfast, by 1790, only five of the twelve burgesses actually resident in the town,[41] and the corporation was ineffective as an instrument of local government. Government, in fact, was left in the hands of the mayor or sovereign, who acted as clerk of the markets, chief magistrate and coroner, as well as

39.   J. J. Monaghan, 'A Social and Economic History of Belfast 1790-1800' (Queen's Univ. Belfast M.A. thesis 1936), pp 179-319. P.R.O.N.I., D.591/62, William Drennan to Mrs M. McTier, 1783, comments: 'I am not very fond of clubs, and were it not for a desire of making acquaintance (though club acquaintances are not generally very lucrative ones) I would wish to avoid these meetings and rather cultivate the domestic parties.'
40.   A. P. W. Malcomson, 'The Newtown Act of 1748: Revision and Reconstruction', *I.H.S.,* xvii (1973).
41.   *Belfast Newsletter,* 9 Nov. 1790.

superintending the paving, lighting and cleansing of the town. As
chief magistrate he was assisted by a panel of magistrates selected
from the leading local merchants.[42] In these circumstances the
initiative in local government came from outside the corporation. A
town meeting to discuss any matter which might affect the welfare
of the town could be called by a public notice signed by a number
of inhabitants and published in the newspapers. The sovereign was
expected to execute its decisions and to summon a general vestry
of the Church of Ireland in order to levy the local rate or cess.[43]
There is no evidence that the sovereign ever refused to requisition
a town meeting as, for example, the seneschal of Newry refused to
do in 1784 on the grounds that he was not satisfied about its
legality.[44]

The town meeting, however, did not concern itself only with
local politics and it was often requisitioned to give voice to Belfast's
sentiments in national politics and to approve petitions to parliament.   Indeed, the town meeting provided the best platform for
political controversy and so the proceedings and resolutions, which
were generally published in the newspapers, display a very lively
political consciousness.[45]   In 1780 the town meeting thanked
King George III for granting Ireland 'a free liberty of trading with
the American colonies' and enthusiastically welcomed the Volunteers, themselves no mean coiners of toasts, addresses and declarations.   In 1782 it opposed the raising of fencibles and supported
Flood against Grattan over renunciation. By 1783-4 it was spear-
heading the Ulster campaign for the reform of parliament. The
collapse of that campaign reduced the level of political activity in
Belfast but it was revived by the constitutional upheaval in France
in 1789.   It was, indeed, a fear of democratic tendencies that
induced Lord Charlemont to propose a scheme for the formation of
a Northern Whig club in Belfast. The club attracted all shades of
reformers in the Belfast region and celebrated the French Revolution in great style on 14 July 1791. In the October following, an
even more radical movement was formed in Belfast, the Society of
United Irishmen.   The tone of their language became more and
more extreme as they deluded themselves with the belief that they
could unite all Irishmen so that even military force would not be
able to resist the voice of the people.[46]   Early in 1793 the govern-

42.   Monaghan, 'Social and Economic History of Belfast', pp 31-2, 33.
43.   *Belfast Newsletter,* 25 Oct. 1793.
44.   P.R.O.N.I., D.591/113, William Drennan to Mrs M. McTier, [autumn 1784].
45.   Many of these were gathered into [Joy], *Historical Collections.*
46.   *Ibid.*, pp v-vii. The confidence of the individual United Irishmen is

ment took action by forbidding 'all seditious and unlawful assemblies', and the United Irishmen were forced to go underground.
They represented the extreme radical wing of the reform movement, and had shed the support of the most influential people in
Belfast.

In Belfast the United Irishmen still believed that the establishment could be overthrown by a national conspiracy, but they
needed to find masses of people to overawe the government. The
problem for the Belfast politicians was to devise a programme that
would appeal to the rural community. A manifesto drafted at
Ballynahinch in 1795 revived all the traditional grievances of the
establishment, notably tithes, hearth-money, excise, county and
church cesses, and tolls at fairs.[47] This appeal was most effective
in south Antrim and north Down, the region from which presbyterian Belfast drew its vitality and strength, where grievances
were played upon by clergy and radical elements until in many
places political excitement reached such a pitch that the more
moderate people did not dare oppose, much less attempt to
control, the extremists. Beyond this region the movement relied for
the propagation of its gospel on local 'societies' which were linked
into a national organization by a hierarchy of baronial, county and
provincial committees. Reports of their meetings by informers
indicate a large membership but few arms and little money. They
reveal the leaders as pathetic amateurs. On 29 May 1798, for
example, a mere ten days before the Antrim rising, delegates to the
provincial committee at Armagh were asked

> If they thought they could disarm the military in their re-
> spective counties: Derry, Donegal and Louth said they could;
> Down, Antrim, Armagh and the upper half of the county of
> Tyrone thought they could not; he then asked them individ-
> ually if they thought the people they represented would act,
> and they all said they would, except Down. Its delegate said
> that he could not exactly answer whether it would or not, but
> he would try and ascertain it by taking the sense of the
> adjutant-generals and colonels.[48]

well expressed in a letter from Sam McTier to William Drennan about
General White: 'I am told he says he has eight regiments that he can bring
together here on very short notice with a suitable train of artillery. What
would this paltry force signify were the people of this country inclined to an
insurrection? Triple the number would not avail — no, nor twice that number
...' (P.R.O.N.I., D.591/386B, [McTier] to Drennan, [c.Feb. 1793].)
47.   *Aspects of Irish Social History*, pp 181-2.
48.   *Second Report from the Committee of Secrecy of the [Irish] House of*

It was small wonder that the United Irishmen collapsed completely in June 1798 after the defeats at Antrim and Saintfield. A loyalist commented on 14 June 1798: 'for some years past there was something brooding in the minds of the Republicans and now that it has broke out and that they could not succeed they will become loyal subjects.' He blamed the presbyterian ministers and rich republican shopkeepers: 'the language these fellows held out to the lower class and the people about them was the principal cause of the present rising and since it has broke out their courage failed and self was predominant.'[49] The '98 in Ulster was not for the rank-and-file a crusade against the British government. Rather, it was a 'turn out' of the restless elements in the countryside, who followed local leaders because their pride would not let them turn back from encounters which turned out to be more bloody than affrays at fairs and markets. The dying embers of a fire had been fanned into a flame, but there was no more fuel. The presbyterians were no longer excluded from local government, and the more democratic mood of the nineteenth century would suit their ambitions.

The troubles which had begun in the mid-1780s in mid-Ulster were completely different in character from those in the east of the province, and were much more serious. Among the manufacturers with their small holdings there was a great need for land, and faction-fighting was rife. Resentments among the weavers gradually focused on the Catholics among them, who formed a considerable section of the community and were improving their social status; Catholic religious pretensions galled them and provided issues for feud.[50] Soon the faction-fighting that was endemic in rural society assumed a sectarian character. In their defence Catholics adopted the organization of the Defenders from north Leinster against the bully-boy tactics of the Peep O'Day Boys, who raided Catholic homes in search of arms.[51] In response to Defender successes the Protestants organized Orange Societies. Since no class of substantial farmers had survived in this region to exercise

Lords (1798), Appendix xiv, p. cxxiv. See also J. L. McCracken, 'The United Irishmen', *Secret Societies in Ireland* ed. T. D. Williams (Dublin, 1973), pp 58-67.
49.   P.R.O.N.I., D.607/F/244 (Downshire Mss.), James McKey to Downshire, 14 June 1798.
50.   J. Byrne, *An Impartial Account of the Late Disturbances in the County of Armagh* (Dublin, 1792). Extracts from this rare pamphlet are printed in *Aspects of Irish Social History*, pp 171-5.
51.   *A Candid and Impartial Account of the Disturbances in the County of Meath in the Years 1792, 1793 and 1794, by a County Meath Freeholder* (Dublin, 1794), pp 1-3, 4.

some sort of social control, the gentry themselves had to intervene, although the sheer scale of the problem made them very cautious.[52] When the magistrates failed to impose their authority through the courts, some minor gentry in the county courted popularity by championing the Protestant cause, and the government was unable to act.[53] As a result many Catholic families from north Armagh and south Londonderry fled from their districts and settled in the west of Ireland.[54]

The Orange troubles were a single response to two contrasting kinds of change in society: social change, in the case of the rise of the Catholics, and economic change, in the decline in the standard of living of the handloom weavers. It is this constant alteration in the system of weights and balances in society that seems to epitomize the situation in late eighteenth-century Ulster, and it set new trends for the ensuing half-century at least. The industrial revolution in Britain had reorientated the Ulster economy so that Belfast became the regional and industrial capital not only of eastern but of central Ulster, while the agricultural revolution promoted the growth of new regional satellites in Ballymena and Portadown, to the detriment of Carrickfergus, Dungannon, Armagh and Downpatrick. The democratic trend would gain ground with the creation of baronial committees to advise grand juries about road-making in 1817, the election of town commissioners as a result of an 1828 act (Belfast gained this system by its Police Act of 1800) and the poor law boards of guardians under the 1838 act. Even the presbyterians were incorporated into the body politic, and under Henry Cooke they would evolve a conservative philosophy. These changes were of profound significance and lasting effect: indeed, their traces can be found even in modern Ulster society.[55]

52. *Aspects of Irish Social History*, pp 173-4, 177-80.
53. H. Senior, *Orangeism in Ireland and Britain, 1795-1836* (London, 1966), pp 32-47.
54. P. Tohall, 'The Diamond Fight of 1795 and the Resultant Expulsion', *Seanchas Ardmhacha*, iii (1958). Mr Martin Davey, who is currently preparing a thesis on the United Irish movement in Ulster, has found evidence of similar expulsions in south Londonderry. I am indebted to him for information imparted in discussions of his work.
55. I should like to thank the Deputy Keeper, P.R.O.N.I., and the following depositors for permission to draw on their material: the duke of Abercorn, the marquess of Downshire, the Misses Emma and Sylvia Duffin, the Viscount Massereene and Ferrard, and Mr Dermot O'Hara.

IRISH REPUBLICANISM IN ENGLAND: THE FIRST PHASE, 1797-9

Marianne Elliott

Ireland's influence on English history is too often ignored by English historians: this fact has been demonstrated once again in the recent debate concerning the extent and importance of revolutionary elements in England's early working-class movements. With much justification the participants in the debate have concentrated on the years 1801-2, when widespread food riots aroused official concern about possible treasonable manipulation of popular discontent.[1] However, a glance at subversive organization at the close of the nineteenth century would clarify many of the problems which have been raised in connection with the later period. In the late 1790s a layer of republicanism had been imported from Ireland and superimposed on a subterranean world of semi-illegal working-class activity in England. The precise extent of collaboration between the two traditions is difficult to establish, but the concept of an English republic, established with the assistance of French arms, was an innovation in the programme of English radicalism. It was carried into England by a splinter group of the United Irish Society, acting in concert with a similar group in the London Corresponding Society. The United Irishmen introduced the organizational framework of the secret and treasonable society, and altered the pattern of working-class radicalism by attaching it to an enlarged United Irish programme of total British revolution and French invasion. Revolutionary activity among the English working class at this period was predominantly an Irish importation, and any discussion of early working-class movements which ignores their Irish dimension is omitting one of the most important pieces of an intricate jigsaw puzzle. The Irish influences in the crisis of 1801-2 have been

---

1. J. R. Dinwiddy, 'The "Black Lamp" in Yorkshire, 1801-1802'; and J. L. Baxter and F. K. Donnelly, 'The Revolutionary "Underground" in the West Riding: Myth or Reality?', *Past and Present*, no. 64 (1974), 113-35. For the continuing debate see J. A. Hone, 'The Ways and Means of London Radicalism, 1796-1821' (Oxford Univ. D.Phil. thesis 1975), especially pp 43-111; J. L. Baxter and F. K. Donnelly, 'Sheffield and the English Revolutionary Tradition, 1791-1820', *International Review of Social History*, xx (1975), 398-423; F. K. Donnelly, 'Ideology and Early English Working-Class History: Edward Thompson and His Critics', *Social History*, no. 2 (1976), 219-238; J. A. Hone, 'Radicalism in London, 1796-1802: Convergencies and Continuities', in *London in the Age of Reform* ed. J. Stevenson (Oxford, 1977), pp 79-101; M. I. Thomis and P. Holt, *Threats of Revolution in Britain, 1789-1848* (London, 1977).

examined elsewhere.[2] The purpose of the present article is to complete the picture of early Irish republicanism in England, and to offer an alternative solution to the vexed problem of English revolutionary activity in the 1790s, by looking at it in an Irish context.

2

The United Irish Society had originated as one of the many British reform associations inspired by the idealism of the French Revolution. However, after the declaration of war between France and England in 1793 the governments of both countries treated the Society as a potential 'fifth column' — long before it had shown any signs of becoming so — and this combination of British fear and French hope eventually transformed the United Irishmen into a republican society.[3] As early as 1793 the Society was approached by a French agent and urged to rebel with the assistance of French arms. This first overture was repulsed, but the war quickly removed the constitutional means of securing reform, and when a second agent was sent from France in 1794, the United Irish Society proved more receptive to the idea of French aid.[4] The mission of the Reverend William Jackson was to ascertain the degree of support in England and Ireland for the idea of a French invasion. His reports from England were unfavourable, but in Dublin he was received enthusiastically by a section of the United Irish Society.[5] Jackson was arrested by the Irish government in April 1794, and convicted of treason the following year. The Irish government hoped to frighten off supporters of the United Irish Society by giving full publicity to the Society's association with Jackson.[6] In the short term the plan succeeded. The Society had been declining steadily since the declaration of war, and few of the moderate

2.   M. Elliott, 'The Despard Conspiracy Reconsidered', *Past and Present* no. 75 (1977), 46-61.
3.   *Parliamentary History*, xxx, 147, 167-8, 231-233, 544; *The Reports of the Committee of Secrecy of the House of Commons on the Papers Belonging to the Society for Constitutional Information and the London Corresponding Society* (Edinburgh, 1974), pp 19, 27, 91; Kent R. O., U. 840 (Camden Mss.), C. 122/5, Pelham to Camden, 30 Oct. 1975.
4.   A.A.E., Corr. Pol. Ang. 587, fos. 167-176, reports on the mission of E. Oswald, June 1793; A.N., AF[iv] 1671, memoir of E. Lewins, c.1802; Lecky, iii, 188.
5.   A.A.E., Personnel, 1[ere] ser., 39, fos. 148-153, 'Jackson'.
6.   T. B. Howell, *A Complete Collection of State Trials* (London, 1811-26), xxv, 783-891; Bod., Burges Deposit, correspondence between Sir James Bland Burges and Lord St. Helens, June 1794.

members returned after Jackson's trial.[7] But the future of the Society was left in the hands of that group of extreme radicals which had negotiated with Jackson, and henceforth its character and strategy were determined by hopes of securing the assistance proffered by the French agents.[8] Many of those implicated with Jackson had fled to France or America, and the government had permitted Theobald Wolfe Tone to voluntarily exile himself.[9] While the numerical strength of the Society had been reduced at home, the main stimulus to Irish republicanism would in future come from abroad.

It is not until the latter months of 1796 that traces of United Irish organization can again be detected. In July Lord Edward Fitzgerald and Arthur O'Connor had travelled to Switzerland and established contact with the French Directory. O'Connor had crossed the French border, and at Angers had made arrangements with General Hoche for a French invasion of Ireland.[10] An English diplomatic official had noticed the two Irishmen in Switzerland, but such was England's ignorance of the new direction in which the old United Irish Society was moving, that he had not considered their presence in Basle sufficiently suspicious to be worth reporting.[11] Within a few months of their return to Ireland, the two agents had re-organized the Society on a republican and a military basis, and the name of United Irishman, which had been obsolete since Jackson's day, was again in common use throughout the country.[12]

Arthur O'Connor was perhaps the most colourful figure of the United Irish saga. A prominent landowner in Cork and member of

7. P.R.O.N.I., T.765/598, 601 (Drennan letters), correspondence between Drennan and Mrs McTier, Mar. 1796.
8. S.P.O., 620/20/27, anonymous information, Feb.–Apr. 1793; W. J. McNevin, *Pieces of Irish History* (New York, 1807), pp 74-5, 99.
9. A.A.E., Personnel, 1ere ser., 65, fos. 57-9, Sullivan to Delacroix, 13 Nov. 1797; P.R.O., T.S. 11/555/1793, the King against W. Stone, 17 Nov. 1795.
10. A.A.E., Corr. Pol. Ang. 589, fos. 249-99, correspondence between Delacroix, Reinhard and Barthelemy, May–June 1796; Archives Municipales de Versailles, 'Catalogue de l'Exposition sur le General Hoche', nos. 52, 153, Hoche to Hedouville, 10, 13, Aug. 1796; A.A.G., Doss. Pers., 2eme ser., G.D. 393, O'Connor. I am indebted to Mlle. A. Joly and the late F. MacDermot for drawing my attention to these documents.
11. P.R.O., F.O. 27/54, vol. ii, C. W. Flint to J. King, 13 July 1799.
12. T.C.D., Ms. 873/774, O'Connor to Dr Madden, 1842; P.R.O., P.C. 1/128/A.62, information of T. Conway, Apr. 1799; S.P.O., 620/18/16, F. Higgins to E. Cooke, Feb. 1797.

parliament for Philipstown, he had commenced his career as an ardent supporter of the government, but turned towards republicanism when his ambition to secure office was thwarted. His vanity, ambition and overbearing self-confidence was later to disrupt the home Society, but ironically to ensure its survival in France long after it had ceased to exist in Ireland.[13] Lord Edward Fitzgerald was a member of one of the oldest Anglo-Irish families, and his social prestige gave the United Irishmen an aura of respectability until his death in 1798. But the driving force behind the revived organization was that of O'Connor, and there can be little doubt that Lord Edward acted chiefly under his guidance.[14]

When Hoche's invasion force arrived at Bantry Bay in December 1796, the re-organization of the United Irish Society had not progressed far enough for any assistance to be offered to the invaders, and a combination of disastrous weather conditions and lack of encouragement from the Irish population had driven the fleet back to France.[15] The attempted invasion had a dual effect on the United Irish leaders. Those who had been actively involved in soliciting French aid greeted the news enthusiastically, and a vociferous minority, led by O'Connor and Lord Edward, urged the necessity of immediate rebellion to assure France of their good faith.[16] But the proximity of a French landing had created fears of French domination among the more moderate leaders, who henceforth were to act as a constant restraining force on the entire movement.[17] By June government circles were reverberating with the news that the United Irish Society was splitting over the issue of a rising.[18] In that month the crisis came to a head. A meeting was convened in Dublin, and delegates attended from all parts of the country. The northern delegates presented their case for an

13. Linenhall Library, Belfast, Joy Mss. (uncatalogued), Joy's annotation of a newspaper article of Jan. 1797; F. MacDermot, 'Arthur O'Connor', *I.H.S.*, xc (1966); M. Elliott, 'The United Irishmen and France, 1793-1806' (Oxford Univ. D. Phil. thesis 1975), pp 253-279.
14. G. Campbell, *Edward and Pamela Fitzgerald* (London, 1904), p. 96; A.A.E., Corr. Pol. Ang. 589, fos. 277-9, Reinhard to Delacroix, 17 June 1796.
15. A.A.E., Corr. Pol. Ang. 590, fo. 266, Reinhard to Delacroix, 22 Apr. 1797; A.H.G., B[11] 1, Grouchy to the Directory, 24 Dec. 1796; E. Desbriere, *Projets et Tentatives du Debarquement aux Iles Britanniques* (Paris, 1900-1902), i, 146-93.
16. S.P.O., 620/10/12/53, information from L. McNally, 18 Apr. 1797.
17. S.P.O., 620/18/14, information from F. Higgins, 23 Sept. 1797; *Report from the Secret Committee of the House of Commons* (Dublin, 1798), p. 23.
18. S.P.O., 620/31/89, Rev. N. Steel Dickson to Pelham, 14 June 1797.

immediate rising. The plan was rejected, but they left the meeting determined to disregard its decision, and the following months witnessed a minor exodus of militant leaders to England and to the Continent. When they left Ireland, the Society's leadership was in disarray. The division on principles had developed into a clash of personalities, adding a bitter note to the quarrel and making it more difficult to heal.[19]

3

The flight of these United Irish militants created the nucleus of a republican party in England. Two of the fugitives, Valentine Browne Lawless and the Reverend James Coigley, were to play a specially important part in its formation. The former took up residence in London where for the next two years he acted as intermediary between France and the Anglo-Irish republicans.[20] Coigley was a Catholic priest of Ulster peasant farming stock, and had studied for the priesthood at the Irish College in Paris. But his progress had been constantly impeded because of his inferior social class, and he had left the seminary after a bitter argument with the president over the allocation of bursaries. The destruction of his father's house and his own library by Orangemen, shortly after his return to Ireland, strengthened his sense of grievance against biased authority, and by 1795 he was already well known as a prominent United Irish militant.[21] In the summer of 1797 he fled to Manchester, and was soon mingling with its working-class population. By the end of that year Coigley had succeeded in extending the United system to Bolton, Stockport, Warrington, Nottingham, Liverpool and Birmingham, and communication had been established between the Lancashire and Scottish republicans. From the outset the English side of the republican movement became a preserve of the militant section in the United Irish Society. Each month it was the Provincial Committee in Ulster, rather than the National Committee in Dublin, which despatched the latest

19. P.R.O., H.O. 100/70/335-7, Camden to Portland, enclosing Turner's information, 9 Dec. 1797; N.L.I., Ms. 54A, fo. 111, G. Dallas to General Dundas, 20 Sept. 1797.
20. W. J. Fitzpatrick, *Secret Service Under Pitt* (London, 1892), pp 35-43; P.R.O., P.C. 1/43/A.152, 'Papers concerning the Society of United Irish in London, Mar. 1799'.
21. S. Simms, *Rev. James O'Coigley, United Irishman* (Belfast, 1937); Rev. B. McEvoy, 'Rev. James Quigley', *Seanchas Ardmhacha,* v (1970). There is some dispute over the spelling of Coigley's surname; I have chosen the version 'Coigley' because it was used by the man himself, *viz. The Life of the Rev. James Coigley, by Himself* (Maidstone, 1798).

United Irish constitution and signs to the United men in England, and the militants' distrust of the moderate Dublin leaders became an essential ingredient of the English movement.[22]

Disaffection was already widespread among the Lancashire textile workers, and this undoubtedly assisted the rapid spread of republicanism. But for the first time the English working classes were to be organized for political ends which were their own, rather than those of upper-class radicals. Coigley's conception of liberty was wider than that of his fellow United Irishmen, and included the formation of a union of all the unprivileged against their social superiors.[23] His first step towards the implementation of these ideas in Lancashire was the foundation of the republican Society of United Britons. Urban-based, and working-class in complexion, it was to prove the most extreme element in both the first and the second phase of the republican movement in England.[24]

When Coigley left Manchester late in the summer of 1797, the nucleus of the United Britons had been established, and on his return the following February delegates came from as far afield as Derbyshire, Nottinghamshire, Cheshire, Yorkshire, Cornwall, Edinburgh and Glasgow to discover the news he had brought from France. He advised them to obtain arms from the Ulster Committee in preparation for the forthcoming French invasion, and announced his own imminent departure for London to meet Arthur O'Connor, in whose hands the final arrangements for the invasion would be left.[25]

The national headquarters for republicanism in England was to be established in London. Here the original corresponding network of old radicalism was utilized by the Society of United Britons, and by January 1798 its secret committee was holding sessions in the cellars of Furnival's Inn, Holborn.[26] The committee was composed of United Irish and London Corresponding Society (L.C.S.) mili-

22. P.R.O., H.O. 100/70/329, Pelham to Grenville, 6 Dec. 1797; P.C. 1/41/A. 136, T. Bancroft to Portland, 24 Nov. 1797, and examination of R. Gray, 23 Mar. 1798; P.C. 1/41/A.139, further information of R. Gray, 17 Apr. 1798; S.P.O., 620/18A/11, W. Wickham to E. Cooke, 13 May 1798.
23. P.R.O., P.C. 1/42/A.143, examination of James Hughes, 17 May 1798.
24. For an account of the second phase of Irish republican activity in England, 1801-3, see Elliott, 'The Despard Conspiracy Reconsidered'.
25. P.R.O., P.C. 1/41/A.136, information of R. Gray, 19 Mar. 1798; P.C. 1/42/A.140, examination of R. Gray, 15 Apr. 1798.
26. S.P.O., 620/18A/14, J. King to E. Cooke, 12 Jan. 1798.

tants, a union which had been facilitated by ruptures between the moderate and militant members of both organizations. The L.C.S. had been declining since the passage of the 'Two Acts' in 1795, and as the number of moderate committee-men decreased, their places were rapidly filled by such republicans as the Irish brothers John and Benjamin Binns,[27] until, by 1798, the original society was unrecognizable.[28]   When Coigley returned from France at the end of 1797 the militants were already in almost total control of the Society, and it only required a change of name to transform it into the republican Society of United Britons. On 18 April 1798 a meeting was convened at the George Tavern in Clerkenwell to perform the re-baptism. Most of the original L.C.S. members stayed away; some attended merely to oppose the decision. The meeting had scarcely begun, however, when both parties were arrested by some Bow Street officers, and the remaining members of the Society were taken up the next day.[29] The arrests marked a major victory for the government, curtailing the organization of the United Britons and terminating the existence of the L.C.S. A few members remained together to organize subscriptions for the prisoners' dependants, but in July 1799 the Society was suppressed by name. By the end of that year the subscriptions had ceased and the L.C.S. was no more.[30]

Like their Manchester brethren, the London United Britons were gradually incorporating the older radical movements; but they were also attempting to establish an executive to co-ordinate the activities of the different parts of the republican movement, in Ireland, England, Scotland and France. As in Manchester, the main impetus behind the London organization had come from Coigley. In the summer of 1797 he had met Benjamin Binns in London, and reinforced the latter's existing republican opinions.   These

27.   T.C.D., Ms. 873/450, B. Binns to Dr Madden, 24 May 1843; E. P. Thompson, *The Making of the English Working Class* (2nd edn., Harmondsworth, 1968), p. 154; B.L., Add. Mss. 27,815, fos. 165-6, letter from div. no. 10 to the President, 2 Aug. 1797; P.R.O., P.C. 1/43/A.152, further examination of Henry Hastings, May 1798.
28.   B.L., Add. Mss. 27,808, fos. 67-79, notes on the L.C.S., 1792-1800; S. Maccoby, *English Radicalism, 1786-1832* (London, 1955), p. 97; B.L., Add. Mss. 27,808, fo. 106, notes by Francis Place; P.R.O., P.C. 1/41/A.138, P.C. 1/28/A.62, accounts of L.C.S. meetings, 1797.
29.   B.L., Add. Mss. 27,808, fos. 92-5, Place's notes; P.R.O., P.C. 1/41/A.136, list of persons taken at the George, Apr. 1798.
30.   Bod., Ms. Eng. hist. c. 196 (Burdett-Coutts Mss.) fo. 17, 'Subscription Raised for the Wives and Dependants, 1798-9'; B.L., Add. Mss. 27,808, fo. 104, Place's notes.

were incorporated in an address composed by Binns and presented by Coigley to the French Directory, after his arrival in Paris. In this Binns claimed to speak on behalf of 'the Chief Revolutionary Committee of England' and he assured the Directory of its support in the event of a French invasion of the British Isles. Almost certainly, Binns was here claiming greater authority than he actually possessed, since there are no references to the existence of such a committee until the end of the year. But the document is an important indication that the alliance between the English, Irish and Scottish republicans was progressing throughout that summer, for Coigley had spoken with a Scottish delegate sent to open discussions with the Irish and English republicans in London.[31]

In Paris, Coigley became involved with a group of United Irish militants who were agitating for the removal of the moderate Edward Lewins as accredited United Irish representative in France.[32] Coigley was despatched to the British Isles in December, with the dual mission of securing a replacement for Lewins, and preparing the British republicans for the arrival of a French invasion force.[33] He immediately contacted the leading republicans in London, Colonel Despard, Lawless, the Binnses and Thomas Evans, and together they set up a republican executive, the Secret Committee of United Britons.[34] The Committee established itself as the Holborn Division of the United Britons,[35] and immediately set about organizing the lower committees in the Irish quarters of London. By the middle of February nine divisions had been established, in Spitalfields, Clerkenwell, Battle Bridge, Somers Town, Southwark and Holborn,[36] and soon several divisions had commenced military exercises in preparation for the French invasion.[37]

---

31. A.A.E., Corr. Pol. Ang. 592, fo. 43, the Revs. Coigley and Macmahon to Talleyrand, 4 Oct. 1797; S.P.O., 620/52/207, 'Copy of Paper Carried by Coigley and in B. Binns's Writing'.
32. *Memoirs and Correspondence of Viscount Castlereagh* ed. Londonderry (London, 1848), ii, 3-5; *Life of Tone*, ii, 100, 461-2, 466-7, 472-3.
33. Simms, *Rev. James O'Coigley*, p. 22.
34. P.R.O., H.O. 100/75/142-3, 174-6, Portland to Camden, 1, 7 Mar. 1798; S.P.O., 620/3/32/24, anonymous information from London (probably from J. Nugent), 5 Jan. 1798.
35. S.P.O., 620/18[A]/14, J. King to E. Cooke, 12 Jan. 1798. The members of the Committee were Despard, Finn, Hamilton, the Binnses, Stuckey, Bailey and Crossfield.
36. S.P.O., 620/10/121/90, McNally to Cooke, 9 Feb. 1798; P.R.O., T.S. 11/122/333, 'Secret Information respecting Quigley, Despard *etc*. Feb. 1798.'
37. P.R.O., P.C. 1/42/A.144, deposition of John Tunbridge, 30 June 1798.

4

Coigley's return from France had introduced a new determination and sense of urgency into the republican movement in London, and the next two months witnessed a frantic effort to organize the disparate elements of republicanism throughout the British Isles. At a meeting in Furnival's Inn, Benjamin Binns was chosen to accompany Coigley to Dublin and explain the new English movement to the United Irish leaders.[38] On 6 January 1798 the two men set off for Dublin, accompanied by another member of the Secret Committee, William Bailey.[39] Three days later they arrived in Dublin, and Coigley immediately arranged an interview with Lord Edward Fitzgerald.[40] What took place at that meeting is not quite clear, but the outcome was a commission for the replacement of Lewins by Arthur O'Connor, and the blessing of at least the militant section of the Dublin leadership for the proposed merger of the English, Irish and Scottish republican movements.[41] The militants welcomed any opportunity of undermining the moderates' authority, since another clash between the two groups had just taken place. In December Lord Edward had received a letter from France urging the United Irishmen to organize some kind of diversion in Ireland to distract the government's attention from a proposed French attack on England. For several months the moderate majority had blocked the militant leaders' demands for an immediate rising, but Lord Edward and O'Connor felt that the letter from France would crush further opposition. They called an urgent meeting of the Leinster Directory, and suggested a rising for Christmas Eve, when the crowds of people going to midnight mass would disguise the gathering of the rebels. The suggestion was decisively rejected; Lord Edward resigned from the Directory, and, 'in a state of impatience amounting to frenzy', O'Connor left for England. The home United Irish Society was now completely in the control of the moderates.[42]

38. S.P.O., 620/18A/14, J. King to Pelham, 6 Jan. 1798; *Parliamentary History*, xxxv, 640-2, report from the Commons' Committee of Secrecy, appendix 8.
39. S.P.O., 620/18A/14, J. King to E. Cooke, 12 Jan. 1798; T.C.D., Ms. 873/450, B. Binns to Dr Madden, 24 May 1843.
40. S.P.O., 620/36/9a, examination of C. Carlton, 13 Mar. 1798.
41. P.R.O., P.C. 1/41/A.136, information of R. Gray, 19 Mar. 1798; A.H.G., Doss. Pers., 2eme ser., G.D. 393, O'Connor; S.P.O., 620/18A/11, memorandum found in Binns's pocket book, Apr. 1798.
42. B.L., Add. Mss. 33,105, fo. 307, Richardson [*i.e.* Turner] to Downshire, 26 Dec. 1797; S.P.O., 620/10/121/86, L. McNally to E. Cooke, 26 Dec. 1797.

O'Connor does not appear at this stage to have contemplated travelling to France. He idled away his time in London, attending concerts at Covent Garden, dining with his friends among the Whig opposition, and to all appearances behaving as an Irish gentleman in London for the season.[43] The return of Coigley from Ireland immediately stirred him into action. John Binns was sent to the Kentish coastal towns in search of transport to the Continent, and O'Connor made hasty preparations for an extended residence abroad.[44] With Benjamin Binns in Ireland, a Committee of United Britons in London, and O'Connor on his way to secure armed assistance from France, it seemed as if Pitt's constant nightmare of a co-ordinated attack by England's external and internal enemies was about to become a reality. 'Already have the English fraternized with the Irish and Scots', was the triumphant claim of the Secret Committee in an address which Coigley was to carry to the French Directory, 'a delegate from each now sits with us ... and United Britain burns to break her chains ... we now only wait with impatience to see the hero of Italy and the brave veterans of the great nation.'[45] But the republican dream was scotched by the hand of authority, and within two months of Coigley's return with O'Connor's commission, all the principal leaders had been arrested.

John Binns's request for a ship to the Continent had created quite a stir at a time when an invasion scare was raging in the coastal towns through which he passed. Anxious about the hostility he had encountered, Binns rushed back to London to warn O'Connor and his travelling companions. But he was too late; they had already left for Whitstable the previous day, 24 February.[46] Three days later, Coigley, O'Connor and his servant O'Leary, John Binns and John Allen, a fugitive United Irishman from Dublin, were all arrested whilst breakfasting at the King's Head in Margate. Coigley had been followed since his arrival from France by the two Bow Street officers who made the arrests.[47] Another officer had followed the movements of Benjamin Binns, and he was also arrested on his return to London. 'Why Mr Binns, I have had a long

43. P.R.O., H.O., 100/75/110, Portland to Camden, 23 Feb. 1798.
44. P.R.O., T.S. 11/689/2187, examination of John Foreman of Whitstable, 8 Mar. 1798; H.O. 100/79/299, A. O'Connor to R. O'Connor, 13 Feb. 1798.
45. P.R.O., P.C. 1/51/A.143, address from the Secret Committee of England to the Executive Directory, 26 Jan. 1798.
46. P.R.O., T.S. 11/689/2187, examination of Thomas Norris, 6 Mar. 1798; *Recollections of the Life of John Binns* (Philadelphia, 1854), pp 87-88.
47. S.P.O., 620/18A/14, J. King to T. Pelham, 21 Jan. 1798; P.R.O., T.S. 11/689/2187, information of Edward Fugion and John Rivett, 1 Mar. 1798.

journey to overtake you', confessed Binns's captor, 'I dare say I have travelled 15 hundred miles after you...I can tell where you have breakfasted, dined, supped and slept for the last 12 months.'[48] It was the first indication of the importance which Whitehall attached to the arrests.

No-one was surprised at the Margate arrests, since the prisoners had scarcely made a secret of their intended mission. On the evening prior to his departure from London, O'Connor had hailed a bye-man on watch, and promised to pay sixpence if he was called up early the following morning. He then aroused suspicion by hurriedly leaving town without paying for the services performed.[49] At Margate he again ill-advisedly attracted much attention, by calling to a fisherman from his hotel window, and enquiring about the different means of travelling to the Continent.[50] After landing from the Whitstable hoy, his luggage was thoroughly searched because of the excessive anxiety he had expressed to the crew about the possibility of just such a search.[51] The large quantity of luggage ill befitted the image of a man who stayed at cheap hotels and haggled over the cost of transport, and it raised many eyebrows in the towns through which the party travelled. Not surprisingly, therefore, rumours that French spies were in the vicinity had circulated even before the arrests were made.[52]

The government was clearly excited by the arrest of such arch-conspirators as O'Connor, Binns and Coigley. The prospect of discrediting the Whigs who had associated with O'Connor was an additional attraction, and both Pitt and Portland took a close personal interest in the affair.[53] At a meeting of the Privy Council one evening, Pitt became so incensed at the refusal of Benjamin Binns to answer questions that he jumped up suddenly from his seat, shook his fist menacingly in the prisoner's face, and demanded his instant committal.[54] The main Irish spies who could help secure the conviction of the prisoners were rushed over to London, and no fewer than eight witnesses were called in to identify

48.   T.C.D., Ms. 873/451, B. Binns to Dr Madden, 24 May 1798.
49.   P.R.O., T.S. 11/689/2187, examination of John Richardson, bye-man on watch, 8 Mar. 1798.
50.   *Ibid.*, examination of Vincent Whaller, 6 Mar. 1798.
51.   *Ibid.*, examination of Jonas King, 6 Mar. 1798, and notes by the Treasury Solicitor on the back of J. Foreman's evidence.
52.   *Ibid.*, examination of Ann Crickett, 6 Mar. 1798, and notes by the Treasury Solicitor on the back of H. Tompsett's evidence.
53.   P.R.O., H.O. 100/75/174-6, Portland to Camden, 7 Mar. 1798.
54.   *Recollections of ... John Binns*, p. 91.

O'Connor's handwriting.[55] O'Connor produced an equally impressive testimony to his good character, and virtually all the leading members of the English and Irish oppositions were called as witnesses for the defence.[56] Events soon took on the appearance of a circus. O'Connor first attempted to bribe the gaoler,[57] then resorted to sending 'anonymous' threatening letters to the Home Office, and finally made an undignified dash from the courthouse when a sympathiser extinguished the lights. Such antics simply confirmed the ministers' belief in his guilt, and they felt confident of a conviction. The opposition, equally convinced of O'Connor's innocence, saw in the forthcoming trials an opportunity of attacking the government's repressive policies. The attack was reinforced by O'Connor's acquittal, and was sustained in parliament throughout the succeeding months.[58] The outcome of the trials was a major defeat for the government, since only Coigley was convicted.[59] There had been enough evidence to convict all five prisoners, but it was not of a nature to be produced in open court, and there was no tangible evidence to prove their intention of travelling to France.[60] By that stage all the incriminating documents were somewhere in the Margate sewerage system, for O'Leary had flushed them down a toilet in the King's Head after an unsuspecting Bow Street officer had permitted him to leave the room.[61] One document, however, had been overlooked. It was the address of the United Britons to the French Directory, which Coigley had carelessly stuffed into his coat pocket at a meeting in Furnival's Inn cellar, and it was on the basis of this paper that Coigley was convicted and executed on 7 June.[62]

Few were satisfied with the results of the trials, and many, even the most ardent of government supporters, felt that Coigley

55. S.P.O., 620/36/9a, 'Witnesses to Prove O'Connor's Writing', 14 Mar. 1798; 620/36/173, 180, letters from J. Pollock to E. Cooke, Apr. 1798.
56. S.P.O., 620/18A/4, J. Pollock to E. Cooke, 20 May 1798; 620/37/14, list of witnesses, n.d.
57. S.P.O., 620/18A/11, W. Wickham to E. Cooke, 15 Apr. 1798.
58. P.R.O., P.C. 1/41/A.139, T. Noble (Maidstone Postmaster) to F. Freeling, 13 Apr. 1798; H.O. 100/76/69-70, W. Wickham to E. Cooke, 15 Apr. 1798; *Parliamentary History*, xxxiii, 1458-81.
59. Howell, *State Trials*, xxvii, 1-254.
60. P.R.O., H.O. 100/75/138-40, 144-7, 150-152, 179-81, exchange of letters between Portland and Camden, Mar. 1798.
61. *The Life, Times and Contemporaries of Lord Cloncurry* ed. W. J. Fitzpatrick (Dublin, 1855), p. 602.
62. T.C.D., Ms. 873/451, B. Binns to Dr Madden, 24 May 1843; Simms, *Rev. James O'Coigley*, p. 33.

had been sacrificed while the main culprits had escaped.[63] Only the opposition seemed happy at their *protege's* acquittal and the government's defeat. However, the following August O'Connor confessed his treason; the Whigs were made to look either fools or liars, and the ministers secured the victory which had eluded them the previous May.[64] Henceforth the opposition became noticeably tamer in parliament, and, with but few exceptions, terminated their association with O'Connor and the United Irishmen.[65]

The republican movement struggled on for some months under the leadership of Valentine Lawless. Periodic meetings took place at Lawless's lodgings and the Royal Oak tavern in Red Lion Passage, and contacts were maintained with France and Dublin.[66] But Lawless was simply performing a 'holding operation' until a decision could be reached about the future of the shattered organization. No attempt was made to effect the ambitious plans of the previous year for amalgamating all the treasonable elements in English society into the Society of United Britons, and Lawless's group confined its attention to plans for individual acts of sabotage in England's dockyards and military depots. It was at a meeting convened to discuss the defection of a number of sailors at Portsmouth that the remaining leaders in London were arrested on 20 March 1799.[67] All signs of an organized republican movement in England disappeared until the release of the leaders in 1801, but the developments of the period between the first government swoop on the United Britons in the spring of 1798 and the second series of arrests in March-April 1799 were crucial for the future development of republicanism in England. The failure of the 1798 rebellion in Ireland introduced into Irish republicanism an element

63. S.P.O., 620/37/175, Pollock to [Cooke], 26 May 1798; P.R.O., H.O. 100/76/285-88, W. Wickham to E. Cooke, 26 May 1798.
64. This is the theme of Gillray's cartoon, 'Evidence to Character — being the Portrait of a Traitor by his Friends and by Himself', 1 Oct. 1798 (Bod., Curzon collection, b. 18/73). See also *Memoirs and Correspondence of Castlereagh*, i, 246-8, 262-4, 309-10, 316-7, correspondence between Castlereagh and Wickham, July-Aug. 1798.
65. A.N., F7 6330, doss. 6988, Mengaud to the Minister of Justice, 14 Feb. 1803; Hants. R.O., 31/M70 (Tierney Mss.), O'Connor to Tierney, 23 Aug. 1802.
66. P.R.O., P.C. 1/43/A.153, 'Papers concerning the United Irish Society in London'; S.P.O., 620/7/74/1-24, secret information from Pollock and McGucken, Jan.-Apr. 1799.
67. Hants. R.O., 38M49/1/38, Pitt to W. Wickham, 27 Feb. 1799; P.R.O., H.O., 100/86/165-6, 198/99, W. Wickham to Castlereagh, 20, 23 Mar. 1799; H.O., 100/87/351, further information of J. P. Murphy, n.d.; A.H.G., MR. 1420, fo. 106, General Bequinot to the Minister of War, 4 Apr. 1799.

of extreme bitterness towards the English nation; until then antagonism had been directed against the English government. The Irish had been disappointed in their hopes of an English insurrection to correspond with their own, and the thousands of rebels who fled to England in 1798 intensified the violently anti-English complexion which Irish republicanism there was rapidly acquiring.[68] The attempted merger of 1798, therefore, never progressed beyond the executive level, and although a certain amount of co-operation continued into the second phase, by 1804 the antagonism and increasing violence of the Irish had alienated most of their English supporters.[69] Despite government fears and United Irish claims, the English working class was not naturally republican in sympathy. Republicanism was an importation which had been continually reinforced from its source in Ireland, and had capitalized on the temporary unpopularity of the war and the government. The tenuous relationship between Irish republicanism and English discontent was destroyed by the emergence of popular patriotism in the face of the Napoleonic threat, and republicanism eventually became the preserve of the most extreme elements of the Irish community in England.

5

The reaction of the English government to the Irish-inspired conspiracy was swift and relatively effective. In the circumstances the Pitt government reacted with a remarkable degree of equanimity. Despite Pitt's personal dread of such a combination between England's domestic and foreign enemies,[70] no systematic 'witch-hunt' or 'reign of terror' was organised against the British 'Jacobins', and legislation such as the Two Acts of 1795 falls into the general pattern of eighteenth-century criminal statutes, with its emphasis on deterrence rather than the strict enforcement of the law.[71] Additional measures had been taken to combat the new threat to law and order in the 1790s, and by 1798 the government was able to call on the assistance of seven public offices established in London the previous year and employing 42 constables and 21

---

68.   P.R.O., P.C. 1/43/A.152, copy of a letter from 'G.S.' [*i.e.* G. Orr] to Wickham, 28 Jan. 1799; A.A.E., Corr. Pol. Ang. 593, fos. 516-19, Thaddeus Sydney to Talleyrand, 1 Sept. 1800.
69.   See Elliott, *'The Despard Conspiracy Reconsidered'.*
70.   *Parliamentary History*, xxx, 231-33.
71.   This general theme is discussed throughout Sir Leon Radzinowicz, *A History of English Criminal Law and its Administration from 1750* (4 vols., London, 1948-68), especially vol. i; and D. Hay, P. Linebaugh, J. G. Rule, E. P. Thompson and C. Winslow, *Albion's Fatal Tree* (London, 1975).

H*

magistrates. In addition, six full-time officers, 68 part-time officers on night patrol and three justices were attached to the original office at Bow Street. However, the London force was frequently reduced when its officers were sent to investigate reports of treasonable activities in the counties, where no effective policing system existed.[72]   The government tended to concentrate its energy on securing the capital and frequently knew little of events in the counties.

Given the limitations of the peace-keeping forces, it proved impossible to enforce legislation against the entry of Irish republicans into England.[73]   Consequently the government became increasingly dependent on its informer network to forestall their schemes on the mainland. Spies have always had a bad press, but in the absence of a national police force an extensive spy-system was essential to the maintenance of order in the country, and its existence as the investigating branch of government was tacitly accepted in official circles.   There is little foundation for the belief that the spies and informers of this period were unscrupulous profit-seekers, who fabricated plots to have the credit of discovering them.[74]   Such a practice would probably have proved fruitless, for the government itself was inherently distrustful of the spies it employed, and would rarely accept their reports until they were corroborated from another source.[75]   Moreover, a career in espionage appears to have been singularly unprofitable, and most spies were kept continually short of money, even for normal expenditure incurred in the course of their employment. The reports of William Barlow, one of the leading spies in the north of England, are representative of the unenviable lot of the conscientious spy.   He travelled around the different industrial centres of Lancashire and Yorkshire, spent large sums of money to secure

72.   *Reports from the Committees of the House of Commons* (London, 1803), xiii, *23rd Report from the Select Committee on Finance, Public Debt and Expenditure ...*, pp 346-7, 375-80; J. Stevenson, 'Disturbances and Public Order in London, 1790-1821' (Oxford Univ. D.Phil. thesis 1972), p. 39; and J. Stevenson, 'Social Control and the Prevention of Riots in England, 1789-1829', *Social Control in Nineteenth-Century Britain* ed. A.P. Donajgrodzki (London, 1977), pp 27-50.
73.   For information on the failure of the passport control regulations in 1798, see S.P.O., 620/36/215, W. Wickham to E. Cooke, 20 Apr. 1798; P.R.O., H.O. 100/66/107, examination of the captain of the *Sweet William*, 3 June 1798; P.C. 1/44/A.161, G. Orr to J. King, 12 Sept. 1799; Hants, R.O., 38M49/1/66, Sir J. Craufurd to W. Wickham, 16 Nov. 1798.
74.   *Parliamentary History*, xxxi, 572; xxxii, 296, 368, 374-5; *Life ... of Lord Cloncurry*, p. 166.
75.   P.R.O., H.O. 100/66/163, T. Bayley to W. Wickham, 7 July 1798; H.O., 100/93/143, J. King to Marsden, 14 Aug. 1800; S.P.O., 620/36a/59, W. Wickham to E. Cooke, 24 Mar. 1798.

information from suspected republicans, and found it impossible to meet his expenses from the spasmodic payments sent up from London. His reports foretell imminent exposure, because poverty was making it difficult for him to maintain his disguise as a travelling tradesman. Nevertheless, despite government stringencies, he never succumbed to the temptation of sensationalising events in order to attract more attention.[76] Most secret-service money was devoted to foreign espionage in these years, and the domestic side suffered as a consequence.

The position of the so-called 'agents provocateurs' is difficult to establish, and the discovery of their true role has been rendered virtually impossible by historians perpetuating the contemporary myth that these agents were to a large extent responsible for fomenting much of the trouble of the 1790s.[77] The only cases which in some way approximate to this stereotype picture are incidents where agents planted information, not to manufacture a plot, but to secure the conviction of persons involved in a known plot.[78] This was a vital part of the spy's work, since his own evidence would have been unacceptable in open court.[79] An act of overt treason could only be proved either by apprehending the suspect in the act, or by discovering incriminating evidence in his possession. This was often where the spy could perform his most useful service. One notable case of a spy planting evidence of this nature led to the arrest of all those who had attended the meeting to launch the Society of United Britons. On 18 April 1798 a stranger interrupted the meeting at the George Tavern in Compton Street, offered several pike-heads for sale, and hurriedly departed before the assembled company could accept or reject the offer. Some minutes later, the entire company was taken up by a Bow Street officer, and the pike-heads subsequently used as proof that those present at the meeting were arming for treasonable purposes.[80] However, the spy could not be accused of encouraging

76. P.R.O., P.C. 1/44/A.161, information of William Barlow, Aug.-Oct. 1799.
77. T.C.D., Ms. 873/451, B. Binns to Dr Madden, 24 May 1843; R.R. Madden, *The United Irishmen, Their Lives and Times* (7 vols., London, 1842-6), ii, 1, 101, 113, 147; B.L., Add. Mss. 27,808, fo. 92, notes by Francis Place.
78. P.R.O., P.C. 1/41/A.136, T. Bayley to W. Wickham, 26 Mar. 1798.
79. For the prosecution evidence at the Maidstone trials, see P.R.O., H.O. 100/100/121, 'Heads of Evidence to be Offered to a Secret Committee', c.1798.
80. Bod., Ms. Eng. hist. c. 196, fo. 130, 'The Particulars of the Arrest and Imprisonment of T. Evans', 18 Apr. 1798; P.R.O., P.C. 1/41/A.136, 'List of Persons Taken at the George Public House, Apr. 1798.'

treason, since most of the men arrested at the George were United Britons, and those who were not were released shortly afterwards.[81]

Because of their suspicion of paid spies, the authorities tended to rely heavily on informers, men who were already involved in treasonable projects and could be depended upon to produce more reliable information than spies, who had to insinuate themselves into the movement. Prisoners were consequently induced to become informers before being committed,[82] and the Maidstone trials produced several timid or repentant republicans who remained in government service for the rest of the period. These United British informers were surprisingly honest in their declarations, and the government consequently obtained more reliable information about the movement than it could ever have expected from the paid spy. Indeed, shock at the increasing violence of the republican movement or a sense of guilt were normally more potent reasons than fear for such changes of colour.[83] In a sharp attack on the ministry, Fox once divided the nation's spy-force into three categories: those who could provide the government with reliable information, those who went to extreme lengths to seek out information and then sold it for gain, and finally those who actively promoted treason in order to betray it.[84] But Fox was wrong in his assertion that most government agents fell within the last two categories, and all the evidence suggests that the information produced by the spy network was of even greater value than the government itself was prepared to accept.

6

In the 1790s republicanism was introduced into England by a group of United Irish militants seeking another area of operation after their defeat at home. Initially they found much support among the existing seditious societies; but the idea of a National Committee, to establish republicanism on a firm basis in England, was crushed at the outset. The strength of the United Britons was therefore potential rather than actual. It was the fanaticism of the leaders, and their ability to capitalize on prevailing popular dis-

81. P.R.O., P.C. 1/3514, 'Persons Apprehended during the Suspension of *Habeas Corpus*'.
82. P.R.O., H.O. 100/87/244-5, Portland to Cornwallis, 4 Nov. 1799; F.O. 27/51, notes of M. Dutheil on E. Devereux, c.Mar. 1797.
83. P.R.O., P.C. 1/41/A.136, examination of R. Gray, 23 Mar. 1798; H.O. 100/70/339, Camden to Portland, 9 Dec. 1797.
84. *Parliamentary History*, xxxii, 374-5.

content, rather than its paid-up membership, which made the United British Society such a potentially destructive force.[85] English support for the movement declined after 1798, but neither the reduction in the number of its English adherents nor the periodic government purges could destroy Irish republicanism in England. Its roots were too firmly established to be removed, and just as the first revival of Irish republicanism in 1801-3 would supply new recruits to the dormant movement in England, so an extension of Irish republican activity to England has accompanied each subsequent revival.

85.   Figures quoted for United British membership are unreliable. Estimates vary, but the figure normally quoted for London would be between 80,000 and 100,000; that for Scotland 30,000; and for such cities as Manchester and Nottingham, 3,000-5,000. See P.R.O., P.C. 1/41/A.136, T. Bayley to W. Wickham, 26 Mar. 1798; P.C. 1/41/A.144, information of J. Tunbridge 11 July 1798; Kent R.O., U.840/0196/2 (Camden Mss.), Downshire to Camden, 4 Apr. 1798.

INDEX

Abercorn, earls and marquess of, *see* Hamilton

Absenteeism, *see* Agriculture

Accounts office, *see* Government and Administration

Act of Parliament, *see* Parliament

Agrarian Disturbances, 183, 190-1, 202-3
See also Law and Administration of Justice

Agriculture, 74, 162-203 *passim*
Absenteeism, 77, 167, 184
Middlemen, 162-85 *passim*
Subdivision, 116, 169, 180, 187, 198

Albemarle, Lord, *see* Keppel, George

Alcohol, *see* Trade and Industry

Allan, Thomas, 102-3

Allen, John, 213

America, 1-2, 17, 94, 113, 130n

Amyand, Claudius, 69

Anglesey, Lord, *see* Annesley, Arthur

Anne, Queen, 40

Annesley, Arthur, 7th earl of Anglesey, 46

Annesley, Arthur, 9th Viscount Valentia and 1st earl of Mountnorris, 117

Annesley, Francis, 23n, 25-6n

Annesley, Francis Charles, 2nd Viscount Glerawly, 113n

Antrim, parliamentary borough, 145

Antrim, Lord, *see* MacDonnell, Randal William

Archdall, Mervyn, 113n, 126n, 129

Ardee, parliamentary borough, 154

Ardglass, countess of, *see* Essex, Catherine

Armagh, archbishop of, *see* Boulter, Hugh; Robinson, Richard; Stone, George

Armagh, County, parliamentary constituency, 59-62, 117, 122, 129, 136

Armed Services
Army, 6-7, 18, 78n, 86, 90, 93, 96, 103, 113
Fencibles, 127-8
Militia, 115-6

Army, *see* Armed Services

Arran, Lord, *see* Gore, Arthur

Athenry, parliamentary borough, 159

Athlone, parliamentary borough, 139, 150n

Augusta, princess of Wales, 84

Bagwell, John, 144, 150n

Bailey, William, 212

Ballast office, *see* Government and Administration

Ballynakill, parliamentary borough, 150n

Baltinglass, parliamentary borough, 153, 158

Baltinglass, Lord, *see* Stratford, John

Bandon, parliamentary borough, 146

Banks and Banking, 69, 75-6

Bannow, parliamentary borough, 138

'Barataria', 94

Barlow, William, 218

Barnard, William, bishop of Derry, 77

Barrington, family, 150n

Bedford, duke of, *see* Russell, John

Belfast, 145, 186-203 *passim*

Belfast, parliamentary borough, 145

Belfast Academy, 199

Belfast Chamber of Commerce, 199

Belfast Charitable Society, 199

Belfast Whig Club, 200
See also Newspapers

Belmore, Lord, *see* Lowry-Corry, Armar

Bentinck, William Henry Cavendish, 3rd duke of Portland, 214

Beresford, family, 139, 141

Beresford, George, 2nd earl of Tyrone, 96

Beresford, John, 154

Bessborough, Lord, *see* Ponsonby, William

Binns, Benjamin, 210-14

Binns, John, 210, 213

Blackwood, R., 113n

Blayney, Cadwallader, 11th Lord Blayney, 34

Blundell, Sir Francis, 25-6n

Bolton, duke of, *see* Powlett, Charles

Bonnell, James, 4, 17, 26

Boulter, Hugh, archbishop of Armagh, 47, 53

Boyle, family, earls of Orrery, 146

Boyle, family, earls of Shannon, 146

Boyle, Bellingham, 66

Boyle, Henry, 1st earl of Shannon, 41, 49, 52-5, 57, 59, 61-2, 67, 81n

Boyle, Henry, 3rd earl of Shannon, 152-3

Boyle, John, 5th earl of Orrery, 146

Boyle, Richard, 3rd earl of Burlington, 146, 151, 175

Index

Holdernesse, Lord, *see* D'Arcy, Robert
Holland House, 66
Holroyd, estate, 184
Hore, family, 154
Hore, William, 143
Howard, Frederick, 5th earl of Carlisle, 121-2

Impeachment, *see* Parliament, Irish
Inchiquin, Lord, *see* O'Brien, William

Jackson, R., 113n
Jackson, Rev. William, 205-6
Jacobite, estates, 4, 9, 16-17, 21-2, 26
Jacobite threat, 41, 58
    See also James II; James Francis Edward; Religious Denominations, Roman Catholics
James I, 138
James II, 3, 6, 10, 79, 83
James Francis Edward, the Old Pretender, 'King James III', 41, 45
Jebb, Rev. John, 130
Jephson, family, 102n
Jephson, Denham, 107n
Jocelyn, Robert, Lord Newport and Viscount Jocelyn, lord chancellor of Ireland, 67
Johnston, Sir Richard, 192
Jones, Theophilus, 89n
Joy, Henry, 132n

Kearney, James, 166, 178
Keightley, Thomas 50
Keppel, George, 3rd earl of Albemarle, 67
Kerry, County, parliamentary constituency, 143
Kildare, bishop of, *see* Moreton, William
Kildare, earl of, *see* Fitzgerald, James
Kildare, County, parliamentary constituency, 137
Killyleagh, parliamentary borough, 151
Kilmaine, Lord, *see* Browne, John
King, Edward, 1st Viscount Kingston of Kingsborough, 165, 184
King, Jane, Lady Kingsborough, 165, 184
King, Sir Robert, 23n, 28-9
King, William, bishop of Derry, 10, 13, 22, 25n
Kingsborough, Lady, *see* King, Jane

Kingsborough, Lord, *see* King, Edward
Kinsale, parliamentary borough, 147
Knox, T., 113n

Lambert, Charles, 102n
Land Settlement, Williamite, 6, 19
Langford, Sir Arthur, 23n
Law and Administration of Justice, 13, 24-5, 46, 62, 64, 68, 74, 77, 82, 100-1, 124, 127
Latouche, family, 144
Lawless, Sir Nicholas, 143
Lawless, Valentine Browne, 208, 216
Lecky, W. E. H., 97-8
Legislative independence, *see* Parliament, Irish, issues in
Leigh, Francis, 152
Leinster, dukes of, *see* Fitzgerald
Lennox, Charles, 3rd duke of Richmond, 130
Lifford, parliamentary borough, 143
Lifford, Lord, *see* Hewitt, James
Lighton, Sir Thomas, 144
Limerick, Treaty of, 3, 10, 19, 43
Limerick, Lord, *see* Hamilton, James
Linen, 75, 77, 179-80, 186-203 *passim*
Lisburn, parliamentary borough, 129, 141, 145
Lismore, parliamentary borough, 146
Lismore, Lord, *see* O'Callaghan, Cornelius
Livestock, *see* Trade and Industry
Local government, *see* Government and Administration
Loftus, Charles Tottenham, 1st marquess of Ely, 99, 155
London, merchant companies of:
    Drapers, 175
    Estates of, 175, 184
    Fishmongers, 175
    Vintners, 175
London Corresponding Society, 204, 209-10
Londonderry, parliamentary borough, 139-40
Londonderry, Port of, 198-9
Londonderry, County, parliamentary constituency, 129, 140
Lord justiceship, *see* Government and Administration, Irish offices
Lord lieutenancy, *see* Government and Administration, Irish offices

Louis XIV, war against, 3
Louth, County, parliamentary constituency, 140, 142
Lowry-Corry, Armar, 1st Earl Belmore, 113n
Lucas, Charles, 72
Lysaght, Nicholas, 107n

Macartney, Sir George, 101-2
Magill, Sir John, 25-6n
McCracken, Professor J. L., 82, 93
MacDonnell, family, 172
MacDonnell, Randal William, 6th earl of Antrim, 113n, 115
McNeill, J. G. S., 97-8
Mahony, family, 172
Malone, Anthony, 55, 59-61, 65-6, 68, 72-3, 80-1n
Management, parliamentary, *see* Parliament, Irish
Manners, Charles, 4th duke of Rutland, 135
Mary, Queen, 5
Massereene, Lords, *see* Skeffington, family
Massue, Henri de, 1st earl of Galway, lord justice, 35
Maxwell, Barry, 2nd Lord Farnham, 113n
Maxwell, Hon. J. J. B., 113n
Maxwell, Robert, 64-5
Meath, bishop of, *see* Dopping, Anthony
Meath, County, parliamentary constituency, 142
Middlemen, *see* Agriculture
Midleton, Viscounts, *see* Brodrick
Militia, *see* Armed Services
Mitchell, Henry, 77
Moira, Lord, *see* Rawdon, John
Molyneux, Sir C., 113n
Monaghan, parliamentary borough, 142
Money bills, *see* Parliament, Irish, issues in
'Monks of the Screw', 118n
Montgomery, A., 113n
Montgomery, G., 113n
Montgomery, N., 113n
Moore, Charles, 6th earl of Drogheda, 150n
Moore, Edward, 5th earl of Drogheda, 96
Moore, Stephen, 2nd earl of Mount Cashell, 150n

Moreton, William, bishop of Kildare, 28n
Morres, Hervey Redmond, 2nd Viscount Mountmorres, 117
Mount Cashell, Lord, *see* Moore, Stephen
Mountmorres, Lord, *see* Morres, Hervey Redmond
Murray, William, 84

Namier, Sir Lewis, 41, 89n
Napier, Colonel George, 137
Nevill, Arthur Jones, 63-4, 73, 78
New Ross, parliamentary borough, 152
Newcastle, duke of, *see* Pelham-Holles, Thomas
Newport, Lord Chancellor, *see* Jocelyn, Robert
Newry, Canal, 189
Newry, economy of, 193-200
Newspapers:
    Belfast Mercury, 199
    Belfast Newsletter, 121, 199
    Dublin Courant, 77
    Freeman's Journal, 97, 100
    Northern Star, 199
    Universal Advertiser, 74
Newtownbutler, Lord, *see* Butler, Theophilus
North, Frederick, Lord, 98, 103, 118-9, 124
    See also Government and Administration, British ministries
Nottingham, Lord, *see* Finch, Daniel

O'Brien, Sir Edward, 74
O'Brien, Sir Lucius, 99, 115n
O'Brien, William, 3rd earl of Inchiquin, 34
O'Callaghan, Cornelius, 2nd Lord Lismore, 150n
O'Coigley, Rev. James, *see* Coigley
O'Connell, family, 172, 180
O'Connor, Arthur, 206-9, 212-16
O'Conor, Charles, 86
O'Hara, Charles, 75, 85, 172, 176-7
O'Leary, manservant to Arthur O'Connor (q.v.), 213, 215
O'Neill, John, 113n, 129, 192
Old Sarum, English parliamentary borough, 137
Orange Societies, 202-3
Ormonde, duke of, *see* Butler, James

Orrery, Lord, *see* Boyle, John
Osbaldeston, Richard, archbishop of Canterbury, 84
Osborne, John, 13, 23, 36

Pakenham, Thomas, 62, 80, 85-6
Parker, William, 169
Parliament:
(i) *British*, 2-3, 5, 8, 25-6, 64, 67, 174
   Acts of:
   Cattle Acts (1667, 1681), 188, 196
   Irish Oaths Act (1691), 2-3n
   Irish Security Act (1690), 2n
   Woollen Act (1698), 43, 75
   Parties in, 4, 14, 22-3, 26, 95-6, 98, 215-6
(ii) *Irish*:
(a) Acts of:
   Act for an Additional Duty (1692), 16n
   Act for taking Affidavits (1692), 16n
   Catholic Relief Act (1793), 164, 182
   Act for Encouragement of Protestant Strangers (1692), 16n
   'Grenville Act' (1771), 146
   Linen Regulating Act (1782), 192
   Militia Act (1793), 136
   Newtown Act (1748), 150n, 199
   Octennial Act (1768), 154, 191
   Place Act (1793), 140-1, 158
   Police Act (1800), 203
   Act of Recognition (1692), 16n
   Revenue Act (1756), 69n
   Vestry Act (1774), 191
   Act of Union (1800), 88, 140, 158-9
(b) *House of Commons, election to,* 59-60, 83, 117, 123, 129, 135, 137-61 *passim*
(c) *House of Lords*, 34
(d) *Impeachment in*, 128
(e) *Issues in*:
   Free Trade, 118-20, 161, 200
   Legislative independence, 79, 88,

94, 118-20, 124, 136, 161
   Money bills, 7-9, 19-21, 24, 34, 43, 55-87 *passim*, 90, 94, 96-100, 103-4
   Reform, 94, 119, 123-4, 130-5, 159, 200
   Renunciation, 125-8
   Wood's Halfpence, 32-3, 51, 74
(f) *Management of (including 'undertakers')*, 32-41, 46, 48, 52-3, 56-7, 62-4, 73, 79, 86, 88-9, 91, 96-7, 99, 101-3, 125, 140, 157, 160-1
(g) *Parties in*, 11-15, 32-4, 41-55, 57-63, 72, 74, 79, 81, 91, 95-6, 98, 100-101, 103, 119-20
(h) *And Poynings' Law*, 2, 5, 7-9, 15, 19-21, 29-30, 32-3, 58, 64, 82, 96
(i) *Procedure in*, 2, 9, 11-12, 21, 24, 29, 33, 58-9, 61, 71-2
(j) *And public opinion*, 120
(k) *Volunteers and*, 113-36 *passim*
(iii) *United*, Acts of:
   Land Acts, various, 176
   Poor Law Act (1838), 203
   Act against Subletting (1826), 169
   Town Commissioners Act (1828), 203
Parsons, Sir Laurence, 2nd earl of Rosse, 166
Parnell, Sir John, 141
Patronage, 90-1, 160-1
Peep O'Day Boys, 202
   See also Agrarian Disturbances
Pelham, Henry 62, 64, 69
Pelham, Thomas, chief secretary, 132-4
Pelham-Holles, Thomas, 2nd duke of Newcastle, 51, 57, 62-9, 80, 84
Pembroke, Lord, *see* Herbert, Thomas
Pennefather, family, 146
Perceval, Sir John, 1st earl of Egmont, 151, 178-9
Pery, William Cecil, 1st Lord Glentworth, 158
Pery, Edmond Sexten, 56, 79, 103-4
Petty, estate, 171
Petty-Fitzmaurice, William, 2nd earl of Shelburne, 92

Sloane, James, 14, 23, 25-6n
Southwell, Edward, 34, 86, 150-1
Southwell, Sir Robert, 172
Spencer, Charles, 3rd earl of Sunderland, 38
Stanhope, Philip Dormer, 4th earl of Chesterfield, 67, 78n
Stanhope, William, 1st earl of Harrington, 72-3, 78n
Stewart, J., 113n
Stewart, Robert, Viscount Castlereagh, 113n, 141
Stone, Andrew, 57
Stone, George, Archbishop of Armagh, 60, 62, 64-5, 67-70, 78n, 80, 83-6
Stokes, Whitley, 168
Strabane, parliamentary borough, 147-50, 156
Strafford, Lord, *see* Wentworth, Sir Thomas
Stratford, family, earls of Aldborough, 145
Stratford, John, 1st Lord Baltinglass and 1st earl of Aldborough, 125n, 158
Stuart, John, 1st marquess of Bute, 95
Subdivision, *see* Agriculture
Sunderland, Lord, *see* Spencer, Charles
Swords, parliamentary borough, 139-40, 146, 149-50
Sydney, Henry, 1st Viscount Sydney, 1-32 *passim*
Synge, Edward, bishop of Elphin, 65-7, 79

Taghmon, parliamentary borough, 154
Talbot, Charles, duke of Shrewsbury, 28n, 39-40, 48, 52
Talbot, Richard, duke of Tyrconnell, 11
Talbot, William, 154, 157
Thynne, Thomas, 3rd Viscount Weymouth, 89
Tighe, William, 164
Tighe, Captain, 83n
Tisdall, Philip, 61, 90
Tobacco, *see* Trade and Industry
Tollet, George, 15
Tone, Theobald Wolfe, 206
Tottenham, Charles, of Ballycurry, 152
Townsend, Horatio, 167
Townsend, Richard, 107n

Townshend, Charles, 93, 95
Townshend, George, 1st Marquess Townshend, 88-112 *passim*
Trade and Industry:
  Alcohol, 57
  Cotton, 193-8
  Livestock, 75, 162-85 *passim*, 196
  Provisions, 75, 188
  Silks, 77
  Tobacco, 57
  See also Economy of Ireland; Linen; Revenues of Ireland
Trench, Frederick, 59
Trench, Robert, 59
Tuam, archbishop of, *see* Vesey, John
Turnpikes, 80
Tyrconnell, duke of, *see* Talbot, Richard
Tyrone, Lord, *see* Beresford, George
Tyrone, County, parliamentary constituency, 142

'Undertakers', *see* Parliament, Irish, management of
United Britons, Society of, 209-10, 215-16, 219-21
United Irishmen, Society of, 200-202, 204-21 *passim*
Upton, estates, 190

Valentia, Lord, *see* Annesley, Arthur, earl of Mountnorris
Vesey, John, archbishop of Tuam, 28n
Volunteers, 113-36 *passim*, 192
  (i) *Companies:*
       Antrim, 115
       Armagh, 114n, 117, 119, 122, 123-4n, 136
       Belfast, 114-5, 121-2, 125-6, 134-5
       Connaught, 131, 134
       Cork, 116
       Doneraile Rangers, 128n
       Ennis, 128n
       Londonderry, 117
       Newry, 119, 135
       Rathfriland, 123n
  (ii) *Conventions:*
       Dungannon (1782), 122-4, 129
       Dungannon (1783), 129-31
       National (1783), 131-3

Waite, Thomas, 60, 65, 94-5n
Wakefield, Edward, 163, 168
Walkington, Edward, bishop of Down and Connor, 30-1
Wallmoden, Amalie-Sophie Marianne von, countess of Yarmouth, 77
Walpole, Horace, 85
Ward, Hon. E., 113n
Ward, Hon. R., 113n
Waterford, County, parliamentary constituency, 146
Watson-Wentworth, Charles, 2nd marquess of Rockingham, 92
Wentworth, Sir Thomas, 1st earl of Strafford, 19, 21
West, Richard, 53
Weymouth, Lord, *see* Thynne, Thomas
Wharton, Thomas, 1st marquess of Wharton, 35, 52
Wilcox and Dawson, bank, 76

William III, 2, 5, 27, 118
Wilmot, Sir Robert, 60, 81
Wilson, James, 191
Wood's Halfpence, *see* Parliament, Irish, issues in
Woodward, Richard, bishop of Cloyne, 133
Wyche, Sir Cyril, 27-8
Wynne, family, 65, 142
Wyndham, Thomas, 53
Wyvill, Christopher, 130

Yarmouth, Lady, *see* Wallmoden, Amalie-Sophie Marianne von
Yelverton, Barry, 118n, 120
Yorke, Philip, 1st earl of Hardwicke, 65, 68, 84-5
Youghal, parliamentary borough, 146, 150-2
Young, Arthur, 163-5, 177, 180-4